After meticulously defi n
epistles, Richard Mayh d
theological instruction. Verse by verse he expounds the epistles with
impeccable precision. Matters of church government, spiritual gifts,
family relationships, church ordinances and future events are examined
through the Thessalonian lens. Having been thus immersed in these
epistles, the reader will be challenged to live out their teachings. That
is the ultimate compliment that can be paid to any sermon or
commentary.

Dr. William D. Barrick
Professor of Old Testament
The Master's Seminary
Sun Valley, California

Richard L. Mayhue's lucid exposition of the Thessalonian epistles is
merely the tip of a very deep iceberg of information. The author
transports us to the past (how these epistles fit within the first century
world), propels us into the future (how the panorama of biblical
prophecy unfolds), and challenges us for the present (how these epistles
equip today's reader). In addition, Mayhue's ability to blend grand
biblical themes yields thirty-three Overviews, which should place this
work on the desk of any student of Scripture.

Dr. W. Gary Phillips
Professor of Bible
Bryan College,
Dayton,
Tennessee

Richard Mayhue, Th.D. is Senior Vice President and Dean of The Master's Seminary in Sun Valley, CA where he also lectures in Theology and Pastoral Ministry. For most of his 25 years of ministry, he has engaged in both pastoring and training pastors. Dr. Mayhue has written, edited, or contributed to over fifteen books including *The Healing Promise* (Mentor), *How to Interpret the Bible* (CFP), *What Would Jesus Say About Your Church?* (CFP), and *Fight the Good Fight* (CFP). He ministers as an elder at Grace Community Church and serves on the boards of Slavic Gospel Association (ministering in the lands of Russia) and Capitol Ministries (ministering in American state capitols).

Dedication

To my sister Linda Benjamin, her husband Jerry, and their daughter Katie who faithfully travel across America and Canada in an itinerant Bible teaching ministry, not unlike that of the Apostle Paul.

To Dr. Homer A. Kent who gave me a love for the Greek New Testament and modeled the precision with which God's Word is to be handled (2 Tim 2:15).

1 and 2 Thessalonians

Richard Mayhue

Christian Focus

© Richard L. Mayhue
ISBN 1 85792 452 5

Published in 1999
by
Christian Focus Publications,
Geanies House, Fearn, Ross-shire,
IV20 1TW, Great Britain.

Cover design by Owen Daily

Printed and bound in Great Britain
by Cox & Wyman Ltd, Reading, Berkshire

CONTENTS

2 THESSALONIANS

OVERVIEWS

1 Thessalonians

2 Thessalonians

Preface

My great love for the Thessalonian Epistles reaches back over twenty years of: (1) writing my doctoral dissertation on the 'Day of the Lord'; (2) teaching these letters in seminary Greek exegesis courses; (3) teaching Bible Institute (English Bible) courses; and (4) preaching through them expositionally verse by verse. They overflow with doctrinal, pastoral, and personal riches.

The biblical text has been interpreted with the consistent use of grammatical-historical principles of hermeneutics (see my *How to Interpret the Bible* in this commentary series). The doubts and spurious theories of Higher Criticism have not been considered for inclusion in this work. A high priority has been devoted to the original Greek text (UBS[4]), history, geography, and culture where appropriate. Special attention has been paid to context, i.e. the immediate text, the Pauline epistles, the New Testament, and ultimately the entire Bible. I have endeavored to provide a balanced treatment by first viewing the individual pieces textually/ exegetically and then as they relate to the entire Bible theologically. The ultimate end of this volume is to produce a doctrinal (what to believe) and ethical (how to behave) exposition of 1 and 2 Thessalonians which will appear in the 'Focus on the Bible' commentary series.

The English Bible text employed (unless otherwise noted) is the *New King James Version*. Footnotes have been used sparingly, except where they will lead the reader to resources which effectively expand a discussion. Of special note are the thirty-three *Overviews* designed to provide exegetical, thematic, or theological summaries, which supply necessary background for understanding how a part in the Thessalonian Epistles fits into the whole of Scripture.

Deep appreciation is extended to Malcolm Maclean, who championed this opportunity for me to publish the fruit from several decades of study and teaching; to The Master's College and Seminary board of directors who granted me a sabbatical leave for writing; to my colleagues at The Master's Seminary who picked up the slack in my absence, especially Dr. Irv Busenitz and Bob White, who also checked all of the Scripture references; to my daughter Lee Carson who faithfully served as the project computer manager; to my son-in-law Mike Carson who did the original artwork on the map of Paul's Second Missionary Journey; and to my dear wife "B" who did whatever was necessary to bring this writing project to a God-honouring conclusion.

May the Lord be pleased to use this commentary in special ways that will be for the spiritual good of His beloved saints and for His great glory.

Richard Mayhue
The Master's Seminary
Sun Valley, CA

rmayhue@mastersem.edu

Helpful Commentaries

Bruce, F.F. *1&2 Thessalonians* in *WBC*, v. 45 (Waco,TX: Word, 1982).

Calvin, John. *Calvin's Commentaries*, v. XXI (Grand Rapids: Baker, rpt. 1989).

Eadie, John. *A Commentary on the Greek Text of the Epistle of Paul to the Thessalonians* (Minneapolis, MN: James and Klock, rpt. 1977).

Frame, James Everett. *A Critical and Exegetical Commentary on the Epistles of St. Paul to the Thessalonians* in *ICC* (Edinburgh: T&T Clark, rpt. 1975).

Hendrickson, William. *Exposition of I and II Thessalonians* in *NTC* (Grand Rapids: Baker, 1955).

Hiebert, D. Edmond. *The Thessalonian Epistles* (Chicago: Moody, 1971).

Milligan, George. *St. Paul's Epistles to the Thessalonians* (Old Tappan, NJ: Revell, rpt. n.d.).

Morris, Leon. *The First and Second Epistles to the Thessalonians* in *NICNT* (Grand Rapids: Eerdmans, 1959).

Thomas, Robert. L. *1,2 Thessalonians* in *EBC*, v. 11 (Grand Rapids: Zondervan, 1978), 229-337.

Wanamacher, Charles A. *The Epistles to the Thessalonians* in *NIGTC* (Grand Rapids: Eerdmans, 1990).

A Time-line of Paul's Ministry*

	Pauline History		*Roman History*
		14-37	Tiberius emperor
c. 33	Paul's conversion		
c. 35	Paul's first post-salvation Jerusalem visit		
c. 35-46	Paul in Cilicia and Syria		
		37-41	Gaius emperor
		41-54	Claudius emperor
46	Paul's second Jerusalem visit		
47-48	Paul and Barnabas on first missionary journey		
48 ?	*Galatians*		
49	Council of Jerusalem and Paul's third Jerusalem visit	49	Jews expelled from Rome
49-52	Paul's second missionary journey		
49-50	Paul and Silas travel from Syrian Antioch through Asia Minor to Macedonia and Achaia		
50	*Thessalonian Epistles*		
50-52	Paul in Corinth	51-52	Gallio proconsul of Achaia
Summer 52	Paul's fourth Jerusalem visit		
52-56	Paul's third missionary journey		
		52-58	Felix procurator of Judea
52-55	Paul in Ephesus		
		54-68	Nero emperor
55-56	*Corinthian Epistles* Paul in Macedonia, Illyricum, and Achaia		
56	*Romans*		
Spring 56	Paul's last Jerusalem visit		
56-58	Paul's Caesarean imprisonment		
		58	Festus succeeds Felix as procurator of Judea
Fall 58	Paul's voyage to Rome commences		
Winter 59	Paul's arrival in Rome		
c. 59-61	Paul under house arrest in Rome *Ephesians, Philippians, Colossians,* and *Philemon*		
		62	Death of Festus; Albinus procurator of Judea
c. 61-64	Paul's final travels		
c. 62-63	*1 Timothy* and *Titus*		
		64	Rome burns
c. 64-66	Roman imprisonment, *2 Timothy,* and Paul's death		

*Adapted from F.F. Bruce, *Paul: Apostle of the Heart Set Free* (Grand Rapids: Eerdmans, 1977) 475.

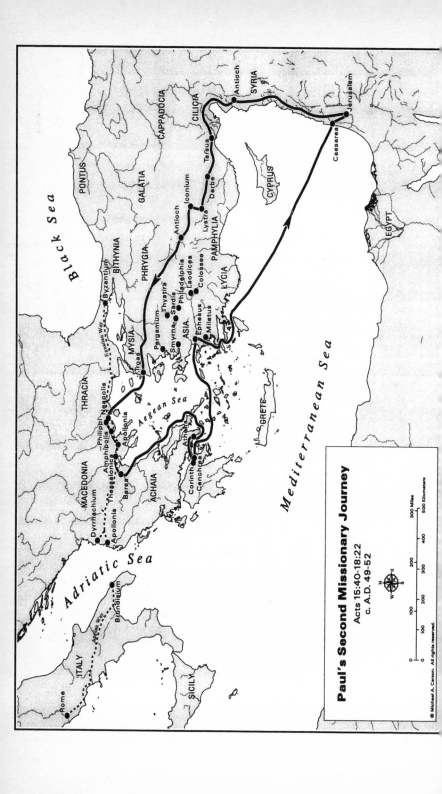

Paul's Second Missionary Journey

Acts 15:40-18:22
c. A.D. 49-52

© Michael A. Carson. All rights reserved.

Futuristic Premillennialism

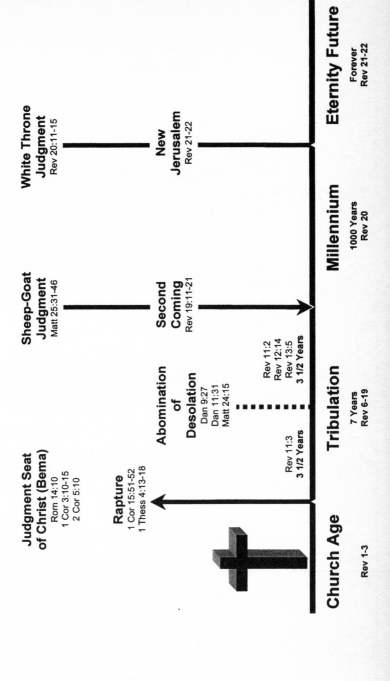

Abbreviations

AD	In the year of our Lord
BC	Before Christ
c.	Circa
cf.	Compare
CFP	Christian Focus Publications
chaps	Chapters
DOC	Day of Christ
DOL	Day of the Lord
EBC	Expositor's Bible Commentary
e.g.	For example
ff.	Following verses
ICC	International Critical Commentary
i.e.	That is
lit.	Literally
LXX	Septuagint
NASB	New American Standard Bible
NICNT	New International Commentary on the New Testament
NIDNTT	New International Dictionary of New Testament Theology
NIGTC	New International Greek Testament Commentary
NIV	New International Version
NKJV	New King James Version
NTC	New Testament Commentary
UBS[4]	United Bible Societies' GNT, 4th rev. ed., 1993
v.	verse
vv.	verses
WBC	Word Biblical Commentary

Introduction

The saga of Paul's Thessalonian experience and the continuing spread of the gospel from Asia to Europe begins in Acts 17, after Paul has traveled from Philippi on his second missionary journey. Resulting from his several month stay in Thessalonica, Paul formed a lifetime relationship with the church as her first pastor. He left the priceless legacy of his two correspondences for churches through the ages to study as a superlative example of evangelism and church planting, biblical shepherding, and doctrinal commitment. These so-called 'eschatological epistles' (because of their prophetic content) are equally rich with intimate insights into the proper relationship between a godly pastor and his committed flock.

Historical Background

The initial reference point for dating Paul's second missionary journey (about AD 49-52) is the Jerusalem Council (Acts 15:6-29) which occurred in early to mid-AD 49. Afterwards, Paul returned to Antioch for a time (Acts 15:30-35) and then decided to revisit the sites of his first journey (Acts 15:36). When Paul and Barnabas could not agree on whether to take John Mark or not (Acts 15:37-38), Barnabas sailed with John Mark for Cyprus (Acts 15:39). Paul afterward selected Silas, who had come from Jerusalem (Acts 15:27, 32, 34), and they set out for Syria and Cilicia (Acts 15:40-41).

When in Derbe, they invited Timothy to join them on their trip (Acts 16:1-3). They returned to the locations of Paul's previous ministry and strengthened the new believers (Acts 16:4-5). At this point, the Lord issued His famous Macedonia call to Paul and redirected the spread of the gospel west to Europe (Acts 16:6-10).

The party set out for Macedonia where they first ministered in Philippi (Acts 16:11-15; 1 Thess 2:2). After encountering severe spiritual opposition (Acts 16:16-18) plus illegal persecution and

imprisonment (Acts 16:19-34), this small band of courageous
ambassadors for Christ departed (Acts 16:35-40). During the
several months' ministry in Philippi, a small assembly of believers
had been established which numbered Lydia and her household,
the Philippian jailer and his family, plus others who must have
believed.

At Thessalonica (Acts 17:1-9)

Paul and his companions set out in late fall AD 49 from Philippi for
Thessalonica, which was an attractive commercial center in the
midst of a politically unique city with a significant Jewish
population. They traveled west on the Egnatian Way which
extended from Dyrrachium to the west on the Adriatic (modern
day Albania) to Byzantium and the Hellespont (Dardanelles Strait)
in the east (modern day Turkey). This stone highway was an
extension of the Appian Way in Italy and linked Rome with the
east, passing through both Thessalonica and Philippi.

They travelled southwest from Philippi to Amphipolis, about a
30-mile journey to this city which was located three miles from the
sea. From there, the journey continued southwest for approx-
imately another 30-35 miles to Apollonia and then west another
30-35 miles to Thessalonica. Overall, the journey was about 100
miles in length and took the better part of a week, if they walked.
Some have suggested that they might have used horses; it is
unknown whether they stayed in each location longer than just
overnight.

They arrived in the seaport of Thessalonica (modern day
Salonika) on the Thermaic Gulf (modern day Gulf of Salonica) at
the northern tip of the Aegean Sea. Thessalonica had been
originally founded by Cassander (one of Alexander's four
generals, cf. the four horns of Dan 8:22) c. 315 BC on or near the
ancient site of Therma and was populated by people from the
nearby villages. He named it after his wife who was Alexander's
step-sister.

In 168 BC, Thessalonica became the capital of the Roman
province of Macedonia. In 42 BC, it was accorded the status of a
'free city' because of loyalty to the Emperor. Thus, no Roman

soldiers were stationed here and the city had self-government (Acts 17:5-6). Because of its important location, the Roman proconsul resided here.

In Paul's day, the population would have approached 200,000. It ranked with Corinth in Achaia and Ephesus in Asia as a major shipping port. Thessalonica was known to the ancient world as 'the mother of Macedonia' and was said to be 'in the lap of the Roman Empire'.

Paul quickly sought out the Jewish synagogue as was his custom (cf. Damascus, Acts 9:20; Salamis, Acts 13:5; Pisidian Antioch, Acts 13:14; Iconium, Acts 14:1; Berea, Acts 17:10; Athens, Acts 17:17; Corinth, Acts 18:4; Ephesus, Acts 19:8) to declare that Jesus of Nazareth was the Old Testament Messiah (cf. Acts 9:20-22). Over a fifteen day span which included three Sabbaths, Paul preached Christ from the Old Testament to show that the Messiah had to suffer and then be resurrected. He did not merely declare the facts, but persuaded some by his reasoning, explanations, and demonstrations from Scripture. Undoubtedly, Paul recounted his personal encounter with the resurrected Christ on the road to Damascus (Acts 9:3-9).

It could well be that Paul's message here was similar to the message he preached at Pisidian Antioch on his first missionary journey (Acts 13:16-41). There he referred directly to Psalm 2:7 (Acts 13:33), Isaiah 55:3 (Acts 13:34), and Psalm 16:10 (Acts 13:35). He might also have quoted from Psalm 22 and Isaiah 53, or used Psalm 110:1 (Acts 2:34-35) as did Peter at Pentecost. The fruit of this two week ministry (Acts 17:4) came from among the ethnic Jews, the Greeks who embraced Judaism, and as usual a number of women (cf. Acts 16:13-15; 17:12, 34).

There seems certainly to have been an unmentioned, but significant, period of ministry to the Gentiles in Thessalonica between verses four and five of Acts 17. Apparently, after three Sabbaths, Paul turned to the Gentiles just as he had done at Pisidian Antioch (Acts 13:46; cf. Acts 9:15; 18:6; 22:21; 26:17; Gal 1:16; 2:7-8). This accounts for Paul's elaboration on his ministry in 1 Thessalonians 1:2-10, especially his comment about their turning to God from idols (1:9).

Some have questioned whether Paul's ministry exceeded three Sabbaths in length. For several compelling reasons, it strongly appears that Paul's ministry lasted about three to six months rather than just several weeks. First, the Philippian congregation had opportunity to send at least one, probably more than one, offering to Thessalonica (2 Cor 11:9; Phil 4:16) which could not have happened in a matter of a few weeks. Second, Paul stayed long enough that he had to work night and day to support himself and probably his whole group (1 Thess 2:9; 2 Thess 3:8). Third, the degree of pastoral care and concern indicated in 1 Thessalonians (cf. 2:1-12) could not have taken place over only three Sabbaths. Fourth, neither could the spiritual maturity of the flock be accounted for in just a few weeks' time (cf. 1 Thess 1:6-10).

At some point after Paul's three Sabbaths ministry in the synagogue and seemingly well into his subsequent ministry to the Gentiles, envy drove the Jews to discredit Paul and disrupt his ministry (Acts 17:5-9). They took evil men, who hung around the market place because they had nothing better to do, and formed a riotous mob with them which set the city in an uproar. Next, they sought Paul at Jason's house, where he apparently dwelt during his stay at Thessalonica. They intended to bring the missionaries out to 'the people' which could refer to the growing mob or possibly, but less likely, to the public assembly of the populace which existed in this 'free city'.

However, not finding Paul, they grabbed Jason (possibly the same Jason in Rom 16:21) and other new Christians. These believers were forcibly brought before 'the politarchs', a group of five-six men who ruled Thessalonica at the time. The charges of revolution, insurrection, treason, and sedition were hurled at these Christian men. First, they said that Paul arrived with a known history of insurrection elsewhere (Acts 17:6). They probably had no knowledge of Paul's past (in light of the long delay in reacting) and certainly used hyperbole for shock value in their highly pejorative charges of the men making trouble (cf. Dan 7:23 [LXX]; Acts 21:38; Gal 5:12). Second, they implicated Jason and the other Christian brethren as acting in complicity with Paul's revolutionary intentions (Acts 17:7). Third, they specifically indicted them for championing another king (or emperor) other than Caesar, in violation of Roman law (Acts 17:7). These false, but serious charges, understandably upset (cf. Matt 14:26; Gal 1:7) the crowd of people who had congregated and the group of city fathers.

Had Paul turned the world upside down? Little did they know with their exaggeration that one day Paul's message would reach Rome (Acts 28:16 ff.), and eventually the whole world. It was true (whether they knew it or not) that wherever Paul went and preached, it usually started trouble (cf. Acts 9 ff.). However, Paul's message was distinctly spiritual, not military, political, or economic in nature.

Had Paul preached Christ as king? Paul is never recorded as referring to Christ as king except in 1 Timothy (1:17; 6:15) which was written more than ten years later. However, he frequently wrote about the kingdom (19 times). Fifteen references are made to the kingdom of God, but four mentions, in varying ways, speak about the kingdom of Christ (Eph 5:5; Col 1:13; 2 Tim 4:1, 18). In light of the strong eschatological content of the Thessalonian epistles and their indication of Paul's initial teaching (cf. 2 Thess 2:5), he obviously talked about a coming king and kingdom from heaven that would ultimately eclipse any power on earth, including the Roman Empire and Emperor. But his message was not one of national revolt, rather spiritual redemption. Paul never advocated insurrection, but always promoted the right place for human government (cf. Rom 13:1-7).

The agitators took whatever (if anything) they knew of Paul's past and his message dramatically out of context in order to strike great concern in the hearts of the people. They did this knowingly in the immediate historical context of a strong anti-messianic spirit prevalent throughout the Roman Empire, which was occasioned by civil unrest at the hands of militant Jewish freedom fighters. Finally in AD 49, due to Jewish disturbances in Rome, the Emperor expelled all Jews from the city (cf. Aquila and Priscilla in Acts 18:2). The Thessalonian instigators used these broader circumstances, now in their 'free city' known for its loyalty to the Emperor, to provoke swift and severe punishment on those who dared to challenge the Jews on a religious basis, much like the Jews in Jerusalem did against Christ (Luke 23:2; John 19:12).

The scheme worked. Having heard the accusations and wanting to return the city to normal as quickly as possible, the politarchs exacted a 'security' from Jason which seemingly guaranteed that Paul and the missionaries would leave town immediately (Acts 17:9). Whether Jason had to put money on deposit, like bail, or make a verbal pledge is unknown for sure. But the outcome was certain; for after Jason and his Christian brothers were released, they immediately sent Paul and his party away by night to Berea (Acts 17:10).

If Paul thought that the Egnatian Way would soon lead him to Rome, his hopes were dashed for now, as he was detoured off the Way southwest to Berea. It would be almost ten years before he would arrive in Rome (Acts 28:16 ff.).

At Berea (Acts 17:10-13)

Having been officially evicted from Thessalonica (Acts 17:9), the party set out for Berea on a three-four day journey that would have covered 50-60 miles in the late winter or spring AD 50 (Acts 17:10). Although Timothy's name is not mentioned, it can be assumed that he came with them to Berea since it is later reported that he was in Berea (Acts 17:14).

When Paul opened the Old Testament Scriptures in the synagogue, he found a much different response than in Thessalonica. The Jews compared what they had in the Old Testament with what they heard from Paul to determine if his message was true or false (Acts 17:11). It appears there was a very fruitful response (Acts 17:12).

However, the news of Paul's success in Berea quickly reached Thessalonica; so the Jews from there rapidly deployed to Berea and provoked trouble as before (Acts 17:13). Apparently, Paul was the main focus of animosity, since he alone had to depart but was able to leave Silas and Timothy behind (Acts 17:14). After Paul safely arrived in Athens, he then summoned his two partners (Acts 17:15).

At Athens (Acts 17:14-34)

After being forced by the Thessalonian Jews to leave Berea, Paul most likely sailed to Athens from the port city of Dium on no more than a few days voyage (17:14). However, after completing the twenty-mile trip to the coast from Berea, he could have possibly walked the coastal highway to Athens, accompanied by his Berean friends. Silas and Timothy were temporarily left behind in Berea (17:14). Apparently, the Bereans who accompanied Paul to Athens returned home with a message for Silas and Timothy to rejoin Paul in Athens (17:15). This would have been springtime AD 50.

In the meantime, Paul being provoked by the idolatry of Athens began to preach in both the synagogue and the marketplace (17:16-17). Luke includes some details in Acts 17:18-31. After they rejected Paul's message (17:32-33) and only a handful of people believed (17:34), he departed to Corinth (18:1), which was about a fifty-mile journey either by sea or land. Paul's stay in Athens probably lasted no longer than several months, if that long.

Silas and Timothy had rejoined Paul in Athens sometime during this gospel ministry. It was from Athens that Paul and Silas dispatched Timothy back to Thessalonica (1 Thess 3:1-2); later Paul sent Silas to Philippi. Sometime afterwards, both Timothy and Silas rejoined Paul in Corinth (Acts 18:5). It is possible that Silas brought a gift from Philippi (cf. 2 Cor 11:9; Phil 4:15).

At Corinth (Acts 18:1-17)

Having either walked (50-55 miles) or sailed, Paul arrived in Corinth which was known for its commerce, but not culture like Athens (18:1), probably in early summer AD 50. Quickly he came across Aquila and Priscilla, fellow tentmakers by trade, who had been evicted from Rome with other Jews by the Emperor Claudius in AD 49 (Acts 18:2-3). As was his habit elsewhere, Paul first went to the synagogue where he reasoned about Messiah from the Old Testament Scriptures (18:4). The Apostle resided in Corinth for at least eighteen months (Acts 18:11).

Sometime early in his stay here, both Timothy (from Thessalonica) and Silas (from Philippi) rejoined Paul to minister with him. During this time, both 1 and 2 Thessalonians were written. Timothy's return with good news about the spiritual faithfulness of the Thessalonians (1 Thess 3:1-8) prompted the first letter. Later, having learned of some difficulties in the church, Paul wrote a second time to encourage, instruct, and confront.

Timothy arrived in Corinth most likely in late summer AD 50 and therefore 1 Thessalonians would surely have been written in that year. Second Thessalonians followed a few months later, and was written in late AD 50 or possibly early AD 51.

While Paul was in Corinth, the Jews brought him before Gallio, proconsul of Achaia, on religious charges. He wisely dismissed the accusation as spiritual wrangling not worthy of his time (Acts 18:12-17). The mention of Gallio is significant for dating purposes. An inscription from the city of Delphi, near Corinth in Achaia, mentions Gallio as proconsul. It was written sometime in the first half of AD 52. Therefore, it has generally been supposed that Gallio's period of oversight would have dated from July AD 51 to July AD 52. Thus, Paul's appearance before the judgment-seat would have been in the latter half of his Corinthian stay and after he had written the Thessalonian correspondence.

Additional Visits

At least four other visits to Thessalonica, after the arrival of 2 Thessalonians, by Paul and/or his companions for ministry purposes are recorded in Scripture. First, in the midst of Paul's third missionary journey while at Ephesus, he sent Timothy and Erastus into Macedonia (Acts 19:22). Both Thessalonica and Philippi would have been the most likely destinations. Paul apparently could not leave Ephesus but was concerned for their spiritual welfare as he had been earlier (Acts 18:5; 1 Thess 3:1-7).

Then, after Paul departed from Ephesus on his third missionary journey, but before he sailed from Philippi for Jerusalem, he visited Macedonia for the first and second times in person since his forced departure in Acts 17:9-10. Even though Paul could not immediately return (1 Thess 2:18), it appeared that after the magistrates of Acts 17 had left office several years later, Paul was once again permitted to visit Thessalonica. At least one of these visits had been anticipated in advance (Acts 19:21). Paul refers to these visits in the Corinthian epistles (1 Cor 16:5; 2 Cor 1:15, 16; 2:13; 7:5; 8:1). After the Ephesian riot had ended, Paul left for Macedonia where it can be assumed he visited Thessalonica (Acts 20:1). Later, having first travelled south to Greece, he returned for another personal visit (Acts 20:3) *en route* home.

Later, during his first Roman imprisonment, Paul hoped for another visit to Macedonia (Phil 1:27; 2:24). It appears from Paul's comments to Timothy (1 Tim 1:3) that Paul made at least one final visit to Macedonia, presumably Philippi and Thessalonica, before his second and final Roman imprisonment. It is most likely then that Paul made at least three personal visits back to Thessalonica for pastoral reasons (cf. 1 Thess 3:1-2, 10). The last known visit by a colleague of Paul does not appear to be prompted by ministry opportunities or concerns. During Paul's second Roman imprisonment, Demas deserted Paul for less than honorable reasons, and returned to what can be assumed was his home in Thessalonica (2 Tim 4:10).

Macedonian Friends
Although Paul must have had numerous friends and traveling companions from Thessalonica, the Scripture names only five. First, there was Jason (the closest Hellenized form of Jesus/Joshua) who gave lodging to Paul and his party on their first visit (Acts 17:5-8) and provided a way for Paul to leave peacefully after the uproar had subsided (Acts 17:9). The Jason in Romans 16:21 is possibly the Jason of Thessalonica.

Second, Gaius of Macedonia (most likely a Thessalonian) was seized along with Paul during the riot in Ephesus (Acts 19:29). This Gaius should be differentiated from Gaius of Derbe (Acts 20:4), Gaius of Corinth (Rom 16:23; 1 Cor 1:14), and Gaius the friend of John (3 John 1).

Third, there was a true Thessalonian named Secundus who accompanied Paul on at least a portion of the third missionary journey (Acts 20:4).

Fourth, Aristarchus (another known Thessalonian) was seized with Gaius and Paul in the Ephesus riot (Acts 19:29) and later travelled with Secundus and Paul during at least a portion of the third missionary journey (Acts 20:4). He also accompanied Paul on his voyage to Rome (Acts 27:2) and was later detained with Paul in his first Roman imprisonment (Col 4:10). It appears he was freed either before or after Paul wrote the Colossian letter (Phile 24).

Fifth, Demas apparently was from Thessalonica and had served Paul well in his first Roman imprisonment (Col 4:14; Phile 24) before he deserted Paul for the things of the world and returned home while Paul was incarcerated for a second and final time in Rome (2 Tim 4:10).

1 Thessalonians

Authorship
The apostle Paul identifies himself twice as the author of this first letter to the church at Thessalonica (1:1; 2:18). Silvanus (Silas) and Timothy, Paul's traveling companions on the second missionary journey when the Thessalonian church was founded (Acts 17:1-9), are also mentioned in Paul's greeting (1:1). Most of the first person plural pronouns in this epistle (we, us, our) refer to all three. However, during Timothy's visit back to Thessalonica, they refer only to Paul and Silvanus (3:1-2, 6).

Paul's authorship has not been questioned until recently by liberal scholars. The attempts of some to undermine the historically reliable acceptance of Pauline authorship fails in light of the combined weight of evidence favouring Paul, such as: (1) direct internal assertions of Paul's authorship (1:1; 2:18); (2) the letter's perfect correlation with Paul's travels in Acts 16–18; (3) the letter's multitude of intimate details regarding Paul; and (4) multiple, early, historical verifications.

Date
Timothy had been dispatched by Paul from Athens back to Thessalonica to check on the flock and encourage them in their faith (1 Thess 3:1-2, 5). Timothy returned to Paul at Corinth (Acts 18:5), bringing good news of their faith and love (1 Thess 3:6-8). In response to Timothy's good news, Paul penned 1 Thessalonians, most likely in fall AD 50, while at Corinth.

There is no indication that Paul is responding to a letter as in 1 Corinthians 7:1. Some have conjectured that Paul wrote from Athens (cf. Acts 17:15-34), but there is no evidence that Timothy returned to Paul at Athens. If Galatians was written before the Jerusalem Council (AD 49), then this is Paul's second epistle. If not, then this represents Paul's first canonical letter.

Audience

While Paul had a brief ministry to the Jews at Thessalonica (Acts 17:1-4), it appears that the broader scope and longer duration focused on the Gentiles (1 Thess 1:9-10). This would lead one to conclude that he wrote primarily to the Gentile converts and would account for the fact that Paul never quotes directly from the Old Testament. However, there are scores of allusions to the only Bible of their day as reference points for Paul's content. A few have suggested that the church was divided into a Gentile group and a Jewish group with 1 Thessalonians going to the Gentiles and 2 Thessalonians intended for the Jews. No credible evidence, internal or external, supports this hypothesis.

Purposes

Paul's reasons for writing flowed from his shepherd's heart which was concerned about the flock from which he had been separated. Some of Paul's purposes clearly include:

- encouraging the church (1:2-10)
- answering false allegations (2:1-12)
- comforting the persecuted church (2:13-16)
- expressing his joy in their faith (2:17-3:13)
- reminding them of the importance of moral purity (4:1-8)
- condemning the sluggard's lifestyle (4:11-12)
- correcting misunderstandings of future events (4:13-5:11)
- defusing potential tensions within the flock (5:12-15)
- exhorting them in the basics of Christian living (5:16-22)

Authenticity

Paul's letter to the Thessalonians is strongly attested to early and frequently. Some of these witnesses include:

1. The *Didache* (c. AD 125)
2. Marcion (c. AD 140)
3. Muratorian list (c. AD 180)
4. Irenaeus (c. AD 180)
5. Tertullian (c. AD 200)
6. Clement of Alexandria (c. AD 200)
7. Origen (c. AD 230)

The canonicity of 1 Thessalonians has never been seriously challenged. Were there other letters written to Thessalonica before this one? There is no evidence whatsoever to that end. It is true Paul corresponded with the Corinthians on more occasions than the two canonical letters (cf. 1 Cor 5:11; 2 Cor 2:3), but he mentioned that fact in his correspondence. There is no parallel in the Thessalonian letters except in 2 Thessalonians 2:15 which most naturally points to 1 Thessalonians.

Major Themes
Six major emphases can be detected in 1 Thessalonians:

1) an apologetic emphasis, i.e. the defense of the behavior of Paul and his co-workers;

2) an ecclesiastical emphasis, i.e. the portrayal of a healthy, growing church;

3) a pastoral emphasis, i.e. the example of shepherding activities and attitudes;

4) an eschatological emphasis, i.e. the focus on future events as the church's present hope;

5) a missionary emphasis, i.e. the importance of evangelism and church planting;

6) a spiritual emphasis, i.e. the centrality of sanctification in the Christian life.

There are several important subjects which Paul might have been expected to address, but in fact did not. They include: (1) church government and offices; (2) spiritual gifts; (3) family matters of the husband, wife, and children; (4) master and slave relationships; (5) church ordinances; and (6) great doctrinal essays such as those found in Romans and 1 Corinthians.

Theological Importance

First Thessalonians makes major contributions in several areas of doctrine:

    1) Bibliology (the study of the Bible), see 1 Thess 2:13;

    2) Ecclesiology (the study of the church), see 1 Thess 1:1–3:13;

    3) Eschatology (the study of future events), see 1 Thess 4:13–5:11;

    4) Soteriology (the study of salvation), see 1 Thess 1:5, 9-10; 5:9-10, 23-24.

In some cases, the contributions encompass clear, undeniable statements about a certain doctrine. At other times, the issues involve passages that at first glance are difficult to interpret. These latter issues are primarily eschatological and include: the coming wrath (1:10; 5:9); Christ's coming (2:19; 3:13; 4:15; 5:23); the events related to the rapture (4:13-18); and the meaning of the Day of the Lord (5:1-11).

2 Thessalonians

Authorship

As in 1 Thessalonians, Paul identifies himself twice as the author of this letter (1:1; 3:17). Silvanus (Silas) and Timothy, Paul's co-laborers in founding the church, are included also (1:1). The evidence, both within this letter and with regard to historical confirmation, strongly points to Paul as the only possible author. Objections to Pauline authorship based on internal factors, such as unusual vocabulary or style of writing, are not weighty enough to overturn this evidence. The substantiation of Pauline authorship is equally impressive in both letters.

Date

The occasion prompting 2 Thessalonians is not as clear biblically as it was for 1 Thessalonians (cf. 1 Thess 3:1-8). Apparently, Paul was aware of the happenings in Thessalonica through correspondence and/or couriers (cf. 'we hear', 3:11). The church had become more effective (1:3), but the pressure and persecution had enlarged as well. So, Paul wrote to his beloved flock which had been discouraged by persecution (ch. 1), deceived by false teachers (ch. 2), and disobedient to Paul's commands (ch. 3). In all likelihood, this letter follows several months after 1 Thessalonians, in late AD 50 or early AD 51.

Paul remained in Corinth when he wrote this second epistle. Some have suggested that Paul penned this from Ephesus (Acts 18:18-21), but his eighteen months stay in Corinth provided ample time for a follow-up letter to be authored.

In recent years, a few scholars have suggested the possibility that 2 Thessalonians was actually written prior to 1 Thessalonians. At least three reasons argue strongly against this. First, 2 Thessalonians 2:15 refers to a previous letter (most likely 1 Thessalonians), while 1 Thessalonians does not. Second, 1 Thessalonians 3:1-8 reports the occasion for the first letter and it is hard to imagine a letter written prior to this. Third, it is far more likely that the church progressed from less persecution to greater persecution with the passage of time, that doctrinal problems were few at the start but expanded with time, and that there were hints of sinful behavior towards the beginning which later grew into major sin requiring direct confrontation. This is, in fact, the progressive pattern when moving from 1 Thessalonians to 2 Thessalonians.

Audience
See discussion on First Thessalonians (page 25).

Purposes
Paul writes to bolster a church which is growing in the midst of painful trials. The purposes of this epistle are:

　　1) to comfort a persecuted church (1:3-12);

　　2) to correct a frightened and falsely-taught church about the future (2:1-12);

　　3) to confront a disobedient and undisciplined church (3:6-15).

Authenticity
Like 1 Thessalonians, this second epistle has impeccable, early credentials of affirmation. They include:

1. Ignatius (c. AD 110)
2. Polycarp (c. AD 135)
3. Justin Martyr (c. AD 140)
4. Marcion (c. AD 140)
5. Muratorian list (c. AD 180)
6. Irenaeus (c. AD 180)
7. Tertullian (c. AD 200)
8. Clement of Alexandria (c. AD 200)
9. Origen (c. AD 230)

Major Themes
Several emphases appear evident:

1) a pastoral emphasis, i.e. encouraging the saints in discouraging circumstances;

2) an eschatological emphasis, i.e. correcting prophetic error taught by false teachers;

3) an ecclesiastical emphasis, i.e. applying church discipline to flagrantly disobedient believers.

Theological Importance
Eschatology dominates the theological issues. It could well be that this letter is referred to later by Peter when he remarks, through Silas, that some of Paul's teaching is hard to understand (2 Pet 3:15-16). Eternal reward and retribution are discussed in 1:5-10 with such general terms that it is difficult to precisely identify some of the details with regard to time. Matters concerning the Day of the Lord (2:2), the restrainer (2:6-7), and the lawless one (2:3-4, 8-10) provide some of the most challenging prophetic material to interpret. One of the clearest statements on the fate of unbelievers is found in 1:9. Church discipline is the major focus of chapter three, which needs to be considered along with Matthew 18:15-20, 1 Corinthians 5:1-13, and Galatians 6:1-5 in order to get a more complete biblical picture.

1 THESSALONIANS

A Compassionate Letter to a Consecrated Church

A shepherd without sheep is like a leader without followers, a coach without a team, a president without an organization, or a captain without a ship. There is a sense of emptiness and a passionate longing to be back at one's station in life. So it was with Pastor Paul when he was painfully forced (2:17) to leave his beloved congregation of relatively new believers behind as a result of Jewish envy over his spiritual success (Acts 17:5-7) and political correctness exercised by the city fathers (Acts 17:8-9).

To ease his agony, Paul sent Timothy from Athens back to Thessalonica on a mission to see how the church had fared since his involuntary departure (3:5) and to strengthen their faith (3:1-2). When Paul's young disciple returned to Corinth (Acts 18:5) with an encouraging report of their faith and love, not to mention growing affection for their exiled pastor, Paul gave thanks to the Lord (3:6-9). Yet, he deeply and passionately beseeched God that he might return, knowing that their spiritual need would continue with passing time (3:10).

But since he could not be with them in the near future, Paul did the next best thing and wrote First Thessalonians as a compassionate letter to this consecrated assembly. In so doing, Paul had two major objectives in mind: first, he expressed himself *personally* over: (1) his affection for them; (2) his reflections on their progress in the gospel; (3) false allegations about his integrity; (4) his concern for their spiritual well being; and (5) his desire to one day return in person (1:1-3:13). Second, the apostle addressed them *pastorally* about issues that Timothy surely must have included in his post-visit debriefing (4:1-5:28).

1. PERSONAL COMMENTS 1:1-3:13

Paul was so overjoyed with Timothy's most encouraging news of a healthy, vibrant church (3:6-8), albeit a persecuted church (2:14-15), that he put pleasure before business and wrote from the heart in the first three chapters of this letter (just about one half of what Paul penned). From 1:1–2:16, he thought back and *reflected* on his prior experiences with them and their subsequent progress in the gospel. Then, he *updated* them on events and his thoughts that had transpired since he departed (2:17-3:13).

A. Paul's Greeting (1:1)

Paul, Silvanus, and Timothy, to the church of the Thessalonians in God the Father and the Lord Jesus Christ: Grace to you and peace from God our Father and the Lord Jesus Christ (1:1).

1:1 This represents a typical salutation in the first century AD (cf. Acts 15:23; 23:26) with three parts: the writer(s); the recipient(s); and the greeting(s). The three chief participants in the second missionary journey appear in Paul's opening words. It would seem apparent that these are the ones whom the Thessalonians would have identified as their first pastors, **Paul** being the leader and thus first in the greeting. The apostle's sense of ministry being a team activity would best account for all three names being included here, rather than the thought that this letter was somehow written by them all.

The ministry of **Paul**, former Saul (meaning 'asked for', cf. 1 Sam 9:2) of Tarsus (cf. Acts 7:58; 8:1-3; 9:1-2), dominates the book of Acts. This man, whose Roman name Paul means 'small', was identified with the Jewish name Saul by which he is known until Acts 13:9 when Luke writes that he was also called Paul. Never again in Acts after 13:9 (except in recounting the past) is he referred to as Saul. Most likely, in accord with the custom of the day and because Paul was a Jew born as a Roman citizen (cf. Acts 22:28), he was given both names at birth by his parents. When he began his ministry to the Gentiles, Paul became the preferred name.

Paul's dramatic conversion (c. AD 33) from a self-righteous, Christian-killing, and church-destroying Pharisee to a true believer in Messiah is recounted three times in Acts (9:1-22; 22:1-21; 26: 1-18). See *A Time-line of Paul's Ministry* (page 11) for a summary of his four missionary journeys, thirteen epistles, and two Roman imprisonments. Other autobiographical details emerge in bits and pieces from his epistles (cf. 2 Cor 11:16-12:10; Gal 1:11-2:21: Phil 3:4-6; 1 Tim 1:12-17).

The apostle's physical stature has been described by one ancient as 'a man of small stature, with a bald head and crooked legs, in a good state of body, with eyebrows meeting and nose somewhat hooked, full of friendliness; for now he appeared like a man, and now he had the face of an angel' (*Acts of Paul* and *Thecla* 3). But, whatever Paul might have lacked in outward appearance, he more than made up for it in natural abilities and spiritual endowments. This man, who called himself the foremost sinner (1 Tim 1:15) and the least of saints (Eph 3:8), stands unique in the annals of Christendom as one who combined the fervor of an evangelist/church planter, the tenderness of a shepherd, the diplomacy of an ambassador, and the intellect of a scholar. In light of his stellar credentials, he surprisingly did not introduce himself as an apostle (cf. 2:7), even though he does in later letters (Rom 1:1; 1 Cor 1:1; 2 Cor 1:1; Gal 1:1; Eph 1:1; Col 1:1) where there was not a prior intimate relationship.

Above all else that could be said about Paul, he was commissioned by God to go to the Gentiles with God's gospel of grace (Acts 9:15; 22:21; 26:20, 23). To the heavenly commission, he proved obedient as demonstrated by his ministry (Acts 13:46-47; 14:27; 15:3, 12; 18:6; 21:19; 28:28) and declared in his letters (2:16; cf. Gal 1:16, 23; Eph 3:8; 1 Tim 2:7; 2 Tim 4:17). Thus, Paul turned to the Gentiles in Thessalonica (cf. 1:9-10) after only three Sabbaths in the synagogue (Acts 17:2).

Silvanus, a Roman name meaning 'woodland' (only in 1:1; 2 Cor 1:19; 2 Thess 1:1; 1 Pet 5:12), is called Silas in his other thirteen New Testament mentions by Luke in Acts. He is first encountered in Jerusalem at the Council which decided on crucial matters relating to Gentiles and the Law (Acts 15:1-29). As a leading man (Jewish by birth) in the Jerusalem congregation (Acts 15:22), he with Judas (both prophets, Acts 15:32) accompanied Paul and Barnabas back to Antioch with a letter declaring the Council's decisions (Acts 15:32).

Silas, also a Roman citizen (Acts 16:37), either remained in Antioch (cf. Acts 15:34) or, after going back to Jerusalem, returned to Antioch and was therefore selected by Paul to go on the second missionary journey (Acts 15:40). He is mentioned by Luke in conjunction with visits to Philippi (Acts 16:19, 25, 29), Thessalonica (Acts 17:4), Berea (Acts 17:10), Athens (3:1; Acts 17:15), and Corinth (Acts 18:5; 2 Cor 1:19). After the second missionary journey, Silas does not appear to have been involved with Paul in ministry again. He apparently later became the secretary to Peter (1 Pet 5:12) which probably accounts for the Apostle's warm words towards Paul in his second letter (2 Pet 3:15).

The final member of this ministerial trio, **Timothy** (meaning 'honoring God'), became Paul's chief disciple (Phil 2:19-22; 2 Tim 2:2; 4:1-8), even though here he is on his first journey with Paul, having been 'well spoken of' by the brethren in Derbe and Iconium (Acts 16:1-3). Since Paul elsewhere speaks of him as 'a true son in the faith' (1 Tim 1:2; 2 Tim 1:2), it is possible that Timothy believed at Paul's preaching on the first missionary · journey (Acts 13-14), even though he was raised by a godly mother and grandmother (Acts 16:1; 2 Tim 1:5; 3:14-15). Timothy's father was an unbelieving Greek (Acts 16:1).

Timothy remained faithful to Paul from the beginning (Acts 16:1-2) to the end (2 Tim 4:21). Paul dispatched him on the second journey to Thessalonica (3:2); on the third journey to Corinth (Acts 19:22; 1 Cor 4:17; 16:10); to Philippi during the first Roman house arrest (Phil 2:19); and to Ephesus during Paul's final travels (1 Tim 1:3). He is named in the salutation, not only in both Thessalonian letters, but also in 2 Corinthians, Philippians, Colossians, Philemon, and even Romans 16:21. Paul also wrote two canonical letters to Timothy. At some time, Timothy was imprisoned and later released (Heb 13:23), presumably after Paul's death.

Paul very specifically identifies the recipients as **the church[1] of the Thessalonians in God the Father and the Lord Jesus Christ** (cf. 2 Thess 1:1). This addresses his beloved flock corporately, geographically, and spiritually.

As a group of people they were **the church** (*ekklēsia*) or, literally, the 'called out assembly'. The word *ekklēsia* can refer to either a secular or religious gathering. It is used in the New Testament: (1) of the riotous mob in Ephesus (Acts 19:32, 39, 41); (2) sparingly of Israel (Acts 7:38; Heb 2:12); (3) frequently of a local church (Acts 5:11; Rom 16:5; Col 4:15); (4) of churches in a geographical region (1 Cor 16:19; Gal 1:2); and (5) of the universal church (1 Cor 12:28; Eph 1:22; Col 1:24).

---

1. See Richard Mayhue, *What Would Jesus Say About Your Church?* (Ross-shire, Scotland: CFP, 1995).

Specifically, this was the company of those who had been called out of sin unto salvation, out of darkness into light, and out of idolatry into worship of the true God (cf. 1:9). With rare exceptions, *church* in the New Testament refers to the gathering of true believers in the Lord Jesus Christ.

Paul very carefully identifies this church geographically as **of the Thessalonians**. A similar designation is used 'of the Laodiceans' (Col 4:16). The local church was made up of those from Thessalonica who had believed in Christ, whether they be Jew or Gentile, free or slave, male or female.

The most important qualification in identifying the group to whom he wrote is that they were **in God the Father and the Lord Jesus Christ**. This would spiritually distinguish them from the Jews of the synagogue who rejected Jesus as Messiah (Acts 17:5) and the civic assembly of the people who believed Christianity to be politically subversive (Acts 17:8-9). These were people who had a special redemptive relationship with both God the Father and the Lord Jesus Christ (cf. John 17:21, 23; Gal 3:3; Eph 1:4, 7, 13). The Father and the Son (cf. 1:10) are inseparable (Matt 11:27-30; John 14:6; 1 John 2:23).

The close proximity of **God the Father** (cf. 1:3; 3:11, 13) and the **Lord Jesus Christ** and His equality with the Father point directly to the deity of Christ. The triune relationship of Father, Son, and Holy Spirit is assumed, since Paul will shortly speak of the Holy Spirit in 1:5.

Paul indicates three truths about the Savior by using His full title, the **Lord Jesus Christ** (cf. 1:3; 5:9, 23, 28). First, He is **Lord** (*kurios*) or Jehovah of the Old Testament, which points to His deity. Next, as **Jesus**, He is declared to be human; His earthly name means 'Jehovah saves' (cf. Matt 1:21). Third, as **Christ** He is the long promised Messiah or Anointed One of the Old Testament (cf. Isa 61:1-2a; John 1:41). Paul's twenty-four uses of **Lord**, sixteen uses of **Jesus**, and ten uses of **Christ** in 1 Thessalonians portray the richness of Christ revealed in His true character.

Having thoroughly identified the recipients of this letter, the apostle briefly, but warmly, greets them with a typical Pauline remark – **Grace to you and peace**. Some Greek manuscripts additionally have the phrase **from God our Father and the Lord Jesus Christ**. It is easier to explain this as a later addition by scribes, since every other Pauline letter gives a similar greeting and states the source of grace and peace, than it is to explain a later deletion, especially in light of Paul's pattern. The same sort of scribal addition appears in Colossians 1:2. However, 2 Thessalonians 1:2 does contain the full greeting.

Grace (from God) or God's unmerited favor is the Divine benevolence by which Christians are saved (cf. Eph 2:8-9) and **peace** (with God) is the fruit of no longer being at enmity with God (Eph 2:16-17) and thus no longer in danger of His eternal wrath (cf. 1:10; 5:9). God the Father is 'the God of peace' (5:23; 2 Thess 3:16); God the Son is 'the Prince of peace' (Isa 9:6); and God the Holy Spirit produces the fruit of peace in the lives of true believers (Gal 5:22). God's peace stands in stark contrast to the counterfeit peace preached by false teachers (5:3). Paul here evokes God's blessing upon this precious congregation.

OVERVIEW

The Thessalonian Church (1:1)

The Apostle's intimate correspondence to the church, which he dearly loved, reveals the basic fibre of the Thessalonian assembly. These letters let one look below the surface, examine the very heart of the flock, and identify twelve important hallmarks.

1. Committed Church

To each of the seven churches of Asia, Christ remarked, 'I know your works'. Just as Jesus commended the church at Ephesus for her 'deeds', 'toil', and 'perseverance', Paul commends the Thessalonians for their work, labor, and steadfastness (1 Thess 1:2-3). The same three Greek words are used in both instances to describe these two churches.

'Faith' in Christ had produced works, just as God had designed the outcome of salvation: 'For we are His workmanship, created in Christ Jesus for good works, which God prepared beforehand, that we should walk in them' (Eph 2:10). As newly redeemed bondservants, they gladly worked on behalf of their Lord Jesus.

'Love' for Christ took their works to a deeper level called labor or toil.

Because of Christ's sacrifice on their behalf, they now sacrificed on His behalf. They spared nothing in their spiritual service, always working to the point of exhaustion.

'Hope' towards Christ's return produced the ultimate level of commitment, i.e. steadfastness or perseverance. They would stay with their kingdom labor on earth until their Lord and Master called them away to be with Him in heaven. They would be found at their Christ-appointed service until the end.

The Thessalonians committed themselves to gospel service. Not satisfied with ordinary or average work, they labored long and hard on Christ's behalf. They intended to do this as long as it pleased Christ.

Their commitment proved genuine. After Paul sent Timothy to strengthen them, he returned with a wonderful report of their 'faith' and 'love' (1 Thess 3:6). Even more telling, Paul commends the Thessalonians in his second letter because their faith was greatly enlarged and their love for one another had grown greater (2 Thess 1:3).

2. Submitted Church

'You became followers of us and of the Lord' (1 Thess 1:6). As Hebrews 13:7 exhorts, the Thessalonians imitated the faith of their spiritual father and his associates. They lived out Paul's admonition to the Corinthian church: 'Imitate me, just as I also imitate Christ' (1 Cor 11:1).

As children submit to and obey their father and mother, so did the Thessalonians to their spiritual parents. But the Thessalonians' submission went a step further. They would have found it easy to submit in good times; however, their submission also came in a time of persecution and hardship.

Paul notes that they received the Word in much tribulation (1 Thess 1:6). The church began with instant spiritual conflict (Acts 17:1-9) and seemingly never knew a moment of peace, but continued in persecution. Because of these obstacles and distractions, the church suffered the same way as did the churches of Judea earlier (1 Thess 2:14). They were submissive at the highest level.

3. Reproducing Church

The Thessalonians took Christ's Great Commission seriously (Matt 28:18-20). Having first been an example to other believers, they then spread the gospel wherever they went (1 Thess 1:7-8). The gospel spread in the city of Thessalonica, the region of Macedonia, beyond to Achaia, and wherever else the Thessalonians travelled outside of their own national boundaries.

Although the text does not explicitly say so, a little sanctified imagination can picture the Thessalonians discipling other believers and evangelizing unbelievers. Undoubtedly, other churches came into being because of their spreading the gospel.

4. Repentant Church

The Thessalonians had turned from the false to the true God in their salvation (1 Thess 1:9). Their 180 degree turn, spiritually speaking, involved completely turning away from idols and completely turning towards God (Acts 11:18; 2 Cor 7:10).

Unlike the church at Sardis, which claimed to be alive although Jesus declared her to be dead (Rev 3:1-2), the Thessalonian church had actually been dead but was now alive. They had been converted by gospel preaching (1 Thess 1:5), then opposed false religion rather than participated in it (Acts 17:5-9), and openly declared their allegiance to the Lord Jesus Christ (1 Thess 1:8).

5. Serving Church

The Thessalonians understood that service to God befitted their new status of being Christians (1 Thess 1:9). Christ is Lord and they were His servants. While they remained on the earth, they were not to attempt to make God their servant or indulge themselves in the wealth of the world. Rather, they now would serve God rather than mammon (Matt 6:24).

Paul's example had been to serve the Lord (Acts 20:19). He instructed the Colossian church, 'For you serve the Lord Christ' (Col 3:24). When one had a perfect Master, the only reasonable and spiritual response was to serve Him.

6. Patient Church

With confident expectancy, the Thessalonians awaited Jesus' return (1 Thess 1:10). He promised 'I will come again' (John 14:3). The angels proclaimed, 'This same Jesus, who was taken up from you into heaven, will so come in like manner as you saw Him go into heaven' (Acts 1:11).

The Thessalonian church was a 'second coming' church. Their hope rested in the glorious thought that one day Christ would return and deliver them from a sin-filled world. The Thessalonian believers, like the believers on Crete, were looking for the blessed hope and the appearing of the glory of our great God and Savior, Christ Jesus (Titus 2:13).

7. Accepting Church

How can we explain such radical change in people's lives as was seen in the Thessalonians? How does a church mature as fast as the Thessalonian assembly? By the power of God's Word working in them (1 Thess 2:13). They began with God's Word (Acts 17:1-3) and they continued in God's Word. They didn't doubt, hesitate, accept some and reject some; rather, they completely accepted Paul's message as God's message.

God's Word is the power of God to save (Rom 1:16; 1 Cor 1:18). God's Word is the power by which Christians grow (1 Pet 2:1-3; 2 Pet 3:18). God's Word goes forth with a promise that it will accomplish God's bidding (Isa 55:11). This power by which God works in us is able to do exceedingly abundantly beyond all that we can ask or think (Eph 3:20).

8. Persecuted Church

No one actively seeks out persecution. While it seemed to purify the church at Smyrna, persecution could not fully cleanse Pergamum. Suffering comes by the will of God (1 Pet 3:17; 4:19) and is not normal for all churches. But persecution quickly found the Thessalonians (1 Thess 2:14-16).

Time did not diminish the pain and conflict. In his second letter Paul writes, 'so that we ourselves boast of you among the churches of God for your patience and faith in all your persecutions and tribulations that you endure' (2 Thess 1:4).

Suffering for righteousness' sake finds favor with God (1 Pet 2:20). Suffering as a Christian glorifies God (1 Pet 4:16); being reviled for the name of Christ brings blessing (1 Pet. 4:14).

This wonderful promise awaits those who now suffer on behalf of Christ: 'But may the God of all grace, who called us to His eternal glory by Christ Jesus, after you have suffered a while, perfect, establish, strengthen, and settle you' (1 Pet 5:10).

9. Staunch Church

When Timothy returned to Paul, he reported that the Thessalonians were 'standing firm' (1 Thess 3:8). The church had started in the midst of spiritual warfare and had grown in the same environment. They were battle-hardened veterans from the beginning. Even though the church had existed for less than a year when Paul wrote, the believers exhibited maturity beyond their years.

The Thessalonians refused any spiritual retreat. They stood their ground without compromise. Because they burned their secular bridges behind them, the only way to go was forward. While the enemy would not always allow them to advance, the Thessalonians purposed not to give up the ground that had already been gained for them by Christ.

10. God-Pleasing Church

Obedient churches please God as did the Thessalonians (1 Thess 4:1). Pleasing God is an important part of salvation's fruit:

> For it is God who works in you both to will and to work on behalf of His good pleasure (Phil 2:13).

> Now may the God of peace who brought up our Lord Jesus from the dead, that great Shepherd of the sheep, through the blood of the everlasting covenant, make you complete in every good work to do His will, working in you what is well pleasing in His sight, through Jesus Christ, to whom be glory for ever and ever. Amen (Heb 13:20-21).

Paul's top ambition was to please the Lord (2 Cor 5:9). Jesus testified, 'I always do those things that please Him' (John 8:29).

11. Loving-the-brethren Church

Loving is the most often mentioned 'one another' in Scripture. On at least ten other occasions the same activity is addressed (Rom 12:10; 13:8; 1 Thess 3:12; 4:9; 2 Thess 1:3; 1 Pet 1:22; 1 John 3:11, 23; 4:7, 11; 2 John 5).

Jesus said, 'By this all men will know that you are My disciples, if you have love one for another' (John 13:35). This contrasting truth is also taught, 'Owe no one anything except to love one another, for he who loves another has fulfilled the law' (Rom 13:8).

Even as well as the Thessalonians must have been doing, Paul exhorts, 'Increase more and more' (1 Thess 4:10). The church needed to grow continually in love towards one another.

12. Praying Church

Paul had great opportunities to preach the gospel. He understood that evangelism needs to be undergirded by effective prayer. So he asked the Thessalonians to pray for his ministry that the Word of God would spread rapidly and be glorified, just as it had been in the beginning at Thessalonica (2 Thess 3:1).

A more important prayer request could not have been rendered. Therefore, one can conclude that the Thessalonians had already demonstrated their faithfulness to an earnest ministry of prayer. Thus, Paul could entrust this supremely important matter to their prayer ministry.

B. Paul's Reminiscences (1:2-2:16)

Paul begins his first letter by remembering what transpired in the few short months he ministered in Thessalonica. He rehearses: (1) the birth and growth of the church (1:2-10); (2) the integrity of his ministry team (2:1-12); and (3) the Thessalonians' faithfulness in his absence (2:13-16). Undoubtedly, this literary journey through the recent past brought much joy to the apostle as he reflected on what God had done. It must have also greatly encouraged him to think that the Lord could do the same kind of things again in spite of his present, difficult circumstances in pagan, immoral Corinth (cf. Acts 18:1-18).

1. The church's birth and growth (1:2-10)

After Paul informs the Thessalonians about his ministry team's current prayers, which were prompted by their past faithful response to the Lord (1:2-4), he then pictures the events which launched the ministry and what had resulted from God's work in their lives (1:5-10). He dynamically describes the complementary, sovereign work of God in salvation (1:4b), the evangelistic ministry of Paul's team preaching the gospel (1:5), and the resulting human response by the elect (1:6-10). Paul's pen paints a real-life picture of what Jesus' Great Commission looks like when it is faithfully obeyed (cf. Matt 28:18-20).

1:2 *Paul and his companions praying* (1:2-4).

We give thanks to God always for you all, making mention of you in our prayers, remembering without ceasing your work of faith, labour of love, and patience of hope in our Lord Jesus Christ in the sight of our God and Father, knowing, beloved brethren, your election by God (1:2-4).

Paul was not exaggerating when he wrote **we give thanks**. Throughout the epistle, Paul primarily talks about 'we', 'us', and 'our' to reflect the fact that he spoke on behalf of Silas and Timothy in truly reflecting their heart attitudes and ministry activities. It was like a father writing on behalf of his family. On rare occasions, he reverts to 'I' when he speaks of something unique to himself (cf. 2:18; 3:5) or when the fact that he actually wrote the letter comes out (5:27). As a ministry team, they lived out their own preaching (cf. 5:18) by engaging in habitual thanksgiving according to the will of God.

Their expression of gratitude did not occur randomly or sporadically and Paul did not embellish the record by writing **we give thanks to God always.** The language and grammar point in the strongest way to the regular habit of giving thanksgiving **to God** by Paul, Silas, and Timothy for the Thessalonians (2 Thess 1:3, 11; 2:13). We can assume it was daily, if not more frequent during the day. This does not indicate an exclusive act nor an unbroken task, but rather a faithful, regular pattern of thanksgiving (cf. 2:13; 3:9; 2 Thess 1:3; 2:13), which included every believer since Paul indicated **for you all.** No one was excluded; nor did they pray only for favorites.

Paul predictably gave thanks to the Lord at the beginning of his letters to churches (cf. Rom 1:8; 1 Cor 1:4-8; Eph 1:15-16; Phil 1:3-5; Col 1:3-6; 2 Thess 1:3). Only 2 Corinthians and Galatians, which are letters of severe correction, lack Paul's usual report of thanksgiving.

The *spiritual occasion* for thanksgiving came during Paul and his associates' **prayers**. It doesn't mean that they didn't express their gratitude at other times, but the most important thanksgiving was given **to God** who enacted and enabled the Thessalonians' conversion (cf. Heb 13:15).

Paul introduces the subject of prayer at least thirteen times in these two letters. On four occasions, he reminds his flock that he has and is praying for them (1:2-4; 3:9-10; 2 Thess 1:3; 2:13). Most frequently (six times), Paul is found praying for his beloved flock (3:11-13; 5:23, 28; 2 Thess 1:11-12; 2:16-17; 3:5, 16, 18). Twice, Paul's need for the church to pray for him surfaces (5:25; 2 Thess 3:1-2). Only once does the pastor instruct his people on how to pray (5:16-18).

On all but one occasion, Paul refers to prayer with the most commonly used New Testament word (*proseuchomai*) because it can versatilely refer to supplication, intercession, praise, or adoration, depending on the context. The one occasion where he deviates in language, Paul uses *deomai* to describe his own urgent, beseeching prayer before God to be able to return to Thessalonica and again resume his pastoral role in person (3:9-10). The apostle prayed with a begging-like passion and intensity.

1:3 The *particular focus* of their thanksgiving was upon **remembering** the fruit of salvation in the Thessalonian assembly. Their recall was **without ceasing** (2:13; 5:17), which meant at frequent intervals but not without cessation. This word was used in ancient literature of someone with a cough. Paul had learned from Timothy that the Thessalonians remembered them in a similar way (cf. 3:6). Their recall was also **in the sight of our God and Father**, which literally means 'in the presence of' (cf. 2:19; 3:9, 13). This can refer to the omniscience of God who would hear their prayer and/or the immanence of God which means He was not detached from life.

He first comments on their **works of faith** or better put, their faith which produced works. Paul speaks here of the ministry which resulted from their personal faith in Christ (1:8; 3:2, 5-7; 5:8) so that they served the living and true God (cf. 1:9). That true faith works fruitful obedience was also taught by our Lord (Matt 13:23; John 15:1-8) and by James (2:14-26). Paul knew that their fruit was not yet complete (3:10) but it was healthy and flourishing (2 Thess 1:3-4).

Next comes their **labor of love** or love which prompted their labor. So intense was their love for God (cf. 1 John 4:10, 19) that they ministered to the point of being exhausted and weary. Paul extols the characteristic of sacrificial love elsewhere (1 Cor 13:1-7). See *Overview* 'True Love' (5:13).

Finally, Paul remembers well their **patience of hope in** the **Lord Jesus Christ** or their hope which produced patience (2 Thess 1:4). Their **hope** in God's promise for eternal life (5:8), as validated by the **Lord Jesus Christ**'s resurrection, energized them to be patient under a heavy load and endure their current hardships and persecutions. That is why they patiently and expectantly waited for God's Son to return to earth from heaven (1:10; cf. John 14:1-3).

Their faith in Christ had been validated by their works; their love of God had been demonstrated by strenuous labor on His behalf; and their hope of eternal life had been expressed by patient endurance in the midst of trial and tribulation. It is no wonder that faith, love, and hope were favorite Pauline subjects (cf. 5:8; Rom 5:2-5; 1 Cor 13:13; Gal 5:5-6; Col 1:4-5).

OVERVIEW

What Does the Future Hold? (1:3)

The Thessalonian letters have been labeled 'the eschatological epistles', and for good reason. About 26% of 1 Thessalonians or 23 of 89 verses deal with the future (1:3, 10; 2:19; 3:13; 4:13-18; 5:1-11, 23). Exactly 40% of 2 Thessalonians or 19 of 47 verses are prophetically related (1:5-10; 2:1-12, 16). Thus, almost one third of these two letters is eschatological in content (42 of 136 verses). God's prophetic promises to the church gave them a future hope which prompted their present patience.

The prophetic content could be outlined in the following manner:

1. KEY PERSONS

A. Christ

1. resurrection	(1 Thess 1:10; 4:14)
2. parousia	(1 Thess 2:19; 3:13; 4:15; 5:23; 2 Thess 2:1, 8)
3. revelation	(2 Thess 1:7)

B. Believers

1. hope	(1 Thess 1:3, 10; 2 Thess 3:16)
2. death	(1 Thess 4:13-16)
3. resurrection	(1 Thess 4:14-16)
4. Bema	(1 Thess 3:13; 5:23 – implied)
5. glorification	(1 Thess 3:13; 5:23)
6. eternity with Christ	(1 Thess 4:17; 5:10)

C. Unbelievers

1. judgment	(2 Thess 1:5-6; 2:12)
2. wrath	(1 Thess 1:10; 2:16; 5:9)
3. everlasting destruction	(2 Thess 1:9)

D. Antichrist

1. revelation	(2 Thess 2:3, 6, 8)
2. activities	(2 Thess 2:3-4, 6, 8-10)

2. KEY SUBJECTS

    A. Kingdom of God   (1 Thess 2:12; 2 Thess 1:5)
    B. Rapture   (1 Thess 4:17; 2 Thess 2:1)
    C. Day of the Lord   (1 Thess 5:2; 2 Thess 2:2)
    D. Daniel's Seventieth Week   (1 Thess 5:2-3; 2 Thess 2:7-12)

Paul's prophetic instruction in this correspondence was not intended to be unabridged or systematic in nature. Rather, Paul applied his eschatology to various life circumstances that the Thessalonians faced and he built on what they already knew (1 Thess 5:1-2; 2 Thess 2:5). Thus, Paul does not deal with (1) the marriage feast of the Lamb (Rev 19:1-9); (2) the Millennium (Rev 20:1-10); and (3) the New Jerusalem (Rev 21:1-22:21).

1:4 Paul concludes the introductory remarks by acknowledging that the *redemptive basis* for their thanksgiving was God's election of the Thessalonian believers to eternal life through faith in the Lord Jesus Christ (5:9; 2 Thess 2:13). The shepherd addresses his flock as **beloved brethren**. The term **brethren** appears nineteen times in 1 Thessalonians (more than any other epistle except 1 Corinthians) and is employed generically, referring to both male and female believers who, like Paul, have been adopted into the eternal family of God (Gal 4:5; Eph 1:5). This is Paul's only elaboration on the nature of the brethren; they are **beloved** (cf. 2 Thess 2:13). It appears from the best Greek manuscripts that the phrase **by God** goes with **beloved**; then, it is implicit that God also elects (see NASB and NIV, although it is explicit in 2 Thess 2:13).

    That which made the brethren so special to Paul is that they were beloved by God as evidenced by their divine **election** (*eklegomai; eklektos; eklogē*) to salvation. This word group for **election** is used frequently to speak of God's initiating, sovereign choice of those sinners whom He would save by His grace (Acts 9:15; Rom 8:33; Eph 1:4; Col 3:12; 2 Tim 2:10; Titus 1:1; James 2:5; 1 Pet 1:1-2; 2 Pet 1:10). Romans 11:5, 7, 28 use this same language concerning the Jews who would be saved as a believing remnant of Israel. God's election is individual, not corporate. Paul's **knowing** came from the Thessalonians' doing (1:6-10;

2:13) as they burst forth with the fruit of true repentance (cf. Matt 3:8; Acts 26:20).

OVERVIEW

God's Role in Salvation (1:4)

Who is responsible for individual salvation – God or the person? Put another way, 'Did God sovereignly elect us and save us? Or did He act in accord with what He knew we would do?' In other words, 'Who makes the first move?'

The following material summarizes what Scripture teaches about God's role in salvation. Look up each passage to sense the overwhelming nature of God being the 'first cause' or initiator of a believer's salvation.

God wills	John 1:12-13; Eph 1:5,11
God draws	John 6:44
God grants	John 6:65
God calls	1 Thess 2:12; 2 Thess 2:14; 2 Tim 1:9; 1 Pet 2:9
God appoints	Acts 13:48; 1 Thess 5:9
God predestines	Rom 8:29; Eph 1:5,11
God prepares	Rom 9:23
God causes	1 Cor 1:30
God chooses	1 Thess 1:4; 2 Thess 2:13; Eph 1:4
God purposes	Eph 1:11
God delivers and transfers	Col 1:13
God saves	2 Tim 1:9; Titus 3:5
God makes us alive	Eph 2:5
God pours out His Spirit	Titus 3:6
God brings us forth	James 1:18
God justifies	Rom 8:30; Titus 3:7
God sanctifies	1 Thess 5:23
God glorifies	Rom 8:3

Paul and his companions evangelizing (1:5).

For our gospel did not come to you in word only, but also in power, and in the Holy Spirit and in much assurance, as you know what kind of men we were among you for your sake (1:5).

1:5 How did the wonderful works among the Thessalonian believers come about from a human perspective, knowing that God had initiated them from the Divine side? Paul recounts the team's evangelistic effort in 1:5 and the Thessalonians' response to the gospel in 1:6-10 as positive proof that God indeed had elected them.

Paul begins with the *message* they preached which he called **our gospel** (cf. 2 Thess 2:14). Paul's gospel was really the gospel given by God (2:2, 8-9) and the gospel about Christ (3:2; 2 Thess 1:8). Paul takes no credit for the gospel other than that he had been entrusted with it by God and endeavored to be a good steward of the Divine trust (2:4). The short version of the gospel is written in 1 Corinthians 15:1-8, while Paul chronicled the detailed version of God's grace in Romans 1–8. The gospel, which generally means 'good news', is that God has made a way in Jesus Christ for those who are dead in their sins (the bad news, Eph 2:1-3) to be made alive for evermore. 'Gospel' is a dominant theme in these two letters, being mentioned eight times.

This gospel was not just another religious or philosophical oration that would **come...in word only** to satisfy their intellectual curiosities like with the Athenians (Acts 17:21). Rather, their **word** (Rom 10:14-17) came with the *manifestation* of Divine authentication which made their gospel preaching effective.

The three manifestations of power, the Holy Spirit, and much assurance would seem to be in reference to the three evangelists. The effects of salvation on the Thessalonians follow in 1:6-10.

All three features would seemingly be linked to the work of the Holy Spirit in the lives of these three as they preached the gospel. Unlike Paul's ministries in Asia (Acts 16:6-7) and in Athens (Acts 17:32-34), which were almost totally devoid of these character-istics, the evidence of God working in them abounded, just like Paul would know at Corinth (1 Cor 2:1-5).

The gospel was preached with **power** (Rom 1:16; 1 Cor 1:18; 2

Cor 4:7; 6:7), such as had been promised to be associated with the **Holy Spirit** (Acts 1:8), so that the evangelists had **much assurance** that God's word would accomplish God's elective will (Isa 55:11). They were not weak in their preaching; they were not devoid of God's Spirit in their ministry; and they had no doubt whatsoever about the positive outcome. Put another way, they boldly preached the gospel in hostile territory, attended by God's abundant blessing. There was no indication in Acts 17, nor is there here, that their ministry in Thessalonica involved signs, wonders, and miracles.

Finally, Paul concludes with their *manner of life* when the evangelists were among the Thessalonians. This subject is expanded in 2:1-12, apparently prompted by gospel enemies attempting to discredit the testimony of the team with charges which included greed and hypocrisy. Paul's reminder of **you know** was enough to settle the issue. The **kind of men** they were was so consistently lived out in public (**among you**) that it made a vivid, unforgettable impression on the church which could not be overturned by false and malicious accusations. Paul, Silas, and Timothy impeccably lived out what they preached so powerfully. Their godly character validated their God-given gospel.

Paul never ministered for self-gain. Rather, it was always for God's glory (1 Cor 10:31) and followed Christ's example of serving for the **sake** of the saints (Matt 20:28; 2 Cor 4:5). All three men were true servants to the church (2:7-11; 3:1-10).

OVERVIEW

Paul's Pastoral Ministry (1:5)

Few would disagree that, humanly speaking, Paul served as a shepherd extraordinaire to many congregations, including Thessalonica, Philippi, and Corinth. The Pauline epistles, along with Acts 13-28, biographically describe the pastoral priorities established by Paul as he labored to extend the church from Jerusalem to Rome. Under-shepherds would do well to emulate his example.

One must recognize the direct relationship between the quality of leadership and the quality of ministry in the church. The writer of Hebrews put it best:

> Remember those who rule over you, who have spoken the word of God to you, whose faith follow, considering the outcome of their conduct (Heb 13:7).

> Obey those who rule over you, and be submissive, for they watch out for your souls, as those who must give account. Let them do so with joy and not with grief, for that would be unprofitable for you (Heb 13:17).

Paul's ministry profile in 1 and 2 Thessalonians outlines the essential elements of effective pastoral ministry. His life among the church illustrates what a shepherd is to be and to do according to God's will. The following summary of responsibilities describes Paul's ministry among the Thessalonians.

1. Praying	1 Thess 1:2-3; 3:9-13; 2 Thess 2:16-17	
2. Evangelizing	1 Thess 1:4-5,9-10	
3. Equipping	1 Thess 1:6-8	
4. Defending	1 Thess 2:1-6	
5. Loving	1 Thess 2:7-8	
6. Laboring	1 Thess 2:9	
7. Modelling	1 Thess 2:10	
8. Leading	1 Thess 2:11-12	
9. Feeding	1 Thess 2:13	
10. Suffering	1 Thess 2:14-20	
11. Watching	1 Thess 3:1-8	
12. Warning	1 Thess 4:1-8	
13. Teaching	1 Thess 4:9-5:11	
14. Exhorting	1 Thess 5:12-24	
15. Encouraging	2 Thess 1:3-12	
16. Correcting	2 Thess 2:1-12	
17. Rebuking	2 Thess 3:6, 14	
18. Rescuing	2 Thess 3:15	

It would be difficult to imagine that a pastor could do any less than this and still be effective. Conversely, if a pastor took these responsibilities seriously, one could not imagine the pastor having time to do much more. These various aspects of Paul's pastoral ministry exemplify the top priorities for each succeeding generation.

Because of Paul's strong sense of pastoral responsibility to God for the church and because of his deep love for the flock, he wrote these two letters as an extension of his ministry to them. Although he could not be with them, he nevertheless consistently thought of the church and desired that they excel.

The Thessalonian church forming and flourishing (1:6-10).

And you became followers of us and of the Lord, having received the word in much affliction, with joy of the Holy Spirit, so that you became examples to all in Macedonia and Achaia who believe. For from you the word of the Lord has sounded forth, not only in Macedonia and Achaia, but also in every place. Your faith toward God has gone out, so that we do not need to say anything. For they themselves declare concerning us what manner of entry we had to you, and how you turned to God from idols to serve the living and true God, and to wait for His Son from heaven, whom He raised from the dead, even Jesus who delivers us from the wrath to come (1:6-10).

1:6 Before the Thessalonians became **followers** of Paul's party and **the Lord**, they had first **received the word** (cf. 2:13; see *Overview* 'The Word of God' [2:13]). There would have been no salvation without a clear salvation message from God's word concerning Christ's death and resurrection (Rom 10:13-17).

The Word is equated with the Old Testament (Mark 7:13). It is what Jesus preached (Luke 5:1). It was the message the apostles taught (Acts 4:31; 6:2). It was the word the Samaritans received (Acts 8:14) as given by the apostles (Acts 8:25). It was the message the Gentiles received as preached by Peter (Acts 11:1). It was the word Paul preached on his first missionary journey (Acts 13:5, 7, 44, 48, 49; 15:35-36). It was the message preached on Paul's second missionary journey (Acts 16:32; 17:13; 18:11). It was the message Paul preached on his third missionary journey (Acts19:10). It was the focus of Luke in the Book of Acts in that it spread rapidly and widely (Acts 6:7; 12:24; 19:20). Paul was careful to tell the Corinthians that he spoke the Word as it was given from God, that it had not been adulterated, and that it was a manifestation of truth (2 Cor 2:17; 4:2). Paul acknowledged that it was the source of his preaching (Col 1:25).

The Thessalonians responded to the gospel by literally

'welcoming it' or **receiving the word**. They accepted the word for what it claimed to be and embraced it without doubt or hesitation (James 1:21). They stood in contrast to those in the future who will perish because they will not receive the love of the truth in order to be saved (2 Thess 2:10).

Paul describes the circumstances of their redemption with two qualities that are not usually associated together. They were **in much affliction** but **with joy of the Holy Spirit**. The **affliction** would most likely refer to the great external difficulty and pressure from all sides exerted by the Jews of the synagogue upon those who were converted, much like they did to Paul, Jason, and the new Jewish converts at the beginning (Acts 17:5-9). Paul makes a point to describe the pressure as intense and frequent. Apparently, these assaults increased with the passing of time (cf. 2 Thess 1:4, 6).

But rather than being discouraged by their circumstances, they possessed a new found **joy**, whose source was the **Holy Spirit** (cf. 4:8; 5:19; 2 Thess 2:13), which authenticated their newly acquired faith in Christ. Just as Paul had preached with the Holy Spirit's power (1:5), so the Thessalonians' conversion was accompanied by the Spirit's **joy** (Gal 5:22).

OVERVIEW

The Joy of the Lord (1:6)

There is a divine joy, i.e. a communicable attribute of God (Neh 8:10; Matt 25:21, 23; John 15:11; 1 Thess 1:6), which He desires to reproduce as a hallmark of godliness in each of His children through the ministry of His Holy Spirit (Gal 5:22-23). As a cardinal Christian virtue, joy involves 'a deep, abiding inner thankfulness and gratitude to God which is not interrupted when undesirable life circumstances intrude'. This heaven-sent joy empowers Christians to rise above the raging battle, to think beyond the painful, to live unfettered to the immediate, and to look with hope at the future. Godly joy appears over 140 times in the New Testament, prompting the most frequent command in Scripture – 'Rejoice!' (5:16).

Joy is rooted in God's trinitarian nature with a view to flourishing, blossoming, and bearing fruit in the Christian's life. God the Father is the object of joy (Pss 35:9; 43:4; 1 Pet 1:8); God the Son mentors joy (Heb 12:2); and God the Holy Spirit prompts joy (Rom 15:13).

Joy contributes one of nine inseparable 'fruit' qualities produced in believers by the Holy Spirit (Gal 5:22-23; cf. in Christ, Luke 10:21; in the disciples, Acts 13:52; and in the Thessalonians, 1 Thess 1:6). To the Roman church, Paul first declared that the Holy Spirit produces joy (Rom 14:17) and then followed by praying, 'Now may the God of hope fill you with all joy... by the power of the Holy Spirit' (Rom 15:13).

Nothing evidences close communion with God more than Spirit-produced joy. One unknown author represented joy as the royal standard flying from the flagstaff of the heart signaling that the King is in residence.

Appropriately, Scripture doesn't speak of divine joy as 'average' but rather in superlative terms like great (Acts 15:3), no greater (3 John 4), exceeding (Matt 2:10), and complete (Phil 2:2). Peter delivered the ultimate statement on joy: 'And though you have not seen Him, you love Him, and though you do not see Him now, but believe in Him, you greatly rejoice with joy inexpressible and full of glory' (1 Pet 1:8).

What Does Joy Look Like?
Fullness of joy is found in God's presence (Ps 16:11), in truth proclamation (1 John 1:4; 2 John 12), in loving obedience (John 15:11), in answered prayer (John 16:24), and in Christ's ministry (John 17:13). Joy should be prompted each new day (Ps 118:24) by the faithful wife (Prov 5:18), by doing good (Eccl 3:12), and by honorable labor (Eccl 11:8). Sin can tarnish salvation's joy (Ps 51:12) but confession and repentance will restore the original luster. If the flock is obedient, joy will be the fruit of spiritual leadership (Heb 13:17). But be warned, Satan can counterfeit joy (Rev 11:10).

The joy of the Lord is the Christian's strength (Neh 8:10) and is an appropriate attitude in prayer (Phil 1:4; Col 1:11), in worship (Lev 23:40; Luke 19:37), over another's salvation (Luke 15:7, 10, 32), over one's own salvation (Luke 10:20; Acts 8:39; 16:34), because of God's salvation (1 Sam 2:1), over presenting the gospel (John 4:36; Phil 1:18), over God's Word (Ps 119:111, 162; Matt 13:20; Acts 13:48; 1 Cor 13:6), over Christian obedience (Matt 25:21, 23; Phil 2:2; 4:1; 1 Thess 2:19-20; 2 Tim 1:4), and over God's ministry (Luke 13:17; Acts 8:8; 11:23; 15:3).

How Is Joy Experienced?
Seeing that joy is both a sovereign act of the Holy Spirit (Gal 5:22-23; 1 Thess 1:6) but also commanded as human responsibility (Phil 4:4; 1 Thess 5:16), how is this produced? To understand, compare Colossians 3:16-17 with Ephesians 5:18-20. One emphasizes the ministry of God's Word; the other focuses on the Holy Spirit, but with the same results. The combination of Scripture intake along with the Holy Spirit produces joy in the believer's life. All believers have the Holy Spirit, but they do not always have equal involvement with the Word.

Compare this spiritual process to starting a car. God's Spirit is the engine, one's will serves as the ignition key, and God's Word acts as fuel. Having an engine without fuel, one can turn the ignition key repeatedly but the car will not start. Without the Word, the power of the Holy Spirit will go unfueled.

One can have the finest engine and the fuel, but until the driver engages the ignition there will be no combustion. The Holy Spirit and the Word remain seemingly dormant without the involvement of the human will.

However, with a top flight engine, a tank of high-octane fuel, and timely ignition, drivers have all the power needed to move. Likewise, with the Holy Spirit, with rich portions of the Word, and with one's will embracing God's will, believers have the spiritual energy needed for joy. All three elements must synchronize for the Holy Spirit to produce joy as a constant companion (Phil 4:4; 1 Thess 5:16).

How Durable Is Joy?
Thankfully, joy is an all-season response to life. Even in the dark times, sorrow enlarges the capacity of the heart for joy. Like a diamond whose radiance is enhanced when seen against a black background, true spiritual joy shines brightest against the darkness of trials, tragedies, and testing. 'Consider it all joy, my brethren, when you encounter various trials' (James 1:2).

Christ commanded rejoicing even in times of spiritual persecution (Matt 5:12). The disciples rejoiced that they had been considered worthy to suffer shame for Christ's name (Acts 5:41). Paul exclaimed, "I am overflowing with joy in all our afflictions" (2 Cor 7:4). Jesus endured the cross for the joy set before Him (Heb 12:2).

As a result of receiving God's word unto salvation (1:6b), the Thessalonians became second-generation **followers of the Lord** (1:6b), with Paul and his partners being the first (**us**). **Followers** literally means 'mimics', or in other words 'disciples', although the normal word for disciple in the Gospels and Acts (*mathētēs*) is not used here or anywhere else in the New Testament epistles. Christians are to imitate God (Eph 5:1), Christ (1 Cor 11:1), the apostle (1 Cor 4:16; 11:1; Phil 3:17), church leaders (Heb 13:7), and other godly Christians (2:14; Heb 6:12). All of this occurred in the context of the local church at Thessalonica (cf. 2 Thess 3:7, 9).

1:7 As a result of receiving the Word and imitating the Lord and Paul, the Thessalonians **became examples** (the textual variant of example [NASB, NIV] or examples [NKJV] are insignificant) *regionally* in **Macedonia** and *nationally* in **Achaia** (see map of *Paul's Second Missionary Journey*). For those **who believe** in Christ, the Thessalonians also made an indelible impression. The word translated **example** (*tupos*) indicates 'the impression made by a blow' such as a seal on wax, an impression struck on a coin, or an engraving on stone. They were so active in their faith that they were used by God to literally shape the lives of **all** other believers in Greece. Put another way, they helped produce a third generation of Christians by leaving their spiritual mark on them. This is the kind of ministry that elders are to teach to their flock (Phil 3:17; 2 Thess 3:9; 1 Tim 4:12; Titus 2:7; 1 Pet 5:3).

1:8 How did this happen? Very simply, **the word of the Lord has sounded forth**! Just as the word came to them from Paul (1:5), just as the word was embraced by them (1:6), so the word had been literally 'trumpeted' or 'reverberated' wherever the Thessalonians travelled, both in Greece (**Macedonia and Achaia**) and **also in every place** their **faith toward God** (1:8) had **gone out**. Thus, their ministry of reproduction had gone beyond their own city, their own region, their own nation, to ultimately have an *international* scope. Their message was like a thunderous echo that continued to sound forth.

In just about one year, a new church with first-generation believers was experiencing a ministry whose proportions matched those of Christ's Great Commission (Matt 28:18-20; Mark 16:15-20; Luke 24:44-49; John 20:21-23; Acts 1:8). First Thessalonians paints an exemplary portrait of how Christ intended to build His church (Matt 16:18) and engage the church in His unfinished work (Acts 1:1-2, 8).

Luke 24 contains the fullest expression of the five key elements to the Great Commission. There is an amazing parallel of all five features in the real life dynamics of 1 Thessalonians 1:5-10. First, the Great Commission rests on the *authority* of God's Word (Luke 24:44-48; 1 Thess 1:6). Second the *message* of the Great Commission is the gospel, i.e. a crucified, resurrected, and coming again Savior (1:5-10; Luke 24:46). Third, the *fruit* of the Great Commission is repentance and the fruits of repentance (1:6-10; Luke 24:47). Fourth, the *extent* of the Great Commission is international in scope (1:6-8; Luke 24:47). Fifth, the *power* behind the Great Commission is from the Holy Spirit (1:5; Luke 24:49). Just as Paul's later ministry in Ephesus reached all of Asia (Acts 19:10), so this ministry reached not only Greece, but beyond (1:8).

The ultimate fruit of this gospel ministry was that Paul did **not need to say anything**. The results were so unimaginable apart from a true work of God and the repentance was so genuine that it could not be self-generated. Thus, the Thessalonians became 'living letters' (2 Cor 3:2-3) declaring to the whole world that Paul, Silas, and Timothy were the true messengers of God who spoke a message that supernaturally transformed lives (cf. Rom 1:8). Therefore, Paul never had to brag about his ministry; the Thessalonians were his 'calling card' (cf. Rom 16:19).

1:9 They themselves refers to those who had encountered the fruit of Paul's ministry and now were continually reporting to them in Corinth the very nature of the earlier ministry in Thessalonica. The **manner of entry** (cf. 2:1) is partially recorded in Acts 17:2-4 and the rest one knows from 1:5-10 and 2:13.

The Thessalonians responded to the gospel and **turned to God** (1:9) **from idols** (cf. Acts 14:15; 26:20). Two New Testament words are used in the context of repentance. First, *metanoeō* which literally means 'to change one's mind' (cf. Matt 3:2; 4:17; 2

Cor 7:10; 2 Tim 2:25). Second, *epistrephō* (used here in 1:9) literally means 'to turn around' (Acts 9:35; 11:21; 14:15; 15:19; 26:18). The first speaks of a mind change which results in the second, i.e. a life change. In Acts 3:19 and 26:20 both words are used to describe the fullest kind of repentance, because both are involved. It is assumed in Scripture that where one is present, the other will be also. Thus, either word can be used as the part that describes the whole.

Now, they turned **from idols**. An idol is anything, any attitude, any belief, or any god that so captures a person's attention and allegiance that God does not have pre-eminence. Both the Old Testament (Pss 96:5; 115:4-8; 135:15-18; Isa 40:18-20) and the New Testament (Acts 15:20; 1 Cor 10:7, 14; Col 3:5; 1 John 5:21) warn against this kind of blasphemy. This would most likely refer to a Gentile conversion, not a Jewish one. The Old Testament teaches that behind the idols were demons (Deut 32:17 with 21; Ps 106:34-39) as does the New Testament (1 Cor 10:19-20).

Having turned away from idols which were dead and fraudulent, they then **turned to** the **God** of Scripture. This accomplished two major objectives – first, that they might serve Him and second, that they might wait for His return in the clouds (1:10) as the angels forecasted in Acts 1:11.

To serve was something a slave did for a master or lord. In the New Testament, it is used in the sense of a person serving God (Acts 20:19; Col 3:24) or a slave serving a human master (Eph 6:5-7; 1 Tim 6:2). Having become imitators of the Lord (1:6) and heralded abroad the word of the Lord, it is easy to see why the master (*kurios*)-slave (*douleuō*) picture is used here.

The **idols** from which they departed were lifeless and counterfeit (Isa 40:18-20; 46:5-7); the **God** they embraced was **living** and **true** (Isa 43:10-11; 44:6; 45:5-7; 46:9-10). They abandoned their illusions in order to identify with reality. They turned their back on that which killed and knelt before the One who gives eternal life. They stopped seeking the emptiness of false religion and started worshiping the fullness of the Almighty. 'My glory I will not give to another, nor My praise to graven images' (Isa 42:8).

1:10 The Thessalonians did not **serve** without an imminent hope nor did they wait inactively without an urgent mission to do the Lord's work (Eph 2:10). The Greek word translated **to wait** is used only here in the New Testament and has the sense of anticipation or expectation (cf. Phil 3:20). It rings with the idea of the prophetic hope that things on earth will not always continue the way they are currently (cf. 'patience of hope', 1:3; also 2 Thess 2:16).

The one whom they await is none other than **Jesus**, God's **Son** who taught His disciples, 'I will come again' (John 14:3). This truth was reaffirmed to the disciples, as they watched Jesus ascend into heaven from the Mount of Olives (Acts 1:11), that He would return **from heaven**. Paul reminded the Philippians of their heavenly hope (3:20). Even the mockers in the last days will acknowledge this Christian hope (2 Pet 3:4), but then deny it. Paul later on teaches that 'the Lord Himself will descend from heaven' (4:16). There is nothing here that specifically points to the superiority of any one eschatological system. The reference is made in a most generic way and should not be used to prove anything doctrinally, other than the truth that Christ will return.

This one who is expected to return had been crucified. Therefore, it was necessary for Paul to remind his readers that **He** (God the Father) **raised** Christ **from the dead**. Without the resurrection, there would be no return of Christ.

OVERVIEW

Christ's Resurrection (1:10)

God has provided many infallible proofs verifying Christ's triumph over death (Acts 1:3). The resurrection is the foundation for Christianity's exclusive claim that there is no other name under heaven given among men whereby we may be saved (Acts 4:12). Those proofs?

1. Old Testament Scripture
'All things which are written about Me in the Law of Moses and the Prophets and Psalms must be fulfilled,' Jesus told His disciples. 'Thus it was written, that the Christ should suffer and rise again from the dead the third day' (Luke 24:44, 46, NASB).

He certainly had Psalm 16:10 in mind, 'For Thou wilt not abandon my soul to Sheol; neither will Thou allow Thy Holy one to see the pit.' Peter (Acts 2:25-28) and Paul (Acts 13:35) both preached Christ's resurrection from this Psalm.

Old Testament Scripture anticipated Messiah's resurrection one thousand years in advance.

2. Jesus Christ's Own Testimony

The four Gospel writers each included the Lord's predictions that He would die but rise again. 'From that time Jesus began to show to His disciples that He must go to Jerusalem, and suffer many things...and be killed, and be raised again on the third day' (Matt 16:21; also Mark 9:9; Luke 9:22; John 2:19).

Even His enemies testified before Pilate, 'Sir, we remember that when he was still alive, that deceiver said, "After three days I am to rise again" ' (Matt 27:63).

Not only did David prophesy the resurrection in Psalm 16, but Jesus unmistakably announced it.

3. The Empty Tomb

What do Buddha, Confucius, Mohammed, Joseph Smith, and Karl Marx all have in common? If signs marked grave-sites, theirs would read 'Occupied'.

Only Christ's grave rates a vacant sign. He arose on the third day, just as He said (Matt 28:6; Mark 16:6; Luke 24:6; John 20:6-7). The empty tomb authenticates the resurrection.

4. Christ's Appearances after the Resurrection

The Lord Jesus appeared on at least ten separate occasions before a multitude of witnesses after He arose.

He showed Himself alive to Mary Magdalene (Mark 16:9), other women (Matt 28:8-10), Peter (Luke 24:34), two on the Emmaus road (Luke 24:13-35), ten disciples (John 20:19-23), eleven disciples (John 20:26-29), seven disciples in Galilee (John 21:1-23), five hundred followers (1 Cor 15:6), James (1 Cor 15:7), and the eleven at the ascension (Acts 1:3-11).

5. Birth of the Church

God's Spirit would only come if Christ arose and ascended to heaven (John 16:7; Acts 1:8; 2:4), and Jesus instructed the apostles to wait for power from on high (Acts 1:4-5).

Pentecost would have been impossible if the Lord had not risen earlier. Christ's Church has annually celebrated His resurrection for centuries.

6. The Apostles' Witness

The major theme of the apostles' preaching was Christ's resurrection. They must have sounded to some like a broken record.

Resurrection preaching dominates the entire book of Acts – Peter proclaimed it (2:32; 3:15; 5:30; 10:40) and so did Paul (13:30; 17:18, 31; 28:31). The apostles, honorable and trustworthy men, unanimously acclaimed the resurrection.

7. A New Worship Day

The early Church revered the first day of the week as unique. On that day, Christ met His disciples in a new intimacy of fellowship (John 20:19), and gave them instruction (Luke 24:36-49).

He ascended into heaven as the 'firstfruits' or wave sheaf (John 20:17; 1 Cor 15:20-23; Lev 23:10-12), and breathed the Spirit on them for a special commission (John 20:22). On the first day of the week, the Spirit descended from heaven (Acts 2:1-4).

8. New Testament Scripture

The New Testament speaks more than one hundred times of the Lord's resurrection. Most convincing are His post-ascension appearances.

Stephen saw Christ standing at the Father's right hand (Acts 7:56). The Lord stood at Paul's side in Jerusalem (Acts 23:11). The beloved disciple John turned to see Him in the midst of seven golden lampstands (Rev 1:12-13).

It is a truth incontestably supported by the entire New Testament.

9. Paul's Conversion

During the nineteenth century, Lord Lyttleton and Gilbert West tried to discredit Christianity by disproving Paul's conversion and Christ's resurrection. After examining the facts, both these outstanding leaders confessed Him as Savior and Lord.

Lyttleton realized that the Church's most ardent persecutor really did have a personal confrontation with the resurrected Lord (Acts 9:1-22; 22:6-21; 26:4-23).

10. Christ's Silent Enemies

The Savior's enemies never built a case against His resurrection. If reasonable doubt existed, they would have seized the opportunity.

Chief priests fabricated a story that while the soldiers slept, Jesus' disciples stole His body (Matt 28:11-15). But how could they have known who stole the body when the only witnesses were asleep?

11. Symbolic Sacraments

Baptism by immersion pictures a believer's death to sin and spiritual resurrection into new life in Jesus Christ (Rom 6:4; Col 2:12). Christ's resurrection provided the imagery.

Paul received instructions for the Lord's Table personally from a resurrected Christ (1 Cor 11:23). The bread and cup regularly remind believers of the Lord's death until He comes (1 Cor 11:26). Only the resurrection allows Him to ascend to the Father and return to gather His own.

12. Christian Doctrine

If the resurrection proves false, Christianity collapses. The resurrection is essential to the gospel. 'That Christ died for our sins according to the Scriptures, and that He was buried, and that He rose again on the third day according to the Scriptures' (1 Cor 15:3-4).

Paul argued that, without the resurrection, his preaching and the Corinthians' faith would be in vain (1 Cor 15:14). He would even consider himself a false witness, the Corinthians would still be in their sins, and deceased loved ones would have perished without hope (vv. 15-18). If Christ had not risen from the dead, Christians, of all people, should be pitied (v. 19).

13. Salvation Message

Claiming to be a Christian while denying the resurrection is a contradiction of God's message to the church. 'If you confess with your mouth Jesus as Lord, and believe in your heart that God raised Him from the dead, you shall be saved' (Rom 10:9).

The resurrection of Jesus Christ cannot be divorced from believing and receiving His free gift of eternal life. Paul inseparably linked the resurrection to salvation.

14. The Church's Confession

Clement of Rome wrote in AD 96, 'Let us understand, dearly beloved, how the Master continually doth showeth unto us the resurrection that shall be hereafter, whereof He made the Lord Jesus Christ the firstfruit, when He raised Him from the dead.'

The historic Westminster Confession (1647) reads, 'On the third day He arose from the dead, with the same body in which He suffered, with which also He ascended into heaven, and there sitteth at the right hand of His Father.'

The last phrase in 1 Thessalonians 1, **Jesus who delivers us from the wrath to come**, needs to be looked at carefully in its context because there are several tough questions to be answered about it. Does Jesus deliver believers out of existing wrath or deliver them from ever experiencing wrath? Is this God's eternal wrath or is this God's temporal wrath in Daniel's seventieth week? Does this passage have any implications with regard to determining the time of the rapture?

The phrase **deliver us from** can be understood in two different ways by comparison with its other New Testament uses. It could refer to *evacuation* from an existing wrath (Luke 1:74; Rom 7:24; Col 1:13; 2 Tim 3:11) or *exemption* from something yet future or possible (2 Cor 1:10; 2 Thess 3:2).

Two New Testament words for wrath/anger are used synonymously in both the LXX and the New Testament. In the few instances where a difference is intended, *thumos* refers to a sudden outburst, whereas *orgē* indicates a premeditated response. *Orgē* occurs only in 1 Thessalonians (1:10; 2:16; 5:9), while *thumos* does not appear at all. Both forms of anger are generally prohibited for humans, appearing side-by-side in Ephesians 4:31 and Colossians 3:8. Because God's wrath is a righteous response, there are no limitations on Him.

These words are used of God to indicate at least five kinds of wrath: (1) sowing and reaping wrath (Lam 2:2,4); (2) cataclysmic wrath (Exod 15:7); (3) abandonment wrath (Rom 1:18,24,26,28); (4) eschatological wrath (Rev 6:16-17); and (5) eternal wrath (Rom 2:5-11). Context determines the exact meaning of 'wrath' in a specific biblical text.

The **wrath to come** could refer to: (1) human wrath (Rom 13:4-5; Col 3:8; James 1:19-20); (2) God's temporal wrath (Rev 6:16-17; 19:15); or (3) God's eternal wrath (John 3:36; Rom 5:9). The wrath spoken of in 1 Thessalonians 2:16 and 5:9 will be considered separately.

Since word usage alone does not answer the previously posed questions, context must serve as the final arbiter. The whole of this chapter has been devoted to remembering the salvation of the Thessalonians. The salvation experience has been particularly detailed here in 1:9-10. Therefore, it is the judgment of this writer that: (1) it does not refer to human wrath; (2) it could refer to God's temporal wrath; but (3) in context, it is best taken as God's eternal wrath. Thus the deliverance is not in the sense of evacuation but rather of exemption (cf. Rom 8:1). Although this writer believes in a futuristic premillennial, pretribulational prophetic hope (see *Overview*, 'The Rapture' [4:17]), it is his opinion that this text does not deal with the issue of the rapture at all. To interpret it so, takes it out of an obvious context of eternal salvation.

To summarize 1:6-10, the Thessalonians were truly regenerate people (1:9-10) who reverberated with the gospel wherever they went (1:8) and thus spiritually reproduced themselves in others (1:6-7). Or put another way, the Thessalonians, having received God's word unto salvation (1:6b), became followers or imitators of Christ (1:6a), thus serving as Christian examples (1:7) by going forth as heralds of the gospel (1:8) and possessing an undeniable testimony of abandoning the false and embracing the true way of God (1:9-10).

2. The shepherds' integrity (2:1-12)

Although the details are not exactly known, it seems apparent from what Paul writes here that there has been an attack(s) on the integrity of the ministry team, or at least Paul is expecting one based on prior experience. So, Paul reminds his flock of the team's *impeccable character* (2:1-7) and their *unimpeachable conduct* (2:8-12).

Memories of their virtuous ministry would quickly neutralize the poison of ill-intentioned criticisms, whether they be issues of the heart or attacks upon their manner of labor.

Pastoral character (2:1-7)

For you yourselves know, brethren, that our coming to you was not in vain. But even after we had suffered before and were spitefully treated at Philippi, as you know, we were bold in our God to speak to you the gospel of God in much conflict. For our exhortation did not come from error or uncleanness, nor was it in deceit. But as we have been approved by God to be entrusted with the gospel, even so we speak, not as pleasing men, but God who tests our hearts. For neither at any time did we use flattering words, as you know, nor a cloak for covetousness– God is witness. Nor did we seek glory from men, either from you or from others, when we might have made demands as apostles of Christ. But we were gentle among you, just as a nursing mother cherishes her own children (2:1-7).

2:1 Most likely, the Jews who had Paul evicted from Thessalonica (Acts 17:5-9) and who then came to Berea causing trouble (Acts 17:13) were now trying to smear Paul's reputation in order to undermine his ministry and destroy the church. Torrential streams of criticism appear to be running across the field of Paul's labor and spiritual erosion is a real danger. So Paul writes to minimize, or even prevent, loss.

In 2:1-7, there is a very obvious grammatical pattern which distinguishes the manner in which Paul handles the charges. Three times Paul uses the combination of **For...But** (2:1-2, 3-4, 5-7). Each **for** introduces his denial of the charge and the **but** opens his defense. They questioned his outward *motivations* by accusing him of being self-serving rather than serving for the good of the people (2:1-2). They challenged his inward *motives* by insinuating that he was out to please men and not God (2:3-4). They also indicted Paul's *methods* by charging that they were too authoritarian, rather than humble and gentle (2:5-7).

Four times in 2:1-12, Paul appeals to the Thessalonians' memory of the recent past with **for you...know** (2:1, 2, 5, 11), just as he had earlier in 1:5. The strongest vindication of Paul and his team would come from the Thessalonians themselves who could easily recall that when he came they were pagan idolaters (1:9), but when he left they had become **brethren** in Christ.

Paul had not been involved in a fraudulent ministry (from the Thessalonians' perspective) which none-the-less had been personally advantageous to him. Using much the same language as he did in 1:9 (**entry** in 1:9 and **coming** in 2:1 are translated from the same Greek word which literally means 'entrance'), Paul states negatively in 2:1 what he had stated so positively in 1:9-10. Paul's ministry in Thessalonica had **not** been **in vain**, empty of true substance, or even fruitless. Later in the letter, he expresses this same concern as the reason for earlier sending Timothy to them (3:5).

Paul invokes three witnesses to deny the charges. First, Paul speaks in his own defense here. Second, he calls on the Thessalonians to deny the charge because of the unforgettable way their lives had been changed by the gospel ministry (2:1). Thirdly, he invites people from all over Greece and beyond to testify that, in fact, Paul had an extremely beneficial ministry in Thessalonica (1:7-8).

2:2 Having obviously been successful in denying the charge in 2:1, he now puts forth, in his defense, a historical note that would convince any remaining skeptics. Not only had there been great spiritual gain to the Thessalonians as a result of his ministry, **but** it had come from one who had already suffered loss for the ministry's sake and was destined to suffer more (Acts 9:16). The path travelled was full of conflict and opposition which yielded little or no self-gain. Only sincerity, never hypocrisy, journeyed that way.

As you know points back in time to Paul's ministry at **Philippi** (Acts 16:12-40). While there, they had **suffered** physically through beatings (16:22-23) and incarceration (16:24; as had Christ, Luke 9:22). They had also been **spitefully treated**, especially in a legal sense (just like their Savior, Luke 18:32). The missionaries were falsely accused (16:20-21), denied due process (16:37), and, as Roman citizens, illegally punished (16:37).

But rather than return home and wait for a better time to preach the gospel (which self-serving men would have done), they continued on to Thessalonica for more of the same. Paul speaks of his ministry there as **conflict**. This word indicates being under great strain in the face of stiff opposition (Phil 1:30; Col 2:1). It could be used of an athletic contest (Heb 12:1). Paul describes his ministry with this term as a 'fight' (1 Tim 6:12; 2 Tim 4:7). The future would hold more of the same at Berea (Acts 17:13), Athens (Acts 17:32), Corinth (Acts 18:12-17), and Ephesus (Acts 19:23-41).

Despite the opposition, Paul continued to preach **the gospel of God** (cf. note on 1:5). His message originated with God, not himself. They were not timid but **bold in...God**, i.e. they spoke out without any internal restraint whatsoever. This style of preaching was characteristic of Paul (Acts 9:27; 13:46; 14:3) but not an easy one, as indicated by his request for prayer regarding wide open evangelism (Eph 6:20).

So, contrary to the charge of being a self-serving, religious fraud, Paul proves just the opposite. His ministry did bear fruit in the lives of those to whom he ministered, and a tremendous price of opposition and pain was paid by him and his colleagues to continue. He ministered with a proper external motivation – sacrifice for the benefit of others.

2:3 Paul moves on to deal with his heart motives for a ministry of **exhortation** which would include preaching the gospel (2:2) and teaching the truth (2 Thess 2:5). His denial is three-fold in nature. First, it was not **from error**. They were not like false prophets whose messages wandered aimlessly (2 Tim 3:13; Jude 11-12). They did not preach a message of heaven that would eventually lead to hell. Their message was truth from God (2:13), not false doctrine from men. The gospel they preached was accurate and authentic.

Second, the message was not preached from **uncleanness** (4:7) or impurity. Paul would later in the letter make God's will in this domain exceptionally clear (4:3-8). Elsewhere, the Scriptures speak out strongly against this sin of the flesh (Matt 23:27-28; Eph 4:19; Col 3:5).

Third, Paul did not speak **in deceit**. They were not wolves in sheep's clothing. The Thessalonians had not been lured towards Christ with a false hope. The gospel had not been set out as a decoy to attract the Thessalonians to their own slaughter. Christ was not the bait used to hook the people on some cult. These men were true, holy, and honest.

2:4 Having categorically denied the charge of improper motives (2:3), in the strongest language of contrast available (**but**), Paul now defends the kind of ministry he conducted. He does so with a 'cause and effect' explanation.

First, **we have been approved by God to be entrusted with the gospel**. The cause of Paul's (along with Silas and Timothy) ministry had been God, not man. He had been personally approved for ordination by God (Acts 9:15; 22:14-15; 26:16-18; cf. Col 1:23, 25). The sense is that he had first been tested (cf. 1 Tim 3:10), passed the test, and now had Divine certification for the gospel ministry. Thus the author of the gospel (**God**) trusted Paul to faithfully preach it and had appointed him to do so (see notes on 1:5; 2:2, 8). Clearly, Paul was not self-appointed or fraudulently sent out by some man-made religious organization.

Second, as a result of God's commission, **so we speak, not as pleasing men, but God**. He walked in the footsteps of Peter who said, 'We ought to obey God rather than men' (Acts 5:29). This would be a frequent theme in Paul's letters (1 Cor 4:4; 2 Cor 4:2; Gal 1:10). He sought to satisfy his Master (cf. 2:15; 4:1) because ultimately he would stand accountable before the Lord (1 Cor 3:10-15; 2 Cor 5:10; Heb 13:17).

OVERVIEW

Pleasing God (2:4)

Paul's highest ambition was to please the Lord (2 Cor 5:9). Jesus testified, 'I always do those things that please Him' (John 8:29). The Scriptures explicitly list at least nine activities that please the Lord. Surely these would have been a consistent part of the Thessalonian church life.

1. Spiritual commitment	(Rom 12:1)
2. Submission	(Col 3:20; Titus 2:9)
3. Walking in God's will	(Col 1:9-10)
4. Spiritual focus	(1 Cor 7:32)
5. Purity	(1 Thess 4:1-3)
6. Doing good	(Heb 13:16)
7. True worship	(Ps 69:30-31; John 4:24)
8. Living by God's Spirit	(Rom 8:6)
9. Preaching the truth	(1 Thess 2:4)

As the final word on his motives, Paul asserts that **God tests their hearts**. Although having first been tested and approved, the examination continued. God monitored their motives as regularly as they spoke. Paul might have alluded to Jeremiah 11:20 here. The message Paul spoke could not be criticized because it was affirmed by Scripture, so Paul's enemies turned on the messengers to discredit them. Ultimately the accusers themselves were discredited, much like Haman (Esth 7:1-10) and the Babylonian satraps (Dan 6:22-24).

2:5 Having brilliantly defended against the charges of being self-serving (2:1-2) and men-pleasers (2:3-4), Paul deals finally with the indictment of being too authoritarian rather than gentle and humble (2:5-7). His method or style of ministry is under attack here. He denies the charge in 2:5-6 and testifies otherwise with 2:7.

He begins by saying that there were no exceptions to his denial, for **neither at any time** did Paul or his colleagues fall into the sins of which they are accused. Not once did they deliver a discourse designed to unrealistically puff up the hearers so that the speaker could take advantage of them – **flattering words** were not a part of Paul's repertoire. He did not resort to the repugnant style of the religious rhetoricians. They were not verbal manipulators in order to gain power or advantage over the flock. Again, Paul appeals to the plain fact that they **know** this to be true.

Next, they did not **use...a cloak for covetousness**. Put another way, they did not give the appearance of being poor in order to get rich or as the NIV states, 'Nor did we put on a mask to cover up greed.' **Covetousness** or greed is condemned in Scripture (Luke 12:15-21; 1 Cor 5:9-10), characteristic of false prophets (2 Pet 2:3, 14) and labeled a form of idolatry (Col 3:5). True men of God, in contrast, are to be free of the love of money (1 Tim 3:3) and not fond of sordid gain (Titus 1:7). Financial gain had nothing to do with why they came to minister, for they were not hucksters nor peddlers of God's word (cf. 2 Cor 2:17).

At this point, Paul calls on the ultimate **witness – God** (cf. 2:4, 10). He will do this again (Rom 1:9; 2 Cor 1:23; Phil 1:8). God is the perfect witness because not only does He know everything (Ps

139:1-6) but He is not like a man and cannot lie (Num 23:19; Titus 1:2). It is impossible for God to perjure Himself and thus His witness is the apex in reliability. Had Paul not been absolutely sure of his assertions, how foolish it would have been to call God as his witness.

2:6 Nor did we seek glory from man. The third and final charge was that Paul was in it for personal glory from the congregation (**you**) or **from others** in previous ministries. Paul taught that God should receive all the glory in all things (1 Cor 10:31; cf. 1 Pet 4:11).

However, Paul was an **apostle of** Jesus **Christ** (Rom 1:1; 1 Cor 1:1; 2 Cor 1:1). Only in Philippians, Philemon, and the two Thessalonian letters does Paul not start with the assertion of apostleship, most likely because of the close relationship he enjoyed with the recipients and the generally positive nature of the letters. He introduces his apostleship here not to **demand** something, but to remind them that he had demanded nothing, although he might have appropriately done so.

Apostles (lit. 'sent ones' with authority) here includes Paul, Silas, and Timothy and thus is most likely not used in the more formal sense of the twelve who personally witnessed the resurrected Christ (Acts 1:21-22). These were men called out by the Holy Spirit and then sent out from and authorized to represent the church of Antioch (Acts 13:2-3), much like Epaphroditus (Phil 2:25), Andronicus and Junias (Rom 16:7), or other associates of Paul (2 Cor 8:23). In so doing, they ultimately represented **Christ**.

They had every right to ask for financial assistance from the Thessalonians in exchange for their ministry (cf. 1 Cor 9:13-14; 2 Cor 11:7-11). Instead, they chose to ask for nothing. Their support came primarily from working night and day (2:9; 2 Thess 3:8) plus an occasional gift from Philippi (Phil 4:15-16). They asked for nothing from the Thessalonians, either financial or non-financial in nature, and willingly gave everything, including themselves (2:8), just as **Christ** did in His earthly ministry.

OVERVIEW

Titles of Christ (2:6)

Outside of being called His Son (1 Thess 1:10), Jesus is always referred to in the Thessalonian letters by some form of the title Lord Jesus Christ (1:1). Elsewhere in Scripture He is called:

Title	Significance	Scripture
Immanuel (God with us)	Stands with us in all life's circumstances	Matt 1:23
Son of Man	Identifies with us in our humanity	Matt 8:20
Holy One of God	Sinless in His Nature	Mark 1:24
Savior	Delivers from sin and death	Luke 1:47
The Word	Present with God at creation	John 1:1
Only begotten of the Father	The unique, one-of-a-kind Son of God	John 1:14
Lamb of God	Gave His life as a sacrifice on our behalf	John 1:29
Son of God	Identifies Christ's deity	John 1:49
Bread of Life	The one essential food	John 6:35
Light of the World	Brings hope in the midst of darkness	John 9:5

Title	Significance	Scripture
Good Shepherd	Provider and caretaker	John 10:11
Prophet	Faithful proclaimer of the truths of God	Acts 3:22
Lord of Glory	The power and presence of the living God	1 Cor 2:8
Last Adam	First of the new race of the redeemed	1 Cor 15:45
Seed of Abraham	Mediator of God's covenant	Gal 3:16
Chief Cornerstone	A sure foundation for life	Eph 2:20
Firstborn from the Dead	Leads us into resurrection and eternal life	Col 1:18
Mediator between God and men	Brings us into God's presence redeemed and forgiven	1 Tim 2:5
Holy Priest	A perfect intercessor	Heb 3:1
Great Shepherd of the sheep	Trustworthy guide and protector	Heb 13:20
Chief Shepherd	Protector, sustainer, and guide	1 Pet 5:4
King of kings, Lord of lords	The Almighty, before whom every knee will bow	Rev 19:16
Alpha and Omega	The beginning and ending of all things	Rev 21:6

2:7 In moving to his defense (**But**), Paul uses an unmistakable human relationship to illustrate the fact that he had not exploited their spiritual vulnerability nor taken advantage of their newness in Christ. He pictures their ministry to the Thessalonians like the love of a mother for her nursing child, i.e. giving everything for the child's good (cf. Gal 4:19; 2 Cor 12:14-15).

A major, controversial textual variant appears here. Should the text read **we were gentle among you** or 'we were babes among you'? One additional letter makes the difference between 'gentle' and 'babes'. Most English translations have opted for 'gentle' although there is strong support for 'babes' among some Greek scholars. I favor 'gentle' for the following four reasons: (1) to make Paul first a 'babe' and then a **nursing mother** in one sentence is a confusing use of metaphors ; (2) Paul elsewhere uses 'babes' in a derogatory sense, which is clearly not the case here; (3) Paul nowhere else uses 'babe' of himself; and (4) 'gentle' fits the context best, since gentleness is to be a pastoral hallmark (2 Tim 2:24).

Paul's imagery might have come from Moses' leadership of Israel. The liberator of the Jews from Egypt pictures himself as a guardian carrying a nursing child (Num 11:12). It is the picture of one who unselfishly **cherishes her own children** just as a mother bird does for her young (Deut 22:6) or Christ does for the church (Eph 5:29).

Paul has concluded his defense against the charge that he and his colleagues were flawed in their character (2:1-7). In fact, they were spotless and without blemish (cf. 2 Cor 1:12). They acted with the right motivation of ministering for the fruitfulness and good of the congregation, not for self interest. Right motives were evident in their desire to please God, not men. Their kindness and gentleness contradicted the accusation of being harsh and domineering. Now, Paul makes a transition from the inward manner of his ministry to its outward appearance.

Pastoral conduct (2:8-12)

So, affectionately longing for you, we were well pleased to impart to you not only the gospel of God, but also your own lives, because you had become dear to us. For you remember, brethren, our labour and toil; for labouring night and day, that we might not be a burden to any of you, we preached to you the gospel of God. You are witnesses, and God also, how devoutly and justly and blamelessly we behaved ourselves among you who believe; as you know how we exhorted, and comforted, and charged every one of you, as a father does his own children, that you would walk worthy of God who calls you into His own kingdom and glory (2:8-12).

2:8 Having transitioned from defending his character to his conduct, Paul now uses four models, or pictures, to describe their proper pastoral leadership: a mother (2:8); a servant (2:9); a family member (2:10); and a father (2:11-12).

So, comparing himself and his colleagues to the nursing mother (2:7), they were **affectionately longing for** the Thessalonians. This word means 'to have a strong emotional attraction'. It is used negatively in the LXX (Job 3:21) of one who suffers and longs for death. In its only New Testament use, here it conveys the most positive, tender sense of a mother's attraction for a child.

As an outpouring of this strong affection, they **were well pleased to impart... not only the gospel of God, but also** their **own lives**. Paul realized that, when he arrived, the Thessalonians were dead in their sins and trespasses (Eph 2:1-2, 5) and enslaved to the kingdom of darkness (Col 1:13). Thus, the evangelists were **well pleased** (delighted) to deliver or **impart the gospel of God**, i.e. living water (John 4:10) and the bread of life (John 6:48), which resulted in eternal life and liberation from sin.

The **gospel of God** would be based on and according to the word of God (2:13). Paul's delivery of the gospel surely would have included: the utter sinfulness or total depravity of humanity (Rom 3:23); Christ's death and resurrection as God's provision for salvation (Rom 10:9); and individual appropriation of salvation by God's grace alone through faith alone in Christ Jesus (Rom 6:23; 10:10). A summary of the gospel is also given by Paul in 1 Corinthians 15:1-4. See notes on 1:5; 2:2, 8.

Not only the gospel did they give, but also their **own lives** (literally, 'souls'). In other words, Paul did not merely preach and then retreat to his study. Rather, he gave of himself all that he had to give, just like a mother to her baby (2 Cor 4:5; 12:15; 2 Tim 2:10). What fueled their sacrificial affection for the Thessalonians?

You had become dear to us. Literally, the Thessalonians were the 'beloved ones' for whom no sacrifice was too great. Those who were first beloved of God (1:4; 2 Thess 2:13) are now beloved by Paul, Silas, and Timothy as their spiritual children in the Christian faith (cf. 3:2-10).

2:9 Now Paul speaks of their efforts as those of a servant. He again appeals to their recent memories (cf. 'you know', 2:1, 2, 5, 11) and their new Christian relationship as **brethren** (cf. 1:4; 2:1) as he recalls their servant-like behavior while preaching the gospel (see 2 Thess 3:7-9 for an expanded version).

Paul had not arrived in town as a 'gospel virtuoso' and demanded celebrity treatment. He was not like Diotrophes (3 John 9), the Pharisees (Matt 23:4), or even Simon Magus (Acts 8:9-24), all of whom acted like pastoral prima donnas. By strong contrast, he and his colleagues worked to the point of exhaustion (**labor**) under difficult working circumstances (**toil**), such as he later writes about in 2 Thessalonians 3:8 and 2 Corinthians 11:27. There was a **night and day** intensity to their **laboring**, much like that of a servant (2 Thess 3:8). Undoubtedly, Paul worked at his trade of tent-making (Acts 18:3).

The missionaries were not there to exchange the gospel for money or anything else. They went out of their way, beyond any normal human expectations, to **not** impose or **be a burden** (cf. 2 Thess 3:8; 2 Cor 2:5) to any of the Thessalonians, without exception. Thus, they **preached...the gospel of God** without any strings attached whatsoever. This is the fifth mention of the gospel so far (cf. 1:5; 2:2, 4, 8). They **preached** as authorized heralds of God, those who had been commissioned to preach a message of good news, i.e. the gospel on **God's** behalf. Thus, the message carried the implications of divine blessing for obedience, but wrath for rejection. See notes on 1:5; 2:2, 8.

2:10 Paul and his party displayed proper family behavior towards these new Christians (**among you who believe**). The Thessalonians (**you**) are **witness** to this and so is **God**. Each of these parties has been appealed to earlier in the letter, but both are now called 'to the witness stand'. The Old Testament law demanded at least two witnesses to adequately corroborate a statement (Num 35:30; Deut 17:6; 19:15-21), as does the New Testament (Matt 18:16; 26:65; John 5:31-32; 8:17; 2 Cor 13:1; 1 Tim 5:19; Heb 10:28). **You who believe** (1:7; 2:13; 2 Thess 1:10) is another way to refer to the church which is elsewhere called 'the multitude of those who believed' (Acts 4:32), referring to the Jerusalem church. The beliefs of the Thessalonian church are described in 1:6-10.

How had they **behaved among** those **who believe**? Paul describes their deportment in three ways. First, with regard to their inward affections towards both man and God, the men had acted **devoutly** or with holiness. Second, with regard to their outward behavior towards both men and God, they acted **righteously** or in conformity to God's revealed standards of behavior. With regard to both categories and in the sight of both witnesses, the Thessalonians and God, they lived **blamelessly** in that no accusations could legitimately be brought against them. They lived openly and consistently as one Christian brother with another.

2:11 The final illustration of spiritual leadership is likened to that of **a father** (2:11-12). As a **father** shows no favoritism to **his own children**, so Paul ministered **like a father** to **every one** of the Thessalonians. The experience had been so recent that Paul could say, **as you know**. Three complementary efforts aimed at one end (2:12) are in view. First, he came alongside and motivated, admonished, or **exhorted** (4:1; 5:14). Next, he also came alongside and **comforted** or soothed (5:14; cf. Jesus with Martha and Mary, John 11:19, 31). Third, he implored or urged them, which seem to be better translation alternatives than **charged**.

2:12 The goal or end result of this pastoral effort would be that the Thessalonians **walk worthy of God**. **Walk** was used to describe one's life, either in a positive (4:1, 12) or a negative fashion (2 Thess 3:6, 11). Here, one's Christian **walk** was to be **worthy of God** (cf. Eph 4:1; Phil 1:27; Col 1:10). Paul speaks of a godly lifestyle which is described with some detail in Ephesians 4:2-3,

Philippians 1:27-28, and Colossians 1:10-12. In his second letter, Paul prays on behalf of the Thessalonians for this suitable kind of life (2 Thess 1:11).

The worthy **walk** was required because of who called them (**God**) and to what He called them, i.e. **His own kingdom and glory**. Paul uses three related New Testament words for *call* forty-four times (*kaleō, klēsis, klētos*). He predominately refers to God's call unto salvation, which is also characteristic of Hebrews and Peter's two epistles. Rarely does the apostle indicate a 'call' to an office or function (Rom 1:1; 1 Cor 1:1). The five references to 'call' in 1 and 2 Thessalonians all refer to some aspect of salvation. Justification appears prominent in 1 Thessalonians 2:12 and 5:24, while 4:7 deals with sanctification. Second Thessalonians 1:11 and 2:14 both refer to glorification. Thus, those whom He elected unto salvation (1:4; 2 Thess 2:13) were expected to be spiritually elegant in the way they lived.

If someone had really known the ministry of Paul, Silas, and Timothy among the Thessalonians, they would not have criticized it but rather commended it. Who could be negative about pastors who were compassionate like a selfless mother to her children (2:8), committed like a devoted servant (2:9), consistent like a faithful family member (2:10), and concerned like a caring father for the spiritual welfare of his home (2:11)? To demean or tear down this ministry meant that the accuser(s) either knew nothing about it or were lying. So in God's sight and before the Thessalonians, Paul and his friends stood innocent, easily acquitted of all the trumped-up charges.

OVERVIEW

The Kingdom of God (2:12)[1]

The idea of a kingdom involves at least three basic features: a realm over which to rule; a ruler with absolute power; the actual exercise of authority.

---

1. This writer has been influenced by Alva J. McClain, *The Greatness of the Kingdom* (Chicago: Moody, 1959).

'Kingdom' in the broadest biblical sense, can be defined as 'the rule of God over His created world and His company of the redeemed'. However, there are multiple aspects of God's kingdom which must be taken into consideration when determining the specific expression of 'kingdom' in a particular Biblical text.

The following kingdom contrasts illustrate the rich diversity inherent in the 'kingdom of God' concept.

1. Certain passages present the kingdom as something which has always existed (Pss 10:16; 145:11-13); yet, elsewhere it seems to have a definite historical beginning (Dan 2:44).

2. The kingdom is described as universal in its scope (Ps 103:19); but it is also revealed as a local rule on earth (Isa 24:23).

3. Sometimes the kingdom is pictured as the direct rule of God (Pss 22:28; 59:13); other times it appears as the rule of God through a mediator (Ps 2:4-6; Dan 4:17, 25).

4. The Bible describes the kingdom as entirely future (Zech 14:9; Matt 6:10), while in other places the kingdom is portrayed as a current reality (Ps 29:10; Dan 4:3).

5. The kingdom of God is set forth as God's sovereign, unconditional rule (Dan 4:3, 34-35); on the other hand, it appears to be based on a covenant between God and man (Ps 89:27-29).

6. God's kingdom is said to be everlasting (Dan 4:3); but God will bring an end to part of His kingdom (Hosea 1:4).

7. The kingdom is not eating and drinking (Rom 14:17) nor can it be inherited by flesh and blood (1 Cor 15:50); yet the kingdom is at times spoken of in an earthly, tangible sense (Pss 2:4-6; 89:27-29).

All kingdom passages can be summarized by recognizing several broad aspects of God's kingdom. First, there is the Universal Kingdom which includes that rule of God which has been, is, and forever will be over all that exists in time and space. Second, there is God's Mediatorial Kingdom in which He rules on earth through a divinely chosen human representative. Third, there is the spiritual or redemptive aspect of God's kingdom which uniquely deals with a person's salvation and personal relationship with God through Christ. Anytime 'kingdom' appears in Scripture, it could refer to any one aspect of the kingdom or several of its parts together. Careful interpretation in context will determine the particulars for a given biblical text.

Some theologians make major distinctions between the 'Kingdom of Heaven' and the 'Kingdom of God'. It is best, however, to view these two phrases as representing basically synonymous kingdom concepts. For example, Luke recounts the 'four soils' parable using the phrase

'Kingdom of God' (Luke 8:10), while Matthew, in presenting a parallel, uses the phrase 'Kingdom of Heaven' (Matt 13:11). To further confirm this conclusion, note that Christ employs 'Kingdom of Heaven' (Matt 19:23) and 'Kingdom of God' (Matt 19:24) interchangeably when describing the difficulty that a rich person experiences in attempting to enter the kingdom. These both deal with the spiritual aspect of God's Kingdom.

Only two texts in the Thessalonian Epistles refer to 'kingdom' (1 Thess 2:12; 2 Thess 1:5). In both instances, Paul refers to the 'worthiness' of the Thessalonian believers to be in the redemptive realm of God's kingdom, with an emphasis on sanctification. Put another way, 'kingdom' in these two instances is to be understood in terms of salvation and a believer's personal relationship with the King of the Universe as evidenced by their spiritual life of obedience to God's commands in Scripture.

---

3. The flock's faithfulness (2:13-16)
Paul completes his remembrances by focusing on the church. He commends their faithfulness to God's Word (2:13) and their faithfulness to Christ in the midst of suffering (2:14-16).

Faithfulness to God's Word (2:13)

For this reason we also thank God without ceasing, because when you received the word of God which you heard from us, you welcomed it not as the word of men, but as it is in truth, the word of God, which also effectively works in you who believe (2:13).

2:13 Paul picks up here where he left off in 1:2-4 with habitual thanksgiving in general to God for all that He had done with the Thessalonians. **This reason** refers back to 1:5-10 which detailed the birth and growth of the church. It was their pattern (**without ceasing**, 1:2) to **thank God** (cf. 1:2) since He was the cause of it all. The powerful working of God through His word drew the praise of Paul, Silas, and Timothy. **Because** indicates the specific point of praise, i.e. the Thessalonians' response to the preaching of the **word of God**.

You received the word of God which you heard from us

OVERVIEW

The Glory of God (2:12)

Being God by definition includes being glorious. Many titles reflect God's glory:

- The Lord of Glory   (1 Cor 2:8)
- The Majestic Glory   (2 Pet 1:17)
- The King of Glory   (Ps 24:7-10)
- The Spirit of Glory   (1 Pet 4:14)
- The Word of Glory   (John 1:14)

God's glory reflected back to Him by us comes through acts of personal devotion and adoration that are God-directed. Please note the activities of personal worship that glorify God.

1. Living with purpose.   (1 Cor 10:31)
2. Confessing sins.   (Josh 7:19)
3. Praying expectantly.   (John 14:13)
4. Living purely.   (1 Cor 6:18-20)
5. Submitting to Christ.   (Phil 2:9-11)
6. Praising God.   (2 Cor 4:15)
7. Obeying God.   (2 Cor 9:13; 2 Thess 1:12)
8. Growing in faith.   (Rom 4:20-21)
9. Suffering for Christ's sake. (1 Pet 4:15-16)
10. Rejoicing in God.   (1 Chron 16:10)
11. Worshiping God.   (Ps 86:9)
12. Bearing spiritual fruit.   (John 15:8)
13. Proclaiming God's Word.   (2 Thess 3:1)
14. Serving God's people.   (1 Pet 4:10-11)
15. Purifying Christ's church.   (Eph 5:27; 2 Thess 1:10)
16. Giving sacrificially.   (2 Cor 9:13)
17. Unifying believers.   (John 17:22)
18. Salvation of the lost.   (Ps 21:5; 1 Thess 2:12;
                                  2 Thess 2:14)

19. Shining Christ's light.   (Matt 5:16)
20. Spreading God's gospel.   (2 Cor 4:15)

implies that Paul and his party arrived and *proclaimed* the truth (cf.
1:5). The Thessalonians listened with interest. The phrase **word of
God** appears over forty-five times in the New Testament (cf. 2 Cor
2:17; 4:2; Col 1:25; Heb 4:12; 13:7; 1 Pet 1:23) to indicate the
divine authority with which Paul preached.

You welcomed it (cf. 1:6) takes the process another step further
by declaring that **the word** they received had now *penetrated* their
hearts. They believed that it had not come from **men** but rather
from **God**. Paul makes this abundantly clear throughout the epistle
that he preached 'the word' (1:5-6, 8; 4:15; 2 Thess 3:1), the gospel
(1:5; 2:2, 4, 8, 9; 3:2; 2 Thess 1:8; 2:14), and the commandments
(4:2). Elsewhere in the New Testament, Paul is always clear about
God being the source of his message (Gal 1:11-12; 1 Cor 11:23;
15:1, 3).

God (Eph 1:11; 3:20; Phil 2:13; Col 1:29), through God's word,
effectively works in those **who believe** (cf. 2:10). God works
powerfully (Rom 1:16-17; 1 Cor 1:18, 24) through His word in the
lives of those who have embraced the gospel, as evidenced by the
Thessalonian experience which was recounted in 1:6-10. In a real
sense, this illustrates the truth of Isaiah 55:8-11 that God's word
will always accomplish His will. Thus, Scripture is central and
indispensable to any true ministry of the Lord (cf. 1 Tim 4:13; 2
Tim 2:2; 3:16-17; 4:2; Titus 2:1, 15). The godly flourish on a
healthy intake of God's word (Ps 1:2-3; Jer 17:7-8; 1 Pet 2:2-3).

Faithfulness in suffering (2:14-16)

For you, brethren, became imitators of the churches of God which are in
Judea in Christ Jesus. For you also suffered the same things from your own
countrymen, just as they did from the Judeans who killed both the Lord Jesus
and their own prophets, and have persecuted us; and they do not please God
and are contrary to all men, forbidding us to speak to the Gentiles that they
may be saved, so as always to fill up the measure of their sins; but wrath has
come upon them to the uttermost (2:14-16).

2:14 The church has known severe opposition, persecution, and
suffering ever since the days of Christ. Some of the greatest
spiritual heroes of the faith have been her martyrs (Heb 11:37). It

OVERVIEW

The Word of God (2:13)

Paul refers to Scripture in the Thessalonian epistles as 'the word' (1 Thess 1:6), 'the word of the Lord' (1 Thess 1:8; 4:15; 2 Thess 3:1), and 'the word of God' (1 Thess 2:13). Elsewhere in the New Testament, Scripture is also called:

the word of His grace	(Acts 14:3; 20:32)
the word of promise	(Rom 9:9)
the word of reconciliation	(2 Cor 5:19)
the word of life	(Phil 2:16)
the word of truth	(Eph 1:13; Col 1:5)
the word of Christ	(Col 3:16)
the faithful word	(Titus 1:9)
the word of His power	(Heb 1:3)
the word of righteousness	(Heb 5:13)

What sort of work does God's Word do? Here's a sample! It...

prospers	(Ps 1:3)	restores	(Ps 19:7)
warns	(Ps 19:11)	rewards	(Ps 19:11)
protects	(Ps 119:11)	counsels	(Ps 119:24)
strengthens	(Ps 119:28)	makes wise	(Ps 119:97-100)
guides	(Ps 119:105)	revives	(Ps 119:154)
confronts	(Jer 23:29)	frees	(John 8:31-32)
sanctifies	(John 17:17)	enriches	(Col 3:16)
teaches	(2 Tim 3:16)	rebukes	(2 Tim 3:16)
corrects	(2 Tim 3:16)	instructs	(2 Tim 3:16)
equips	(2 Tim 3:17)	judges	(Heb 4:12)
saves	(1 Pet 1:23)	nourishes	(1 Pet 2:2)

has been said down through the ages that 'the blood of the martyrs is the seed of the church'. The same anti-Christian sentiment of Paul's day exists in many parts of the world at the start of the twenty-first century.

Paul's **brethren** (the fourth of nineteen mentions, cf. 1:4; 2:1, 9), the Thessalonians, were **imitators** (this same Greek word was translated **followers** in 1:6) of Paul and Christ but also of **the churches of God...in Christ Jesus** (see notes on 1:1). He particularly had the churches **in Judea** in mind (cf. Acts 1-12). **Judea** is the Greco-Roman name for the land of Judah and comes from the word 'Jewish' which was used of the Babylonian captives who returned to Israel during the Persian rule (cf. Ezra and Nehemiah). It extends from Gaza, on the coast, north to Caesarea (where the Judean governor lived in Paul's day), and from the Mediterranean on the west to the the Dead Sea in the east.

However, Paul is not referring to **imitators** here in the sense of disciples, but rather that they **also suffered** (cf. 2 Thess 1:5). The Christians at Thessalonica had experienced **the same things from** their **own countrymen** (the Thessalonian Jews) **as did** the Jerusalem and surrounding churches **from the Judeans** (Jews). This had been true in Judea from Pentecost and following (cf. Acts 2:13; 4:1-21; 5:17-41; 6:9-15; 7:54-8:4; 9:1-2, 29; 12:1-19). Paul addresses increased persecution in 2 Thessalonians 1:4-10.

Paul could write as one who intimately knew and could empathize with **suffering**. From the beginning of his ministry, Paul had been told he would suffer (Acts 9:16). He mentioned the suffering periodically in his letters (cf. Phil 1:29; 2 Tim 1:12). Obviously, what the Thessalonian Jews began in Acts 17:5-9, they had continued up until the time Paul wrote. Little did they realize that the suffering which they inflicted would work towards the accomplishment of God's will. The Thessalonians would be purer, stronger, and wiser as a result of what the Jews intended for evil (cf. Gen 50:20).

2:15 The Judeans were the ones who **killed...the Lord Jesus**. The evidence in the gospels and Acts abundantly testifies to this truth (Matt 16:21; 26:3-4, 59, 66; 27:1; Mark 8:31; 10:33-34; 14:1, 55,

OVERVIEW

Who Killed Jesus? (2:15)

'Who killed Jesus?' arguably stands as the most provocative question in human history. To answer it in part introduces tragic error which produces the worst of tempers, the most hellish of outcomes, and extremely distorted accounts of history. Millions of Jews have wrongly died at the hands of the Crusaders, in the Inquisitions, and throughout history they have been accused of killing Christ.

Let's set the record straight. The Jews did have a major hand in the death of Christ, but they were not alone. There were at least six groups/persons who in some way participated in the crucifixion of the Lord Jesus Christ.

First, there was Judas, in league with Satan, who betrayed Christ (Luke 22:3-4; John 13:27). Second, Jewish religious leaders condemned Him (Luke 24:20; Acts 4:8-10; 13:27-28). Third, Roman political leaders acquiesced to the demand of the Jews, and their agents, the Roman soldiers, carried out the crucifixion (Matt 27:27, 35; Luke 18:32-33; 23:1-25; Acts 4:27). Fourth, the Jewish populace cried out, 'Let Him be crucified!' (Matt 27:22; Mark 15:14). The historical record is clear on these four, rather obvious groups. However, the final two are often overlooked, but they actually participated just as much as these four.

The fifth group encompasses the whole world, all of whom were conceived as sinners at enmity with God (Pss 51:5; 58:3; Rom 3:23; Eph 2:1, 5). Throughout the Scriptures, Christ's death on behalf of the world is made clear (1 Tim 2:6; 4:10; Heb 2:9; 1 John 2:2; 4:14). For unbelievers, His death brought God's common grace in this life. For believers, it brought eternal life.

Finally and shockingly, God the Father, by His predetermined plan and for His redemptive purposes, killed His own Son. Put another way, without God's plan and permission, Christ would never have died on the cross (Isa 53:10; Acts 2:23; 4:28).

64; Luke 9:22; 22:2; 24:20; John 5:16, 18; 7:1, 19, 25; 8:37, 40; 11:53; Acts 2:23; 3:15).

The Judeans also **killed...their own prophets** (Matt 23:37; Luke 11:47; 13:34; Acts 7:51-53). The words **their own** are not in the oldest and best Greek manuscripts, but the idea is evident by the context. They killed **both** Messiah and those who came to announce His coming. The Jewish leaders sought to seize Jesus when He taught the parable of the vineyard (Matt 21:33-46; Mark 12:1-12; Luke 20:9-18) in which He accused them of killing both the prophets and, in a short time, Him (cf. Acts 13:27).

Additionally, the Judeans **persecuted** Paul and Silas (**us**). What Paul once did to the church (Acts 9:4-5; 22:4; 26:11; Gal 1:23; 1 Cor 15:9; Phil 3:6; 1 Tim 1:13), the Jews now did to him and those who stood with him (Acts 9:23-25; 13:50; 14:5-6, 19). Persecution for Paul was foretold (Matt 5:10-12; Acts 9:16). Paul hints at it in the epistles (1 Cor 4:12; 2 Cor 4:9; Gal 5:11; 6:12). Persecution should actually be the expectation of all who live godly lives in Christ Jesus (2 Tim 3:12; cf. Phil 1:29-30).

To persecute Christians was to persecute Christ; to persecute the Son was to persecute the Father. Therefore, this **did not please God** (see *Overview*, 'Pleasing God' [2:4]) because they acted in the flesh (Rom 8:8) and they killed the One who always does the things that please God (John 8:29). Additionally, the Jews were **contrary to all men** in the spiritual sense of being hostile or against them, spiritually speaking.

2:16 The greatest example of their displeasure with God and animosity toward men occurred in their **forbidding** Paul (**us**) to **speak to the Gentiles that they may be saved**. These men attempted to silence God's spokesmen. What could be more horrible than withholding a life-saving message from people who otherwise will die? It was God's will that all men be saved through the gospel of Christ (1 Tim 2:4; 2 Pet 3:9), but the Jews wanted no one to find salvation in Jesus, even though He came to save His people (the Jews) from their sins (Matt 1:21). In effect, they attempted to gag God.

As a result, they sinned at the most severe level so that their cup of transgression and guilt was full **of their sins**. Nothing could do this more directly or fully than persecuting the preachers of the gospel. As a Divine result, **wrath has come upon them to the uttermost**. There is no direct mention that it is God's wrath, but given the context, it can be assumed.

What kind of **wrath** is this? (See notes on 1:10; 5:9.) It has been understood in four possible ways. First, it could refer historically to the Babylonian captivity (sixth century BC). However, that seems too far removed from Paul's day. Second, it could refer prophetically to Jerusalem's destruction in AD 70, although it is difficult to see how this would affect Jews outside of Judea. Third, it could be speaking of Christ's coming in eschatological judgment, but that would be limited only to the Jews alive at the time. A fourth alternative seems more likely, i.e. Paul speaks in soteriological terms of God's eternal wrath in exactly the same way as the Apostle John (John 3:18, 36). The outcome is so certain, it is spoken of as a present reality (**has come**). Context strongly favors this view. Those who reject the gospel or refuse to let it be preached will know the eternal wrath of God to the extreme, while those who believe the gospel will be rescued altogether from experiencing God's wrath.

C. Paul's Updates (2:17-3:13)

Having walked down memory lane with the Thessalonians and (1) rejoiced over what God had done to give birth to a presently thriving church (1:2-10), (2) rehearsed pastoral integrity (2:1-12), and (3) rewarded their faithfulness with words of praise (2:13-16), Paul now fills them in on what has happened since he departed (Acts 17:10). He expresses his great desire to come and regrets that he was unable (2:17-20). He then explains why he sent Timothy from Athens back to Thessalonica (3:1-5). Finally, Paul delights over what he heard from Timothy when he reunited with Paul in Corinth and brought good news about the flock (3:6-13; cf. Acts 18:5).

1. Paul's desire (2:17-20)

Absence had actually made Paul's heart for the Thessalonians grow fonder. He had deep-seated pastoral concerns for their ongoing spiritual welfare and strongly wanted to return, but could not.

But we, brethren, having been taken away from you for a short time in presence, not in heart, endeavoured more eagerly to see your face with great desire. Therefore we wanted to come to you – even I, Paul, time and again – but Satan hindered us. For what is our hope, or joy, or crown of rejoicing? Is it not even you in the presence of our Lord Jesus Christ at His coming? For you are our glory and joy (2:17-20).

2:17 We refers to Paul, Silas, and Timothy, all of whom departed Thessalonica for Berea under protest. **Having been taken away from you**, or literally 'orphaned', fits **brethren** better than the previous 'mother' (2:7) and 'father' (2:11-12) pictures. Paul was hurting or bereaved over their brutal, non-voluntary separation from their Christian family in Thessalonica (cf. Acts 17:5-10).

It had been months since he was in Thessalonica, but Paul considered it just **for a short time**, or literally 'for a season of one hour' (cf. Luke 8:13; 2 Cor 7:8). This understatement was used to emphasize the fact that, while he was not there in personal **presence**, he was there in **heart**, i.e. he had not forgotten them nor had his affections diminished. It was as if he had only been gone **for a short time**. For Paul, out of sight was certainly not out of mind.

With a passionate **desire to see** them again (**your face**), Paul and his friends spared no effort to return (**endeavored more eagerly**). Paul wanted them to understand that they were not forgotten nor abandoned. The pastor desperately wanted to be by their side but, in spite of herculean efforts to return at the time, they were unsuccessful in their many attempts.

2:18 They literally 'wished' (**wanted**) **to come** (Paul interjects here his own personal desire – **I, Paul**) on many occasions (**time and again**). Most likely, they explored possibilities to return when they were in Berea, Athens, and now Corinth, but to no avail.

OVERVIEW

Satan (2:18)

Satan first appears in Scripture at Genesis 3:1, approaching Eve in the garden and passes off the earthly scene to hell in Revelation 20:10. Throughout world history, he has energetically and ingeniously attempted to (1) ascend to the place of God's power and glory and (2) command the allegiance and obedience of the human race. He is mentioned twice in the Thessalonian correspondence by his most frequent and familiar name 'Satan' which means 'adversary' (1 Thess 2:18; 2 Thess 2:9). He is also referred to as 'the tempter' (1 Thess 3:5) and 'the evil one' (2 Thess 3:3).

Elsewhere in Scripture, Satan is called by many other names.

Serpent	(Gen 3:14; Rev 12:9; 20:2)
Devil	(Matt 4:1)
Enemy	(Matt 13:25, 39)
Ruler of the demons	(Mark 3:22)
Murderer	(John 8:44)
Liar	(John 8:44)
Ruler of this world	(John 12:31)
Evil One	(John 17:15)
God of this age	(2 Cor 4:4)
Roaring Lion	(1 Pet 5:8)
Dragon	(Rev 12:7, 9; 20:2)
Deceiver	(Rev 12:9)
Accuser	(Rev 12:10)

Satan's chief activity and goal in the lives of Christians is to cause them to think differently than God's Word and consequently act disobediently to God's will (Prov 23:7; 2 Cor 2:11; 10:4-5; 11:3; Eph 6:11, 16). He attempts to accomplish this end through four basic strategies:

1. By distorting or denying the truth of God's Word (Matt 4:1-11).
2. By discrediting the testimony of God's people (Acts 5:1-11).
3. By diminishing or destroying a believer's zeal to accomplish God's work (2 Cor 12:7-10).
4. By diluting the effectiveness of God's church (Luke 22:3-6).

Paul knew the Thessalonians would be curious to know why they could not return, so he tells them that **Satan hindered us**. There is no question here that Paul is referring to the infamous **Satan** of Scripture and not merely to some human adversary, although frequently he works through people since he is neither omnipresent nor omnipotent.

Hindered, used in a military sense of breaking up or cluttering up a road so as to make it impassable to the opposing army, describes Satan's activities in opposition to Paul. To him, this was intense spiritual warfare and the enemy was lying in ambush to attack them (Eph 6:10-12). How did Satan thwart Paul's effort? Most likely through the hostile Jews in Thessalonica. Either the potential violence which would be incited by their return or the pledge given by Jason at their departure (Acts 17:9) served as the barrier through which they could not move. Some have also suggested Paul's physical problems (cf. Gal 4:15), but this would seem to be foreign to the context.

Someone has said, 'When God is at work, Satan is surely alongside.' What Christ was building (Matt 16:18), the devil was committed to destroying. It is not surprising then to see **Satan** so visible in so many New Testament churches, e.g. Jerusalem (Acts 5:1-10), Corinth (2 Cor 2:1-11), Ephesus (1 Tim 3:6-7), Smyrna (Rev 2:9-10), Pergamum (Rev 2:13), Thyatira (Rev 2:24), and Philadelphia (Rev 3:9).

Paul had been able to discern between God closing a door to ministry and Satan blocking the way. Earlier in the journey, at the outset, they were forbidden by the Holy Spirit to speak the Word in Asia (Acts 16:6) and the Spirit did not permit them to go into Bithynia (Acts 16:7). This was clearly not the case here, yet God would triumph. Had Satan not prevented their return, potentially these two canonical letters would not have been written and the church would have been deprived of their treasures. Because of the circumstances, everyone reached a new level of spiritual purity and strength.

2:19 In a sudden burst of energy, Paul breaks out in hallelujahs over the Thessalonians. To demonstrate the ultimate in commitment and love, Paul asks one question in three parts. **For what is our hope, or joy, or crown of rejoicing?**

Paul had many spiritual hopes which were all bound up in the will of the God of hope (Rom 15:13). In one way or another, all of these hopes related to the believers' progress towards ultimate salvation or being with the Lord. He hoped in: the glory of God (Rom 5:2; Col 1:27); righteousness (Gal 5:5); salvation (5:8; Col 1:5); Jesus Christ (1 Tim 1:1); eternal life (Titus 1:2; 3:7); and the eschatological blessed hope (Titus 2:13). Here his **hope** is focused on God's work in the Thessalonians' lives (cf. 2 Cor 10:15). Paul and company had paid a dear price personally for the Thessalonians' spiritual progress and had high hopes that one day salvation's work would be completed in a final sense.

They were also the ministry team's **joy**, much like John who found no greater joy than seeing his children walk in truth (3 John 4). See *Overview*, 'The Joy of the Lord' (1:6) for a full discussion of joy. He speaks of the Philippians in much the same way (Phil 4:1).

Paul was **rejoicing** in few things or better, 'boasting in'. They included: the Lord (1 Cor 1:31); the hope of the glory of God (Rom 5:2); the cross of Christ (Gal 6:14); and the lives of those to whom he ministered (2 Thess 1:4; 2 Cor 9:2).

He pictured this as a **crown**, not a royal diadem (Rev 19:12), but the simple garland or wreath worn by a victor as the prize in an athletic contest. In Scripture, this crown (*stephanos*) points to various aspects of man's salvation. It is spoken of in terms of:

1) the imperishable wreath that celebrates salvation's victory over corruption (1 Cor 9:25);

2) the righteous wreath that celebrates salvation's victory over unrighteousness (2 Tim 4:8);

3) the unfading wreath of glory that celebrates salvation's victory over defilement (1 Pet 5:4);

4) the wreath of life that celebrates salvation's victory over death (James 1:12; Rev 2:10); and here

5) the wreath of exultation which celebrates salvation's victory over Satan's and mankind's persecution of believers.

The answer to Paul's question is **you** – the Thessalonians. While not a formal part of Paul's defense earlier (2:1-12), the sentiment still spills over as he updates the Thessalonians on what has recently transpired. They were not 'here today, gone tomorrow' in Paul's mind; they would be prominent to the end as indicated by these expressions of spiritual endearment.

When will Paul's **hope, joy,** and **crown of rejoicing** come to full fruition? When Paul is **in the presence of** the **Lord Jesus Christ at His coming**.

OVERVIEW

Christ's Coming (2:19)

Christ's eschatological 'coming' is frequently referred to in the New Testament by the simple word *parousia* which literally means 'to be alongside'. This term was frequently used in ancient literature to describe: (1) the arrival of the king or high-ranking government official; (2) the military invasion of a country; or (3) the visitation of deity. There seems to be no significant difference between the secular and biblical meaning of *parousia*.

Of the twenty-four New Testament uses of *parousia*, only six are in a non-eschatological context (1 Cor 16:17; 2 Cor 7:6, 7; 10:10; Phil 1:26; 2:12). All seven appearances in the Thessalonian epistles are prophetic in nature – six times of Christ (1 Thess 2:19; 3:13; 4:15; 5:23; 2 Thess 2:1, 8) and once of the Antichrist (2 Thess 2:9). There are eleven other New Testament uses (Matt 24:3, 27, 37, 39; 1 Cor 15:23; James 5:7, 8; 2 Pet 1:16; 3:4, 12; 1 John 2:28).

Parousia can be employed in the varying senses of: (1) anticipated arrival (Phil 1:26); (2) fact of arrival (1 Cor 16:17); or (3) presence after arrival (Phil 2:12). Eschatologically speaking, *parousia* can refer to (1) Christ's rapture of the church (1 Thess 4:15); (2) Christ's arrival in wrath to judge the earth (Matt 24: 27, 37, 39); or (3) the 'day of God' when the heaven and the earth will be burned up (2 Pet 3:12). Whether these three events occur in close proximity time-wise or are three distinct events separated by significant periods of time will generally be determined by one's prior prophetic convictions. It is this writer's opinion that *parousia* in 1 Thessalonians 2:19; 3:13; 4:15; 5:23; and 2 Thessalonians 2:1 all refer to the time of the rapture. The use of *parousia* in 2 Thessalonians 2:8 refers to the coming of Christ in judgment immediately prior to the millennium. See notes on 2 Thessalonians 1:7.

For this writer's prophetic convictions see *Appendix 1*, 'Various Millennial Views' and *Appendix 2*, 'The Time of the Rapture' (4:17). In light of these biblically based beliefs, then the time that Paul most likely has in mind here, in context and in this writer's opinion, is at the rapture of the church.

2:20 For you are our glory and joy. Paul and his companions were distinctly different from most religious leaders of the day. He was primarily focused on them (**you**) not himself (cf. 1:2, 5; 2:8, 12). He measured his ministry by the spiritual or eternal blessings received by those to whom he ministered, not the earthly and temporal. The Thessalonians were a **glory and joy** to God, so they were also an obvious **glory and joy** to Paul and his friends (cf. Phil 4:1). See *Overview*, 'The Joy of the Lord' (1:6) and *Overview*, 'The Glory of God' (2:12). They had surely set their affections on the things above, not on the earth (Col 3:1-2); they had stored up treasure in heaven where neither moth nor rust destroys and where thieves do not break in or steal (Matt 6:20).

2. Timothy's visit (3:1-5)
Paul's alternative plan was to send Timothy in his place to Thessalonica. Since Timothy was the youngest member of the team and thus the least prominent, there was the smallest possibility that Satan's blockade of Paul would be applied to him. The apostle was most concerned to build up their faith (3:1-2, 5a), to bolster their courage (3:3-4), and to block or neutralize any temptation from Satan (3:5b).

Therefore, when we could no longer endure it, we thought it good to be left in Athens alone, and sent Timothy, our brother and minister of God, and our fellow labourer in the gospel of Christ, to establish you and encourage you concerning your faith, that no one should be shaken by these afflictions; for you yourselves know that we are appointed to this. For, in fact, we told you before when we were with you that we would suffer tribulation, just as it happened, and you know. For this reason, when I could no longer endure it, I sent to know your faith, lest by some means the tempter had tempted you, and our labour might be in vain (3:1-5).

3:1 By the time that Paul, Silas, and Timothy had all reached **Athens** (Acts 17:15-16), they were tortured with such intense pain over their separation from the Thessalonians that they **(we) could no longer endure it**. They must have prayed for God's wisdom in this matter (James 1:2-5). As a result, they **(we) thought it good to be left in Athens alone**. While there were multiple advantages to the team in being together, the unselfish decision of sending someone was made. See *Historical Background* in the *Introduction* for a chronology of events when the missionaries were in Athens and Corinth.

3:2 So they **sent Timothy** (cf. Phil 2:19-24 when Paul sent Timothy to Philippi). It seems clear that Paul and Silas dispatched Timothy. As if to justify why he sent the junior member of their team, Paul describes him in three ways. First, Timothy was **our brother**, a true believer in the Lord Jesus Christ. Second, he was a **minister of God**. There is a major textual variant here with one option being to drop **minister** out altogether. However, this writer prefers to retain it since Paul uses this phrase elsewhere (Rom 13:4; 2 Cor 6:4; Col 1:7). Thus, Timothy would be serving God by returning to Thessalonica. Third, he was termed a **fellow laborer in the gospel of Christ**. Paul refers to Timothy in the same manner elsewhere (Rom 16:21) as he also does of Titus (2 Cor 8:23), Epaphroditus (Phil 2:25), and Philemon (Phile 1). So Timothy was highly qualified as a brother in Christ, a minister of God, and a fellow worker with Paul and Silas in the **gospel**. See notes regarding the gospel on 1:5, 2:2, 8.

Timothy was to **establish** or strengthen the Thessalonians **(you)**. This word was literally used in regard to buttressing or reinforcing a building. Normally, this is a ministry reserved for God (3:13; Rom 16:25; 2 Thess 2:17; 3:3). However, Paul desired this kind of ministry with the Romans (Rom 1:11; cf. 1 Thess 3:10) and Timothy would at Thessalonica. Closely related, Timothy would also **encourage** them, i.e. come alongside the flock to exhort or beseech them. Both of these activities would be done **concerning** their **faith** (cf. 3:5-7, 10). This was a common ministry practice of Paul (cf. Acts 14:22; 15:32; 18:23).

Faith could refer to doctrine (Jude 3) or the ability to believe Christ (Eph 2:8). Here, it is better taken as the whole spectrum of the Christian life (cf. 2 Thess 1:3). Paul is inquiring as to their entire Christian walk – both what they believe and how they behave. Paul was not concerned about their health, wealth, self-esteem, or ease of life, but rather their spiritual quality of life.

3:3 Paul's concern for their ongoing faith seems to be linked to his suffering and **afflictions** (cf. 2 Cor 4:7-11; 11:24-28; Col 1:24). Somehow, he believed that they would be less committed to their faith or be discouraged in their faith by misunderstanding what he had endured. It could be that his opponents were telling the Thessalonians that God's plan was not working out as evidenced by Paul's troubles, or that Paul's afflictions evidenced God's displeasure with him and his teaching (cf. Job's counsellors). Thus, they ought not to follow Paul's teaching.

To think this way about Paul would be to be potentially **shaken** or beguiled in one's faith. The flock would have been deceivingly alarmed and upset (cf. 2 Thess 2:1-2). So, Paul reminded them that they knew ahead of time, because he had taught them, that he had been **appointed** to **afflictions** (3:3). The Greek word translated **appointed** literally means 'to lie down'. Here it is used figuratively of someone who has been laid or sat down, i.e. appointed (by God specifically, Acts 9:16, or generally, 2 Tim 3:12) for these tough times (cf. Luke 2:34; Phil 1:16).

3:4 These experiences of **tribulation** for Paul were not just by chance, bad luck, or even an uncontrollable conspiracy. He knew and they knew that God had allowed this to happen and it would work out according to His sovereign will. Just as Jesus warned the disciples ahead of time concerning His crucifixion (John 13:19; 14:29), so Paul had alerted the Thessalonians (cf. 4:2; 2 Thess 2:5; 3:10). Christians who don't experience persecution or affliction are the exception, not the rule (John 16:33; Acts 14:22).

3:5 Paul picks his thoughts back up again from 3:1, **when I could no longer endure it**. Here he expresses his own personal agony at not knowing how the Thessalonians were doing in regard to their

faith (cf. 3:2). So, Paul **sent** Timothy to find out and report back to him.

Of first concern was that **the tempter** (Satan) had **tempted** them (**you**). See *Overview*, 'Satan' (2:18). The word translated 'tempt' can be neutral in the sense of 'test' or negative in the sense of 'lure'. Because Paul is speaking of Satan (cf. 2 Thess 2:9; 3:3), the intent is obviously to disable the Thessalonians' faith by deceitfully drawing them into sin, by testing them with malicious intentions. Satan is elsewhere said to tempt (1 Cor 7:5) and is found in Matthew 4:3 tempting Christ. While Paul fulfilled his human responsibility by sending Timothy, God is the ultimate help in the moment of temptation (cf. 1 Cor 10:13; 2 Pet 2:9).

Had the Thessalonians actually succumbed to Satan's temptations, Paul was concerned that his wearying **labor** would have been in **vain**. It had not initially been empty (cf. 2:1) and he did not want it to ever be without impact. Paul was not ignorant of Satan's schemes (2 Cor 2:11), nor vulnerable to his methods (Eph 6:11), nor naive about his intent (1 Pet 5:8), so he takes decisive action by sending Timothy to block Satan's expected attack. Paul's chief ministry priority at this point was to see the Thessalonians continue to mature in their walk with God. It is uncertain if the Thessalonians had actually been tempted or not, but Paul's concern was justified in light of their temptation in 2 Thessalonians 2:2.

Paul did not underestimate the power of Satan. He knew that what had occurred in Eden could also occur in Thessalonica. He most likely suspected that if Satan was thwarting his own return to the flock (2:18), that it was because Satan intended to tempt them and he did not want any spiritual intervention. If Satan had been successful, the Thessalonians would have sent forth the perception that God's power was weak and Paul's ministry was frail. Nothing could have been further from the truth and reality, yet nothing could have disabled the Thessalonians more.

OVERVIEW

Defeating Satan (3:5)

God has prepared the true believer to not be defeated by Satan. Here are eleven means by which the spiritual battle can be won.

1. The Savior's victory at Calvary (John 12:31; Heb 2:14; Rev 12:11).
2. The overcomer promise (1 John 2:13; 5:4-5).
3. The intercessory ministry of Christ (John 17:15).
4. The protection of Christ (1 John 5:18).
5. The knowledge of Satan's tactics (2 Cor 2:11).
6. The believer's spiritual armor (Eph 6:10-17).
7. The Holy Spirit's indwelling power (1 John 4:4).
8. The believer's prayers (Matt 6:13; Eph 6:18-20).
9. Biblical instructions for defeating Satan (James 4:7-8).
10. Shepherds who strengthen and encourage (1 Thess 3:2, 5).
11. The encouragement of ultimate victory (Rev 20:10).

---

3. Timothy's return (3:6-10)

Having explained why Timothy had been sent to the Thessalonians (3:1-5), Paul now rejoices greatly at the positive report with which Timothy returned to Paul in Corinth (Acts 18:5). Undoubtedly, Timothy's return with good news of the flock prompted Paul to write this letter as an immediate outlet for his personal joy over their spiritual progress.

But now that Timothy has come to us from you, and brought us good news of your faith and love, and that you always have good remembrance of us, greatly desiring to see us, as we also to see you– therefore, brethren, in all our affliction and distress we were comforted concerning you by your faith. For now we live, if you stand fast in the Lord. For what thanks can we render to God for you, for all the joy with which we rejoice for your sake before our God, night and day praying exceedingly that we may see your face and perfect what is lacking in your faith? (3:6-10).

3:6 Paul would know the pain of people trying to destroy his ministry. Judaizers came in after him in Galatia with a false gospel (Gal 1:6-10). Some people in Corinth turned on him (2 Cor 12:19-21). A certain group of Christians schemed to make Paul miserable in Rome (Phil 1:15-18). Would it be a sad day when Timothy returned from Thessalonica? Would they still love their pastor? Would they have withstood Satan's temptations?

When **Timothy** returned (**has come to us**) to Paul at Corinth **from** Thessalonica (**you**), he brought **good news** of their **faith and love**. This is the only time in the New Testament where the word usually translated 'gospel' is employed for general good news. Paul had (3:2, 5) and would continue (3:10) to be concerned about their **faith** and their **love** (4:9-10). There is no significance to the fact that Paul does not include 'hope' here as he had in 1:3 (cf. 2 Thess 1:3 where faith and love are combined). **Faith and love** taken together would represent the totality of the Christian life – internally and externally, beliefs and behavior. Perhaps Paul has in mind their **faith** towards God and their **love** for the brethren as he did in Colossians 1:4. See *Overview*, 'True Love' (5:13).

There was no question that Paul wanted to see the Thessalonians again (2:17-3:5). But did they want to see Paul again? Like Paul's remembrances of them (1:3), they **always** had a **good remembrance** of Paul, Silas, and Timothy (**us**). What had started well, now continued even better. Just as Paul could not get the Thessalonians out of his mind (1:2), so they also **always** had **good** thoughts about their first pastors.

The relationship had grown so strong that they **greatly desired** to be reunited, i.e. **to see** each other. Paul speaks of this strong yearning in the same terms as a babe desiring mother's milk or his own longing later to see Timothy (2 Tim 1:4) and other churches (Rom 1:11; Phil 1:8).

3:7 Through the good news from Timothy about the **brethren** in Thessalonica (**therefore**), Paul and his friends were **comforted** to hear of their healthy **faith**. Although it was not perfect, as evidenced by Paul's exhortations in this letter, their faith had endured Satan's temptations and the Jews' assaults. Their faith was not stagnant nor was their love for Paul merely lukewarm. Their faith proclaimed fruitful works, their love resulted in strenuous and sacrificial labor, and their hope made them patiently endure (1:3).

This good news could not have come at a better time. Paul faced **affliction**, literally 'a calamity', in Corinth along with **distress** (translated 'affliction' in 3:3). Both words are used together in Job 15:24 (LXX) of one who is terrified and overpowered. It is no wonder then that the Lord appeared to Paul in a vision at Corinth saying, 'Do not be afraid, but speak, and do not keep silent; for I am with you, and no one will attack you to hurt you; for I have many people in this city' (Acts 18:9-10; cf. 1 Cor 2:3). In the midst of intense pressure over preaching the gospel, the good news from Thessalonica **comforted** Paul and brought great joy.

3:8 As a result, Paul seemingly shouts, **Now we live**. The good news not only has comforted (3:7) but also refreshed, rejuvenated, and energized. It is likely that he has a new lease on life because a heavy burden of concern for the Thessalonians has been lifted (cf. 2 Cor 11:28).

Paul speaks of this whole episode in military terms. He was hindered by Satan from returning to Thessalonica (2:18). The Thessalonians were in danger of being ambushed by Satan's temptations (3:5). Paul was weighed down in Corinth (3:7) and could send only one man as a reinforcement to Thessalonica (3:2, 5).

Then, he gets Timothy's battlefield report (3:6-7) and announces, **you stand fast in the Lord**. They had faced the enemy and refused to retreat. The **if** here would be better translated 'because', in light of the Thessalonians' resolve. This is certainly the language of spiritual warfare as evidenced by three mentions of *stand* in the context of putting on the spiritual armor of God and waging war against the spiritual forces of darkness in Ephesians 6:11, 13-14. **Stand fast** (or 'firm') is a frequent exhortation by Paul to the churches (1 Cor 16:13; Gal 5:1; Phil 1:27; 4:1; 2 Thess 2:15). So Paul's small, newly-trained band of militia had withstood the well-equipped and expertly-prepared army of hell to win the battle. Now their spiritual general, Paul, shouts the victory. Paul's desire that they walk worthy of God (2:12) had surely been achieved by their immoveable commitment to Christ.

3:9 Paul asks an interesting question in 3:9-10. His **joy** is so great over what **God** has done in and through the Thessalonians (**for your sake**), that he inquires (**before our God**) how their **thanks** to **God** could ever match or repay God for the **joy** that He has provided to them. Paul sees himself as a debtor to God for the spiritual fruit He has provided in Paul's ministry (cf. 2 Thess 1:3 notes). As a result, Paul pours out a never-ending stream of prayer, adoration, and thanksgiving as an offering to God, knowing that he will never be able to fully repay the obligation. The psalmist expressed the same idea, 'What shall I render to the Lord for all His benefits toward me?' (116:12). Paul here expresses that same joy as did John when his children walked in truth (3 John 4).

OVERVIEW

The Names of God (3:9)

The psalmist exuberantly exclaimed, 'O Lord, our Lord, how majestic is your name in all the earth!' (Ps 8:1). Actually, Scripture reveals not one but hundreds of names for God the Father, God the Son, and the Holy Spirit, such as 'the Rock' (Deut 32:15), 'Everlasting Father' (Isa 9:6), 'Faithful and True' (Rev 19:11), and 'the Word of God' (Rev 19:13).

This priceless treasure portrays God's character ('the Father of compassion', 2 Cor 1:3), God's deeds ('the deliverer', Rom 11:26), God's roles ('the righteous Judge', 2 Tim 4:8), God's relationships ('the good shepherd', Ps 23:1), and God's rank ('God of gods', Psalm 136:2). In the future, God the Father will bestow upon God the Son 'the name that is above every name' (Phil 2:9).

The Meaning of 'Name'
Reflecting this richness, the Bible uses God's name in several different ways:

1. *Name* refers to God Himself as in 'those who love your name' (Ps 5:11) or 'those who believe in His name' (John 1:12).

2. *Name* can be used to represent God's reputation, as in Psalm 106:8, 'for His name's sake'.

3. 'In the name of the LORD' (Ps 118:26) and 'whatever you ask in My name' (John 14:13) indicate God's authority.

4. God's presence is referred to by 'your Name is near' (Ps 75:1).

5. 'Everyone who is called by My name' (Isa 43:7) and 'your people bear your Name' (Dan 9:19) indicate divine ownership.

Prominent Names

Here are some of the key names of God:

Elohim or God (*Theos* in the New Testament) means He is supreme above people and all things (Gen 1:1). He is the creator; everything has been made by Him (Isa 40:28).

El-Elyon, 'the Most High', reflects God's unique authority over creation (Deut 32:8).

El-Shaddai, God Almighty, points to God's invincibility and His omnipotence (Gen 17:1-2). Nothing is too hard for God, and no enemy will ever defeat Him because He can do all things. God is also called 'the Mighty One' (Ps 132:2, 5).

Adonai means Lord or Master (Deut 10:17), indicating authority and ownership.

YHWH (rendered 'Jehovah' or 'Yahweh' in some Bibles) or LORD occurs over 6,800 times in the Old Testament and speaks of God's eternal and unchanging nature. God used this name, which literally means I AM, to instruct Moses (Exod 3:13-15). Christ confounded the Pharisees when he said, 'Before Abraham was born, I am!' (John 8:58).

El-Olam, 'the Eternal God', also points to God's foreverness (Gen 21:33).

Jehovah-Jireh, 'the LORD Will Provide', is a name Abraham memorably learned about when God substituted the ram sacrifice to replace Isaac (Gen 22:14). The name pictures God's divine provision of the right supply at just the right time. His omniscience or all-knowingness and wisdom are on display.

Jehovah-Rapha points to God as the healer (Exod 15:26). The Shepherd's mercy, compassion, and lovingkindness are center stage.

Jehovah-M'kaddesh, which means 'the LORD who sanctifies', depicts God's holiness (Lev 20:7-8). He stands as our Redeemer and the one who sets believers apart from sin. A synonym is 'the Holy One' (Isa 40:25).

Jehovah-Shalom, signifying the quality of peace that is central to God's nature, is also the name given by Gideon to an altar he built (Judges 6:24).

Jehovah-Tsidkenu, or 'Jehovah our righteousness', is more closely associated in a redemptive sense (Jer 23:5-6).

Jehovah-Rohi, 'The LORD is my shepherd' (Ps 23:1) and *Jehovah-Shammah*, 'the LORD is there' (Ezek 48:35) describe God's presence to guide, protect, and make provision for our needs.

Jehovah-Sabaoth or LORD Almighty ('LORD of hosts', NASB, NKJV) refers to God's command of all His creation, which ensures divine victory over every enemy (Jer 11:20).

Jehovah-Nissi, 'the LORD is my Banner', triumphantly pictures that God's presence and promise of deliverance will continually identify His people (Exod 17:15).

3:10 In spite of, and perhaps also because of, this exhilarating news concerning the Thessalonians, Paul more than ever wanted to return to **see** their **face**, i.e. to be there in person. He speaks about his **praying** to this end in two ways. First, as to persistence and frequency, he prayed **night and day**. Since he also labored night and day (2:9; 2 Thess 3:8), he must have prayed while he worked because he could not get the Thessalonians out of his mind (much like the needy widow in Luke 18:1-8). Second, as to fervency, Paul was **praying** at the extreme, highest level, i.e. **exceedingly**. Using the same Greek word on the Divine side, Paul would later write that God is able to do 'exceedingly, abundantly above' all we are able to ask or think (Eph 3:20). His prayers overflowed all known boundaries as he flooded heaven with this request. The word Paul uses for prayer (*deomai*) indicates a begging-like passion for God to supply an urgent need. See the survey of Paul's prayer life in the notes on 1:2.

His chief desire behind such intense prayer was to minister to the new converts whom he longed to see face to face. He would **perfect what** was **lacking** in their **faith**. Paul is not being critical of the church, but rather acknowledging that they had not yet reached their full potential. **Perfect** describes: (1) setting a broken bone; (2) healing a wounded relationship (Gal 6:1); (3) mending a torn net (Matt 4:21); or (4) supplying a military operation, which is the sense employed here. It is not difficult to understand that a church which is hardly a year old would be **lacking in their faith**. Paul strongly wanted to come and minister to their needs with his spiritual supply. Having now explained how and for what he would pray, Paul actually prays (3:11-13).

4. Paul's pastoral prayer (3:11-13)

Paul concludes his Personal Comments (1:1-3:13) with a wonderful pastoral prayer. For the present, he prays that God will allow the ministry party to return to Thessalonica (3:11) and that the Thessalonians will grow in their faith (3:12). Regarding the future, Paul prays that their salvation will be made complete at the coming of Christ (3:13). He has written about his prayer life (1:2-4; 3:9-10); now he prays for the first time in the epistle. His intercession is uncomplicated, but profound.

Now may our God and Father Himself, and our Lord Jesus Christ, direct our way to you. And may the Lord make you increase and abound in love to one another and to all, just as we do to you, so that He may establish your hearts blameless in holiness before our God and Father at the coming of our Lord Jesus Christ with all His saints (3:11-13).

3:11 Paul's prayer overall bears four general characteristics: it is directed to God; it is focused on others; it is spiritual in content; and it acknowledges his utter dependence on God. He is depending on **God** the **Father** and the **Lord Jesus Christ** (see notes on 1:1, 3 for the significance of the two being mentioned together) to overpower the one who thwarted Paul's return to Thessalonica. He confesses, in effect, his own inability to do what needs to be done (2:17-3:5, 10) and appeals to his omnipotent God to overcome any and all obstacles. **Direct** is always used in the New Testament in the context of prayer (Luke 1:79; 2 Thess 3:5). Put another way, Paul is asking God to navigate a straight course (**our way**) for Paul **to** Thessalonica (**you**) without frequent stops or detours, i.e. to remove the hindrances previously erected by Satan (2:18). Paul has already disclosed his reason for wanting to come (3:10). Paul's prayer was answered in due time (Acts 20:1, 3-4; 1 Tim 1:3). See 'Additional Visits' under *Historical Background* in the *Introduction* for details.

3:12 To **increase and abound in love** is not something that can be humanly willed by merely increasing the emotional output of the flock. **Love to one another and to all** is something that takes the **Lord** to **make** happen. It is the fruit of the Holy Spirit's work in the life of a believer (Gal 5:22).

Paul is not praying for infrequent or barely noticeable **love**, but rather love that is increasing (2 Thess 1:3) to the point that it abounds (cf. 4:1, 10). Paul uses these two growth words together in 2 Corinthians 4:15 and Philippians 4:17-18. See *Overview*, 'True Love' (5:13) for all of the components that make up Divine love dispensed through Christians by God. He wanted the Thessalonians to rise to the same intensity of love as he had for them (**we do to you**; cf. 2:1-12; 3:1-5).

Their **love** would be expressed broadly (**to all**) and more narrowly (**to one another**). God's redemptive overture of love in Christ was to all men (John 3:16; 1 Tim 2:4; 4:10; Titus 2:11; 2 Pet 3:9). Thus, the redeemed should respond in love to all with peace (Rom 12:18; Heb 12:14), goodness (5:15; Gal 6:10), patience (5:14; Phil 4:5), prayer (1 Tim 2:1), consideration (Titus 3:2), and honor (1 Pet 2:17). Even more important, the redeemed should respond to each other in love. God answered Paul's prayer rather quickly (cf. 2 Thess 1:3).

OVERVIEW

New Testament 'One Anothers' (3:12)

Family behavior in the body of Christ starts with 'Love one another'. Our Lord told the disciples, *By this all will know that you are My disciples, if you have love for one another* (John 13:35).

The epistles refer to this overarching principle more than ten times (Rom 12:10; 13:8; 1 Thess 3:12; 4:9; 2 Thess 1:3; 1 Pet 1:22; 1 John 3:11, 23; 4:7, 11; 2 John 5).

From this general statement, the epistles then specifically explain the various features of 'one another' ministry in the church. They are numerous and, in general, self-explanatory.

Be devoted	(Rom 12:10)
Honor by giving preference	(Rom 12:10)
Be of the same mind	(Rom 12:16; 15:5)
Build up	(Rom 14:19; 1 Thess 5:11)
Be at peace	(Rom 14:19)
Receive/accept	(Rom 15:7)
Admonish/comfort	(Rom 15:14; 1 Thess 4:18; 5:11)
Greet	(Rom 16:16; 1 Cor 16:20; 2 Cor 13:12;1 Pet 5:14)
Care	(1 Cor 12:25)
Serve	(Gal 5:13)
Bear burdens	(Gal 6:2)
Forbear, be patient	(Eph 4:2; Col 3:13)
Be kind	(Eph 4:32)
Submit	(Eph 5:21)
Esteem highly	(Phil 2:3)
Forgive	(Col 3:13)
Seek the good	(1 Thess 5:15)
Stimulate	(Heb 10:24)
Confess sins	(James 5:16)
Pray for	(James 5:16)
Be hospitable	(1 Pet 4:9)
Be humble	(1 Pet 5:5)
Fellowship in the light	(1 John 1:7)

Not only are Christians to add positive responses to their lifestyle, but they need to eliminate or avoid other responses which Scripture prohibits. Here is a look at the 'do not' side of the 'one anothers'.

Owe anything but love	(Rom 13:8)
Judge	(Rom 14:13)
Defraud/deprive in marriage	(1 Cor 7:5)
Devour/consume	(Gal 5:15)
Provoke/challenge	(Gal 5:26)
Envy	(Gal 5:26)
Lie	(Col 3:9)
Hate	(Titus 3:3)
Speak against/complain	(James 4:11; 5:9)

Whether it be a marriage, a family, or the body of Christ, when these mature behavior patterns consistently color life, great harmony and peace will be the experience.

3:13 So that He may establish your hearts blameless in holiness looks forward towards the end in conjunction with **the coming of the Lord Jesus Christ**. This would be to the Bema or judgment seat of Christ (2 Cor 5:10; cf. Rom 14:10; 1 Cor 3:10-15) before which all believers will appear. There, the inner man (**hearts**; cf. 2:4) is **establish**ed (3:2; 2 Thess 2:17; 3:3) as **blameless in holiness** (cf. 5:23). In other words, this is a part of the believer's glorification (Rom 8:17, 30). This would occur immediately after the rapture of the church (4:13-18), **before** (in the presence of) **God** the **Father** in heaven (cf. John 14:1-3). Paul uses **coming** here in the same sense that he did in 2:19.

Paul prays that with regard to **holiness** there will be no grounds of accusation (**blameless**) towards unholiness. This is a major New Testament theme (cf. 1 Cor 1:8; 2 Cor 11:2; Eph 5:25-27; Jude 24). It is God's supreme wish that believers be holy even as He is holy (Lev 20:26; 1 Pet 1:15-16).

All of this occurs in tandem with **the coming of** the **Lord Jesus Christ**. This is the second of four mentions (cf. 2:19; 4:15; 5:23) in this letter. In light of what happens, this **coming** would refer to the rapture (4:15) and immediately subsequent events. See *Overview*, 'Christ's Coming' (2:19) for further details and the discussion of 'coming' in the notes on 2:19.

With all His saints raises two major questions: Who are the saints? What are the saints doing? Three possible answers have been given to the first question: believers; angels; or both. Those who favour angels point to Old Testament texts (Ps 68:17; Dan 7:10) which picture Christ surrounded by angels, as well as New Testament texts (e.g. Matt 25:31). While this is true, it does not deal with **His saints** in this Pauline text. The phrase, literally 'His holy ones', is repeatedly used by Paul in at least nine of his epistles to refer to believers. Never does Paul elsewhere use the phrase to refer to angels. Even in all of the New Testament, there is only one possible use referring to angels (Jude 14). Therefore, this writer prefers the interpretation of **His saints** as 'believers in Christ'. The phrase really cannot accommodate both believers and angels, especially if there is no other evidence for it.

If **His saints** are believers, then in what activity are they engaged? Some suggest that they are part of Christ's royal entourage at the parousia. It could be that the spirits of deceased believers return with Christ to receive their resurrected, glorified bodies at the time of the rapture (cf. 4:14), but that is unlikely. A better view, in this writer's opinion, is that it refers to His people who join the Thessalonians at the Bema. The verse could easily be translated, 'So that He may establish your hearts blameless in holiness **with all His saints** before our God and Father at the coming of our Lord Jesus Christ.' Given the context and Pauline word usage, this approach to both the time and nature of the event seems to make the most reasonable sense. Some manuscripts end with 'Amen', although this is likely a later scribal addition.

Thus, Paul's first (Personal Comments; 1:1-3:13) of two major sections in this letter ends with Paul praying that God would fully complete in the future (3:13) what He first began (1:5-10) just about twelve months earlier regarding the Thessalonian believers. He now moves to the second and last section of the epistle (Pastoral Comments; 4:1-5:28) where he deals with doctrinal and behavioral issues.

2. PASTORAL COMMENTS (4:1-5:28)

One now encounters a decided shift in Paul's letter away from Personal Comments (1:1-3:13) to Pastoral Comments (4:1-5:28) which complete the letter. The apostle deals with doctrinal issues such as the resurrection in relationship to the rapture (4:13-18) and the day of the Lord (5:1-11). He also addresses ethical subjects like sexual purity (4:3-8), interpersonal relationships (4:9-12), and church harmony (5:12-15).

A. Paul's Exhortations (4:1-5:22)

Exactly who or what raised the topics that Paul engages is not exactly known for sure. Was there correspondence from the Thessalonians carried back to Paul by Timothy? While that is a possibility, there is no hint of such a letter. Did Paul intuitively know, like a spiritual father (2:11-12), what the Thessalonians needed to hear? This could be, but nothing in the letter points to this

explanation. Most likely, he wrote in response to Timothy's report
when he returned to Paul at Corinth from Thessalonica (3:1, 5;
Acts 18:5). None of the situations mentioned in the rest of 1 Thessalonians seems to have reached an extreme stage, since Paul's
exhortations appear to be either proactive or just mildly corrective.

1. In general (4:1-2)

Finally then, brethren, we urge and exhort in the Lord Jesus that you should
abound more and more, just as you received from us how you ought to walk
and to please God; for you know what commandments we gave you through
the Lord Jesus (4:1-2).

Finally then, brethren makes a major transition in Paul's
thoughts. It could also be translated 'as far as the rest goes' or 'in
addition' (cf. 2 Thess 3:1; Phil 3:1). Paul continues to remind his
readers (**brethren**) that they share a common bond in the
redemption of Jesus Christ that makes them part of God's family.
This is the eighth of nineteen uses in this epistle alone. Paul's
overall exhortation here picks up scattered mentions of the same
theme in earlier remembrances and prayers (1:3, 9-10; 2:12; 3:6-8,
10, 12-13). These two verses should be understood as a general
introduction to the specific exhortations that follow.

4:1 Paul is eager that the Thessalonians mature in the faith, so he
intimately appeals (**urge**) and firmly nudges (**exhort**) them to that
end. This is the only time that Paul uses this combination of words
in either epistle to be candid about the spiritual direction which
they should take. Further adding to the importance of the subject,
Paul writes first as one brother to another which is the idea behind
urge, while he is also writing as a representative of the **Lord Jesus**
who is now conveying the Savior's will for them. His main point is
that they should **abound more and more**. In other words, avoid
spiritual lethargy or complacency. While the church had an
amazing beginning, one year later they had not yet arrived at the
finish line. Interestingly, nowhere does the epistle ever discuss the
number of people in the church (quantity), but Paul continues to
encourage their advance in quality.

Paul's instruction centered on how they **ought to walk and to please God** (see *Overview*, 'Pleasing God' [2:4]). They had already **received** this kind of instruction from the men (**us**) when they were in Thessalonica (2:13). Paul's exhortation is not new in content, but rather a reminder of fact and a motivation to reach new levels of spiritual excellency (cf. Eph 5:10). There is a textual variant which the NKJV does not include, **just as you are actually walking**, which seems to be genuine. It would indicate that Paul is not rebuking them for disobedience, but rather affirming them in their Christian walk and encouraging them to continue their growth pattern. Everything else in the epistle would indicate that this is a true picture of the Thessalonians' spirituality.

4:2 For you know what commandments we gave you reminds them of the Divine authority (**through the Lord Jesus**) behind their teaching (cf. 4:15; 5:27; 2 Thess 3: 6, 12). The precepts were not optional but mandatory; the heavenly responses would be blessing for obedience or God's displeasure and chastisement for disobedience. The past instructions (cf. 3:4; 2 Thess 2:5; 3:10) had been delivered by Christ's representatives and were binding on the Thessalonians. These Christian marching orders are obligatory because they ultimately come from the Lord. In a sense, then, these commandments formed their 'Manual of Arms' or fighting instructions for the spiritual battle ahead.

2. Sexual purity (4:3-8)

The Greek culture of Paul's day openly celebrated immorality and could be characterized as highly sensual. Since the apostle writes from Corinth, he would have daily, explicit reminders of the reigning debauchery, not only from daily life in the city, but also from the over 1500 feet-above-sea level Acro-Corinth, a sanctuary devoted to Aphrodite the love goddess, which housed over 1,000 male and female courtesans who fronted as religious servants of the temple. While Thessalonica did not have the sexual reputation of Corinth, it was a major seaport and trade center, which attracted lewd practices. Therefore, it is not surprising that Paul begins with a call to pursue purity.

For this is the will of God, your sanctification: that you should abstain from sexual immorality; that each of you should know how to possess his own vessel in sanctification and honour, not in passion of lust, like the Gentiles who do not know God; that no one should take advantage of and defraud his brother in this matter, because the Lord is the avenger of all such, as we also forewarned you and testified. For God did not call us to uncleanness, but in holiness. Therefore he who rejects this does not reject man, but God, who has also given us His Holy Spirit (4:3-8).

4:3 For this is the will of God abruptly commences this section by declaring an absolute, i.e. God's will for everyone. Paul is about to answer one of the most often asked questions in Christian circles – 'What is God's will for my life?' – with a direct statement.

OVERVIEW

The Will of God (4:3)

Christians ought to make God's will the practice of their life – nothing more, nothing less, and nothing else. There are at least ten specific statements of God's particular will in the Bible for true believers.

1. Salvation	(1 Tim 2:4; 2 Pet 3:9)
2. Sacrifice	(Rom 12:1-2)
3. Spirit-control	(Eph 5:17-21)
4. Sanctification	(1 Thess 4:3-4)
5. Submission	(1 Pet 2:13-15)
6. Satisfaction	(1 Thess 5:18)
7. Seeking	(1 John 5:14-15)
8. Serving	(Ps 103:21)
9. Suffering	(1 Pet 3:17; 4:19)
10. Shepherding	(1 Pet 5:2)

The **will of God** here is **your sanctification**, being set apart for holy living (cf. 2 Cor 7:1; Heb 12:14; 1 Pet 1:15-17). Paul begins to elaborate on the general subject of holiness for which he prayed in 3:13. In 4:3-4, 7, he refers to present or progressive sanctification in this life, especially sexual purity. In 5:23, he prays in a similar sense to 3:13 regarding final or ultimate sanctification at the time of glorification. In 2 Thessalonians 2:13, Paul mentions the activity of the Spirit in sanctification in the initial sense of salvation. It is the Holy Spirit (1:5-6; 4:8) then who produces saints (lit. 'holy ones'). To be holy is to emulate God's highest quality (Isa 6:3).

This is one of the most socially relevant passages in Scripture. It touches on homosexuality, pornography, trans-sexuality, bestiality, incest, adultery, premarital and extramarital sex, sexually transmitted disease, abortion, trial relationships, and casual sex, just to mention a few expressions or ramifications of **sexual immorality**. Obedience to this part of God's will has enormous implications for good and prosperity.

Paul answers the first question, 'What does this sanctification involve?' **That you should abstain from sexual immorality**. The word translated **abstain** means 'to hold oneself off of' (cf. 5:22; 'Abstain from every form of evil'). The Thessalonians were to respond to sexual temptation like Joseph who refused the overtures of Potiphar's wife (Gen 39: 7-12). Paul stresses the Christian's human responsibility when confronted by **sexual immorality**. The Greek word (*porneia*) is a broad, all-inclusive term for both the married and the single that has any connection with sexual impropriety, even one's thought life (see Matt 5:27-28). There are no exceptions whatsoever in this realm of life.

OVERVIEW

Biblical Sexuality (4:3)

The Bible is not at all silent about human sexuality which is portrayed as good when not tainted by sinful perversion (Gen 1:31). God created the human race male and female, with two distinctly different sets of sexual characteristics, who were to be righteously joined for propagation of the human race (Gen. 1:27-28; 9:1) and mutual pleasure for husband and wife (Prov 5:15-21; 1 Cor 7:1-5).

Tragically, with the fall of Adam and Eve into sin (Gen 3:1-7), the most vile distortions of God's will quickly took over in the realm of sexuality. Polygamy was practiced by Lamech (Gen 4:19). Abraham engaged Hagar in adultery (Gen 16:3-4). Sodom and Gomorrah became synonymous with homosexuality (Gen 19:4-10). Lot's daughters initiated an incestuous relationship with their father (Gen 19:30-38). Shechem raped Dinah (Gen 34:2). Judah engaged the services of a prostitute (Gen 38:12-19).

Without looking at every biblical text on the subject, I will suggest that the whole of scriptural truth on the subject can be summarized in three principles. If one's sexual practices conform to these, then it is a righteous act. However, if any part of the three is violated, then one has sinfully tarnished that which God intended to be positive and pure.

Principle One: Sexual activity is to be between a man and a woman (Gen 2:24). This rules out the extreme perversions of bestiality (Exod 22:19; Lev 18:23; 20:15-16; Deut 27:21) and homosexuality (Lev 18:22; 20:13; Rom 1:24-27; 1 Cor 6:9; 1 Tim 1:10; Jude 7). This principle definitively answers the question of 'who?'

Principle Two: Sexual activity is to be after marriage and not before (Heb 13:4). This prohibits any premarital sex and addresses the inquiry of 'when?'

Principle Three: Sexual activity is for mutual gratification between legitimate marriage partners (1 Cor 7:3-5). This forbids incest (Lev 18:6-18; 20:11-14, 17-21; Deut 22:30; 27:20, 22-23; 1 Cor 5:1-5) and adultery (Lev 20:10; Deut 23:17-18; Prov 2:16-22; 1 Cor 6:15-20). It answers the question 'why?'

4:4 'How does one abstain?' is the next question Paul answers in both a positive (4:4) and negative sense (4:5). There are two distinct choices in the translation and interpretation here. Both 'to acquire his own wife' and **to possess his own** body (**vessel**) have been offered as the intended meanings. This writer prefers the latter for seven reasons.

First, while the verb when it is in the present tense is usually translated 'acquire' and in the perfect tense is translated 'possess', there is abundant evidence in the papyri documents that it could also mean 'possess' in the present tense. There is a strong possibility that this verb in the present tense means 'possess' also in Luke 18:12.

Second, although the noun *skeuos* (wife or body) is translated 'wife' in Ruth 4:10 (LXX) and associated with 'wife' in 1 Peter 3:7, it is always intended to mean 'body' or 'person' in the New Testament when not taken in its literal sense (cf. Acts 9:15; Rom 9:21, 22, 23; 2 Cor 4:7; 2 Tim 2:21; 1 Pet 3:7; Rev 2:27).

Third, being married is no guarantee of sexual purity, but having one's body under control does.

Fourth, there is no evidence that Paul is talking to men only. Rather, it is assured that he is addressing both men and women and thus 'possess one's body' would be preferable.

Fifth, never in the New Testament are believers commanded to marry, but they are commanded to be sexually pure by having one's body under control.

Sixth, to take this as referring to marriage only would be unbiblically derogatory toward the single state (1 Cor 7:32-35).

Seventh, it would make Paul a poor example since he was single. If each person, male or female, married or single, would **possess** one's body **in sanctification and honor**, then each would **abstain from sexual immorality**.

4:5 Paul contrasts the sanctification and honor of the believer (4:4) with **passion of lust like the Gentiles**. **Lust** is translated from a word that can be taken positively (2:17) or negatively depending on context. In the New Testament, it is frequently used in the context of sinful practices (cf. Rom 1:24; Gal 5:16; Eph 2:3; 4:22; Col 3:5; Titus 2:12). **Gentiles** would be better translated 'heathen' or 'nations' to indicate non-Christians. Paul's point is that Christians should be able to control their bodies in contrast to unbelievers whose passions run wild and out of control. Paul is writing about the heathen (both Jew and Gentile) as confirmed by his description that they **do not know God** (cf. 1 Cor 1:21; 2 Thess 1:8). This phrase probably has its origin in the Old Testament (cf. Ps 79:6; Jer 10:25).

4:6 'Why should one be concerned about sexual purity?' is the third question with which Paul deals. **That no one should take advantage of and defraud his brother in this matter**. This is not a **matter** of inappropriate behavior in the business world but rather the illicit results of immoral behavior in the sexual realm. To engage in sexual immorality is to sinfully 'over step the boundaries' (**take advantage**) and to **defraud** (cf. 2 Cor 2:11, this is what Satan does to believers). **Brother**, in this context, would indicate another human being, not just another Christian. Those who are cheated could include: the sexual partner; parents; other family members; present or future marriage partners; and present or future children.

At this point, Paul gives three compelling reasons to avoid sexual immorality. The first one is found here in 4:6b, because God will judge the immoral. Apparently, Paul had taught them this when he was among them (**we also forewarned you and testified**), as he also says in 2 Thessalonians 2:5. Believers are not to take personal revenge for a wrong done (Rom 12:19), but they are to wait on the **Lord** who, in both the Old Testament (Deut 32:35; Ps 94:1) and the New Testament (Rom 12:19; 2 Thess 1:8; Heb 10:30), is characterized as the One who will take the appropriate revenge to right a wrong. As the avenger, God will work out justice.

4:7 The second reason Christians are to abstain from sexual immorality is that **God called** them (**us**) **in holiness**, not **uncleanness** (cf. 2:3). Consult the notes on God's call in 2:12 and holiness/sanctification in 4:3. The **uncleanness** is in the context of sexual sin (cf. Rom 6:19; Gal 5:19; Eph 5:3; Col 3:5). Holiness is contrary to and is the opposite of immorality. Christians have been called out of such darkness into the light of God's holiness. Nothing so dishonors God as dishonoring Him with the body (cf. 1 Cor 6:15-20).

4:8 The third reason for embracing sanctification is that to **reject** holiness is to **reject God who has also given us His Holy Spirit**. This would be just the opposite of their previous experience in 2:13. It is a standing truth that God has gifted all Christians with the Holy Spirit at their conversion (Rom 5:5; 1 Cor 3:16; 6:19; 2 Cor 1:22; Gal 4:6; 1 John 3:24). The one who actively engages in unholy behavior has rejected **God**. The word translated **reject** is a strong word that indicates 'rejection with finality'. This seems to be the picture of one who claims to be a Christian, but demonstrates a pattern of behavior which indicates that the profession of faith was counterfeit (cf. Matt 13:20-22; Heb 6:4-8). The outcome is that the fornicator **rejects God, not man**.

The one who continues to live immorally rejects God's Spirit, rejects God's will, rejects God's call, rejects God's Word, and rejects God's pleasure. To put it simply, they reject God. When King David repented of his sexual sin with Bathsheba, he confessed, 'Against You, You only, have I sinned, and done this evil in Your sight – that You may be found just when You speak, and blameless when You judge' (Ps 51:4).

3. Interpersonal relationships (4:9-12)
Paul is concerned that these Christians have a right relationship with one another (4:9-10) and with unbelievers in the community (4:11-12). Love and discipline are the keys to fulfilling these responsibilities.

But concerning brotherly love you have no need that I should write to you, for you yourselves are taught by God to love one another; and indeed you do so toward all the brethren who are in all Macedonia. But we urge you, brethren, that you increase more and more; that you also aspire to lead a quiet life, to mind your own business, and to work with your own hands, as we commanded you, that you may walk properly toward those who are outside, and that you may lack nothing (4:9-12).

4:9 With **but concerning brotherly love** (*philadelphia*), Paul changes the immediate subject from sexual purity to loving the brethren, both of which are within the larger category of ethical behavior. **Brotherly love** in secular use referred to a blood relationship. Here, it speaks of one Christian's relationship with another believer established by the blood of Jesus Christ (cf. Rom 12:10; Heb 13:1; 1 Pet 1:22; 2 Pet 1:7). Paul has family behavior in mind.

Unlike other issues (e.g. the death of loved ones, 4:13-18), the Thessalonians had **no need** (cf. 5:1) for Paul to **write** by way of instruction because they were **taught by God**, which is one word in the Greek text and used only here in the New Testament. It evidences a personal relationship with the teacher. An almost exact statement is made in Isaiah 54:13 and quoted in John 6:45. A similar idea is contained in the New Covenant promise of Jeremiah 31:33-34. This appears to be the ministry of the Spirit spoken of by John (1 John 2:20, 27). The Thessalonians obviously prayed, 'Teach me your statutes,' just as the psalmist had repeatedly asked (Ps 119:12, 26, 33, 64, 66, 68, 108, 124, 135) and the Lord had so responded.

The issue is **to love one another** (3:12; 2 Thess 1:3). See *Overview*, 'New Testament "One Anothers"' (3:12) and notes on 3:12. Since God is love (1 John 4:16), since his love has been poured out in our hearts by the Holy Spirit (Rom 5:5), and since love is part of the spiritual fruit produced by the Spirit (Gal 5:22), the Thessalonians had all the examples, teaching, and resources necessary to obey this most frequently mentioned of the New Testament 'one anothers'. The Old Testament root for the New Testament fruit is found in the Leviticus 19:18 command to love your neighbor (cf. Matt 22:39). Jesus taught that love for one another provided the signature sign of one's Christianity (John 13:34-35).

4:10 Another reason Paul did not have to write is that the Thessalonians obeyed what God had taught them. **Indeed you do so toward all the brethren who are in all Macedonia**. They understood that love was not limited to one person, one church, or one city, but was to be extended to **all the brethren**, both **in all Macedonia** and beyond. This would have included the congregations in Philippi and Berea.

In typical Pauline fashion, they (**we**) **urged** them (**you, brethren**) to do even better. He repeats his exhortation from 4:1. Looking ahead at the second letter (2 Thess 1:3), it appears that they heeded his admonition because God answered his previous prayer (3:12). **Increase more and more** looks back to 4:9-10 and also ahead to 4:11-12.

4:11 The subject shifts from godly behavior among believers to one's lifestyle before the unredeemed community. Paul moves from a characteristic that would flourish (2 Thess 1:3), i.e. love of the brethren, to one which would deteriorate with time, i.e. disciplined living (see notes on 2 Thess 3:6-15). He challenges them to **aspire** (to aim, to hope as an honorable ambition) to three qualities in their daily lives (cf. Rom 15:20; 2 Cor 5:9). First, **to lead a quiet life** (cf. 2 Thess 3:12; 1 Tim 2:2). By this, he means a life that is peaceful, not turbulent. A related word is used to describe the wife with a quiet spirit in 1 Peter 3:4. It is a life that does its best to avoid unnecessary contention and to be at peace with all men in so far as it is humanly possible (cf. Rom 12:18; 14:19; Heb 12:14).

Second, they were **to mind your own business**. This was intended for the busybody and meddler who had more time to interfere with other people's lives than to make sure their **own business** was in order.

Third, they were also **to work with your own hands**. Greek culture looked down on manual labor, but here Paul exalts it (cf. Eph 4:28). The emphasis is **to work** in contrast with loafing or the sluggard's lifestyle (cf. Prov 6:6-11; 13:4; 15:19; 19:24; 20:4; 21:25; 22:13; 24:30-34; 26:13-16). The quality of their life was to be quiet; the focus of their life was to be on their own affairs; and a priority of their life was to work.

Paul finishes off these three exhortations with **as we commanded you**. Paul's authority to command came from God who appointed him to speak on His behalf (2:4) and from his message which really was God's message (2:13). As an apostle (2:6), Paul had the right to command holy behavior for believers. As one who was over them in the Lord (5:12), Paul exercised his responsibility and obligation to teach the truth and confront misbehavior. Only here and in 2 Thessalonians 3:4, 6, 10, 12, where the context is 'disciplined living', does Paul use the strong language of **command** (cf. 4:2, 'commandments'). In light of the major sin he addresses in the second letter (2 Thess 3:6-15), it is probable that even now this was a minor problem which Paul thought could be corrected with this mild, but direct admonition. While the Thessalonian church in almost all ways was a model church, it did have several flaws.

OVERVIEW

Thessalonian Weaknesses (4:11)

Thessalonica is not often thought of in the same league as Ephesus (Rev 2:1-7), Pergamum (Rev 2:12-17), or Thyatira (Rev 2:18-29). But just as Christ both commended and condemned these three churches, so Paul also has some words of correction for the Thessalonians. While the areas of weakness were not many, had they been left unchecked the Thessalonian church would have quickly been corrupted.

Undisciplined Living
Paul had alluded to a possible problem in 1 Thessalonians 4:11-12. Apparently his instructions were ignored because later he addressed this as an escalating issue of sin in 2 Thessalonians 3:6-15.

The situation seemed to be that a group of people in the church, for unknown reasons, refused to work and take care of their own needs (2 Thess 3:8, 10-12). Paul instructed the Thessalonians to deal with this undisciplined idleness as sin and to initiate church discipline in the hope of restoring these brethren to a productive life (2 Thess 3:6, 14-15). See *Overview*, 'Church Discipline' (2 Thess 3:6).

False Teaching
They had also succumbed to false teachers (2 Thess 2:1-2). Apparently, some heretics had come in the name of Paul and taught something false that the church naively believed to be true. But rather than providing comfort, it disturbed them and shook their spiritual composure.

Paul gave two rules by which to prevent this from happening again. First, remember the truth (2 Thess 2:5). By comparing the future teaching with already affirmed truth from the past, the true can be distinguished from the false. By setting the new alongside the true, false teaching can be exposed.

Second, be sure the message is from Scripture. Paul made a significant effort to point out the distinguishing or authenticating mark of his own handwriting (2 Thess 3:17). Without this sign, no letter was to be received as a genuine apostolic letter from Paul.

4:12 A life characterized by the qualities of 4:11 would achieve two important results. First, **you may walk properly toward those who are outside**. Paul has referred to their **walk** or Christian lifestyle previously (2:12; 4:1) as one which should be worthy of God and bring pleasure to Him. Later, he will condemn some of the Thessalonians for a disorderly **walk** (2 Thess 3:6, 11). Paul desires that the Thessalonians live honorably and honestly (**properly**; literally 'in good form' [cf. Mark 15:43; Acts 13:50; 17:12; Rom 13:13]) in their city and among their neighbors who are **outside** of the faith (cf. 1 Cor 5:12-13; Col 4:5; 1 Tim 3:7). In other words, they were to have a good testimony for the gospel's sake among the unbelievers in their community.

The second result would be **that you may lack nothing** (cf. 1 Tim 5:8). This was not so much for the material well being of the person as it was for the clear testimony of the person who obeyed the Scriptures regarding work and thus knew the provision of God through exercising proper human responsibility. The Christians who lived dishonorably and depended on unbelievers for their daily necessities because of an undisciplined life would have been a shame and a displeasure to God, plus a contradiction to the gospel. The brightest testimony to the power of God would be evidenced most convincingly by one with an industrious walk and an independent life.

Some have theorized that this undisciplined living was prompted by the eschatological expectation of Christ's soon return which resulted in people abandoning their productive life to wait for Christ. While this could be true, there is no evidence of this kind of cause and effect relationship in either epistle. It could very well be that there were just some lazy, indolent people in the flock who refused to obey in this area of their life. In light of Paul's approving testimony about the Thessalonians in 1:9-10, it would be this writer's opinion that a wrong application of prophetic teaching is not the cause for the undisciplined circumstances which Paul here addresses.

4. The 'dead-in-Christ' (4:13-18)

Apparently a question came up in the congregation regarding the future of Christians who died before the rapture of the church. Will they be left behind? Will they miss out on spiritual blessings received by those who are alive at the Lord's coming? Paul writes, not to teach the nuances of eschatology, but rather to give informed hope to those who are concerned. In the midst of his answer, he reveals more details about the rapture of the church than can be found in any other portion of Scripture.

But I do not want you to be ignorant, brethren, concerning those who have fallen asleep, lest you sorrow as others who have no hope. For if we believe that Jesus died and rose again, even so God will bring with Him those who sleep in Jesus. For this we say to you by the word of the Lord, that we who are alive and remain until the coming of the Lord will by no means precede those who are asleep. For the Lord Himself will descend from heaven with a shout, with the voice of an archangel, and with the trumpet of God. And the dead in Christ will rise first. Then we who are alive and remain shall be caught up together with them in the clouds to meet the Lord in the air. And thus we shall always be with the Lord. Therefore comfort one another with these words (4:13-18).

4:13 The Thessalonians knew much, but not all they needed to know. Paul did not want them to be **ignorant** (uninformed) **brethren** so he tells them about **those who have fallen asleep** (4:14-15; 1 Cor 15:51). **Those who...sleep** are the Thessalonian Christians who have died since Paul left town. In most cultures, the idea of sleep is a euphemism for death (cf. Matt 27:52; John 11:11; Acts 7:60; 13:36), just as it was in Macedonia. This did not represent some kind of 'soul sleep', as taught by Jehovah Witnesses or Seventh Day Adventists, that the spirit or soul after death is in an unconscious state. When a Christian dies, the body is committed to the grave (1 Cor 15:42), but the spirit is in the presence of the Lord, very much awake (2 Cor 5:8). Take Stephen, for instance, who in Acts 7:59 delivered up his spirit to the Lord Jesus and in 7:60 fell asleep, i.e. he died. Or the thief on the cross, who after death, would be very much alive and awake in Paradise (heaven) with Christ (Luke 23:43).

Paul wanted them to know about the future of their dead

brethren so that they would not **sorrow as those who have no hope**. 'Sorrow' here is heavy, painful distress like that of one who suffers unjustly (1 Pet 2:19; 4:16) or like Paul's sorrow over Israel's rejection of Christ (Rom 9:2). Those who are sorrowful over death like that are those who have no hope, i.e. unbelievers whose eternal destiny is completely unknown because they have not gone to heaven and those they left behind have no awareness of heaven either. It was not to be that way for Christians, as Paul goes on to explain. While the Greeks did not believe in resurrection (Acts 17:32), the Christians did.

4:14 We believe that Jesus died and rose again defines the basis of the gospel message (cf. Rom 10:9; 1 Cor 15:3-4). **If** that is so, which it is, then one day, at the resurrection, **God will bring with Him those who sleep in Jesus,** i.e. the dead in Christ (4:16). Just as Jesus was raised from the grave to be in heaven, so will all who have believed in Him and then died (see 1 Cor 15:12-49, 52 for a much fuller explanation). This answers the question, 'How do those who died in Christ rejoin their body?' Paul answers in effect, 'Through the resurrection!' See *Overview*, 'Christ's Resurrection' (1:10).

OVERVIEW

Facts about the Resurrections (4:14)

Fact 1
Daniel 12:2, John 5:28-29, and Romans 2:5-8 speak about two results from resurrection without regard for their timing. There is a resurrection of life (John 5:29), eternal life (Rom 2:7), or everlasting life (Dan 12:2). There is also a resurrection of judgment (John 5:29), wrath and indignation (Rom 2:8), or everlasting contempt (Dan 12:2). These passages speak of resurrection in a compressed sense, i.e. without regard for the dimension of time, much like Isaiah 61:1-3 speaks of the two comings of Christ (cf. Luke 4:17-22).

Fact 2
The Bible nowhere speaks clearly of only one general resurrection of the redeemed.

Fact 3
Revelation 20:4-5 speaks of two resurrections. Verse 4 speaks of a resurrection of saints before the millennium, while verse 5 speaks of a resurrection after the millennium. The term 'first resurrection' refers to a resurrection of the redeemed.

Fact 4
The rest of the dead, i.e. the unrighteous (Rev 20:5), come to life to stand at the white throne judgment (Rev 20:11-12) where they will be sentenced to the second death (Rev 20:13-15). This is the general resurrection of all the unrighteous from all time.

Fact 5
1 Corinthians 15:23-24 speaks of at least three different resurrections: (a) Christ, the first fruits; (b) the resurrection at His coming; (c) the resurrection that will occur at the end when He delivers up the kingdom to His Father.

Fact 6
Since I believe that the rapture is pretribulational, I then understand that His one coming is in two parts, and thus resurrections are associated with each: (a) a resurrection just prior to the tribulation (1 Cor 15:23, 50-58; 1 Thess 4:13-18); (b) a resurrection at the end of the tribulation (Rev 20:4-5).

Fact 7
The Bible gives a definite time for the resurrection of Old Testament saints (Ezek 37:12-14; Dan 12:2). This seems to occur at the end of the tribulation since the next expected event is the long-awaited Jewish hope of Christ's millennial kingdom.

Conclusions
  1. The Bible speaks of the resurrection of the redeemed as 'the first resurrection' (Rev 20:5), or 'resurrection of life' (John 5:29), or 'eternal life' (Rom 2:7), or 'everlasting life' (Dan 12:2).
  2. This 'first resurrection' of the redeemed occurs over time in three parts: (a) Christ the first fruit (1 Cor 15:23); (b) Church saints (1 Cor 15:23, 50-58; 1 Thess 4:13-18); (c) Old Testament saints (Ezek 37:12-

14; Dan 12:2) and Tribulation saints (Rev 20:4).

3. Nowhere does the Bible use the term 'second resurrection', but rather the Bible refers to the resurrection of the unredeemed as 'a resurrection of judgment' (John 5:29) or 'the second death' (Rev 20:6, 14; 21:8).

4. There is no Biblical warrant to conclude that there is only one general resurrection of the righteous which occurs at the end.

5. There are four recognized times of resurrection in Scripture: (1) Christ's resurrection (1 Cor 15:23); (2) Church saints' resurrection (1 Cor 15:23, 50-58; 1 Thess 4:13-18); (3) Old Testament saints' (Ezek 37:12-14; Dan 12:2) and Tribulation saints' (Rev 20:4) resurrection; and (4) the unredeemed of all time resurrection (Rev 20:5).

4:15 If someone were to ask Paul, 'How do you know this?', he would answer, **By the word of the Lord**. It was by Divine revelation that he received this word. It could additionally be asked, 'Where did you get this from the Lord?' Was it from the Old Testament, or from the agrapha (sayings of Jesus which were not recorded canonically; Luke 1:1-3; John 21:25; Acts 20:35), or by direct revelation? This writer prefers the explanation of direct revelation given in one of Christ's appearances to Paul (cf. Acts 18:9-10 in Corinth). This kind of detail is not found in the Old Testament, although the hope is expressed (Job 19:25-26). Most likely, neither Matthew nor Mark would have been written yet. Nevertheless, as he does elsewhere (2:13), Paul claims that the source and authority for his message is God. See *Overview*, 'The Word of God' (2:13).

He begins in 4:15b-17 to describe with some detail the sequence of events at the time of the rapture (cf. 4:17, 'caught up'). He explains that **we who are alive and remain until the coming** (2:19; 3:13) **of the Lord will by no means precede those who are asleep** (dead in the grave). They who remained would be encouraged to know that their deceased loved ones, instead of being left behind, would actually precede them in the resurrection. Paul uses a double negative to emphatically express this certainty (**by no means**). This occurs at **the coming of the Lord**, i.e. the *parousia* (cf. 1 Cor 15:23). See *Overview*, 'Christ's Coming'

(2:19). This answers the question, 'When will the resurrection of believers occur?' It is the opinion of this writer that these three mentions of the *parousia* (2:19; 3:13; 4:15) all refer to the time of the rapture and the events that immediately follow, i.e. the return to heaven and the Bema.

4:16 Paul begins to answer the question, 'What will be involved?' It all starts when **the Lord Himself will descend from heaven** (cf. 1 Cor 15:50-57), as forecast by the angels on the Mount of Olives when He ascended to heaven (Acts 1:11) and as Jesus taught the disciples (John 14:1-3). The King is coming unexpectedly, personally, suddenly, visibly, audibly, and spectacularly. It will be **with a shout**, i.e. an authoritative command (cf. John 5:28-29) from the Lord. Then will be heard **the voice of an archangel**, most likely Michael (Jude 9). Very little is known for sure about angelic organizational structure other than (cf. Col 1:17) they are led by archangels (Dan 10:13 hints of more than just Michael). See *Overview*, 'Titles of Angels' (2 Thess 1:7). Finally, the **trumpet of God** announces His arrival (cf. Pss 47:5; 98:6). This is distinctly the trumpet associated with the rapture and is not to be equated with other trumpets appearing in another prophetic passage unless context warrants it, e.g. 1 Corinthians 15:52.

In response to this Divine summons, **the dead in Christ will rise first** as previously mentioned (4:15). This will be the final step in their redemption with the resurrection of their body (Rom 8:23). Some have said that this will be a 'secret' event. But it seems incredible to this writer that something so spectacular and global would be considered 'secret'. In any case, although Paul termed it a mystery (1 Cor 15:51), it has now been revealed in Scripture.

4:17 As if to answer the question, 'What about those still living?', Paul addresses **we who are alive and remain**. Paul uses **we** in the sense that if it happened in their lifetime, if it happened before they died, this would be the sequence for them. The living **shall be caught up** or raptured. Rapture actually comes from the Latin *raptura* which translates the Greek word *harpazō*, which literally means to be snatched away (cf. John 10:28; Acts 8:39; Rev 12:5).

First Corinthians 15:52 adds that it will happen 'in a moment, in the twinkling of an eye'.

When will the rapture occur? In the opinion of this writer, 1 Thessalonians 4:13-18 clearly establishes the fact of the rapture, but does not determine its timing in relation to Daniel's seventieth week. *Appendix 2* attempts to answer the question of time by looking at many other passages which are more helpful than this one.

Having been **caught up**, there will be a reunion together **with them** (the resurrected dead) **in the clouds**. The Lord does not actually come to the earth here, but rather is above the earth **in the air**. The purpose of both the resurrection and the rapture is **to meet the Lord**. The word translated **to meet** was used in the ancient world of the citizens of a city going out to greet a coming king or dignitary to escort him back to the city for a royal visit. Is that the case here? Posttribulationists would impose that idea on this text to make their point, although it is nowhere to be found. In all likelihood, this is the picture of the king who has come and gathered all of his loyal followers from among a primarily rebellious population and returned temporarily to his home base (heaven, cf. John 14:1-3) before he later returns to soundly defeat the enemy and claim the kingdom (Rev. 19:11-21).

In the opinion of this writer (see *Appendix 1*, 'Various Millennial Views'), there is a seven year period, spoken of in Daniel 9:24-27 and Revelation 6–19, between the rapture taught here and Christ's arrival later. There are at least five distinct differences in these two events which demand that they occur at separate times. At the rapture: (1) Christ gathers His own (4:16-17); (2) resurrection is prominent (4:15-16); (3) Christ comes to reward (4:17); (4) believers depart the earth (4:15-17); and (5) unbelievers remain on earth.

In total contrast, at the revelation (Matt 24-25; 2 Thess 1:7, i.e. the end of Daniel's seventieth week just prior to the millennium): (1) angels gather the elect (Matt 24:31); (2) there is no mention of any resurrection; (3) Christ comes to judge (Matt 25:31-46); (4) unbelievers are taken away (Matt 24:37-41); and (5) believers remain on the earth. These dramatic differences demand that they describe two very unique events at two separate times.

One other issue about the rapture is worth discussing. Some have suggested that this is a partial rapture, i.e. participation in the rapture is conditional upon deserving conduct. This theory rests on the New Testament passages that stress obedient watching and waiting (e.g. 5:6 ff.; Matt 25:1-13; Heb 9:28). The result would be that only part of the church is raptured and those who are not will endure through part of or the entire seventieth week of Daniel. These texts are best understood as differentiating between true believers and merely professing ones. This theory fails for numerous reasons, some of which include: (1) 1 Corinthians 15:51 says 'all' will be changed; (2) a partial rapture would logically have to be paralleled by a partial resurrection, which is nowhere spoken of in Scripture; (3) this would eliminate the need for the judgment seat of Christ; (4) it creates a purgatory of sorts on earth for disobedient believers; and (5) it is nowhere clearly taught in Scripture. Therefore, this writer believes that Paul is teaching a full, complete rapture, not one that is partial.

Paul concludes that **we shall always be with the Lord**. This process is irreversible. All believers will be together forever in the presence of the Lord after the resurrection/rapture. No wonder Paul wrote, 'Maranatha' (1 Cor 16:22) and John, 'Even so, come, Lord Jesus!' (Rev 22:20). This will be the greatest of reunions. Christians will be rejoined with believing family members, among others.

4:18 Paul did not write this section to satisfy the prophetic curiosity of the people or to present some spectacular doomsday scenario. Actually, he wrote to the Thessalonians who were uninformed and worried. So he says **comfort one another with these words**. They would be comforted by: (1) the fact of these events; (2) their certainty; (3) their order, with the dead being resurrected first; (4) the expectation of reunion; (5) the irreversibility of these events; and (6) the eternal prospect of these events. See *Overview*, 'New Testament "One Anothers"' (3:12). Their hope was comprised of a coming resurrection, known by a revelation from the Lord, at the return of Christ, when the bodies of the dead would be redeemed from the grave and then the living church would be raptured to be reunited with fellow believers and the Lord forever. This must be 'the blessed hope' (Titus 2:13) which explains why the Thessalonians were patiently waiting for God's Son from heaven (1:10).

5. Spiritual watchfulness (5:1-11)

Prophetic matters continue to occupy Paul's instruction in 5:1-11, but the introductory phrase, **But concerning**, introduces a contrast in topic within the same general subject matter, i.e. future events. This represents the first of two discussions by Paul dealing with the Day of the Lord. It is interesting to note that the embryonic mention of disciplined living in 4:11-12 is later expanded to a full chapter in 2 Thessalonians 3. Also, what Paul dealt with briefly here – the Day of the Lord – subsequently becomes the point of major concern in 2 Thessalonians 2. Paul first acknowledges that the Thessalonians do not need more revelation about the Day of the Lord (5:1-3) and then proceeds to expound on their spiritual responsibility in light of what they know to be true (5:4-11).

The Thessalonians' revelation (5:1-3)

But concerning the times and the seasons, brethren, you have no need that I should write to you. For you yourselves know perfectly that the day of the Lord so comes as a thief in the night. For when they say, "Peace and safety!" then sudden destruction comes upon them, as labour pains upon a pregnant woman. And they shall not escape (5:1-3).

5:1 Paul begins with **the time and the seasons**. **Time** refers to the quantity or measurement of time, while **seasons** (epochs) refers to the quality or character of time. These terms are used together in Ecclesiastes 3:1-8 and Daniel 2:21 in the Old Testament and Acts 1:7 in the New Testament. They refer to both the specific and the general aspects of time respectively.

The Apostle then asserts that **you have no need that I should write to you**. It would appear that Paul is answering their question, 'When will the Day of the Lord occur and what will be the signs of the time, so that we can be prepared?' This would not be unlike the questions that Jesus' disciples asked Him (Matt 24:3; Acts 1:6). Paul responds that they did not have a need for him to address either aspect of the question. First, they did not need instruction on the **times** because no one knew the exact time, i.e. Paul could not help them because he did not know either (cf. Matt 24:36; Acts 1:7). Second, neither did they need to know any more than they already knew (5:2-3) about the **seasons**. They knew enough of what was knowable to produce a godly lifestyle (5:4-11). This is an entirely different discussion, not a continuation from Paul's teaching on the *parousia* and rapture in 4:13-18. For perspective, see *Appendix 1*, 'Various Millennial Views' and *Overview*, 'Christ's Coming' (2:19).

5:2 The Thessalonians were not completely ignorant on the subject (cf. 2 Thess 2:5). What they knew, they knew **perfectly** (accurately). This is not surprising because **the day of the Lord** was a frequent Old Testament teaching, mentioned explicitly at least nineteen times in eight Old Testament books. Paul would have taught them this from the Old Testament prophets.

OVERVIEW

The Day of the Lord (5:2)

Old Testament
The term 'Day of the Lord' appears nineteen times in the Old Testament. The expression occurs only in the prophets and is distributed among six minor and two major prophets.

The data appears as follows:

Prophet/Text		Writing Date
Obadiah	15	c.845 BC
Joel	1:15	c.835 BC
	2:1	
	2:11	
	2:31	
	3:14	
Amos	5:18	c.755 BC
	5:18	
	5:20	

Isaiah	2:12	c.700 BC
	13:6	
	13:9	
Zephaniah	1:7	c.630 BC
	1:14	
	1:14	
Ezekiel	13:5	c.580 BC
	30:3	
Zechariah	14:1	c.480 BC
Malachi	4:5	c.430 BC

New Testament

There are four generally agreed upon uses of the Day of the Lord in the New Testament. In Acts 2:20, Luke records Peter's sermon on Pentecost in which he quotes Joel 2:31. Paul uses the phrase twice in the eschatological sections of the Thessalonian epistles – 1 Thessalonians 5:2 and 2 Thessalonians 2:2 (see notes). The third New Testament author to use the term is Peter who speaks about the cleansing of heaven and earth at the the Day of the Lord (2 Peter 3:10). Because there is a contested textual variant at 1 Corinthians 5:5, it has not been included in this database. To this writer, the more likely reading is 'the day of the Lord Jesus' following 1 Corinthians 1:8 and 2 Corinthians 1:14 (see notes on 5:4).

Observations

The Hebrew concept of time was normally orientated towards quality not quantity and the Day of the Lord is no exception. The Day of the Lord was presented by the prophets as a day of undetermined length which uniquely belongs to the Lord for judgment.

The Old Testament uses of the Day of the Lord involved the near prophetic and far eschatological perspectives. At times they were compressed together into one text. The context alone enables the interpreter to separate the multiple fulfillments.

Day of the Lord prophecies were fulfilled in various ways. These included: (1) the Assyrian deportation of Israel c.722 BC (Amos 5:18, 20); (2) the Assyrian invasion of Judah c.701 BC (Joel 1:15; 2:1, 11); (3) the Babylonian exile of Judah c.605-586 BC (Joel 1:15; 2:1, 11; Zeph 1:7; Ezek 13:5); (4) the Babylonian defeat of Egypt c.586 BC (Ezek 30:3); (5) the demise of Edom (Obad 1-14); (6) the eschatological judgments of the tribulation period (Obad 15; Joel 2:31; 3:14; Isa 2:12; 13:9; Zech 14:1; Mal 4:5); and (7) the final Day of the Lord experience which ushers in the eternal state (Zeph 1:14-18).

Obadiah and Joel serve as the classic texts in this study. This following model describes what the Bible teaches about the Day of the Lord.

1. The Day of the Lord at times combines near and far eschatological truth in one context.

2. The Day of the Lord involves a singular national application in the near view.

3. The Day of the Lord involves an international application in the far view.

4. The Day of the Lord consists of judgment and destruction to the godless.

5. The restoration of Israel is a result in the far view, but is not experienced in the near.

6. The near view includes a preview of what the far will involve and heralds its occurrence.

7. The Day of the Lord argues from the lesser (near) to the greater (far).

8. The prominent mention of the Day of the Lord in both Testaments refers to the posttribulational event.

9. The establishment of God's kingdom and eternity future, respectively, promptly follow the last two expressions of the Day of the Lord.

The New Testament picks up where the Old concluded. Because the near fulfillments were then history, Luke, Paul, and Peter did not mention them. They did focus on the far fulfillments which conclude both the tribulation period and the millennium. In 2 Thessalonians 2, Paul added significant new material to that already known about the Day of the Lord from the Old Testament. Peter's second epistle introduced the final Day of the Lord occurrence which ends the millennium and prepares for eternity future. Therefore, no basis exists for beginning the Day of the Lord with the rapture nor for extending it through the millennium. Future expectations involve two fulfillments, each of which will be God's judgment. The blessings that follow in each instance are logical progressions, but not inherent features.

Five precursors to the Day of the Lord are revealed by Scripture.

1. Stellar Signs   (Joel 2:31)
2. The Valley of Jehoshaphat   (Joel 3:14)
3. Elijah's Coming   (Mal 4:5)
4. The Apostasy   (2 Thess 2:3)
5. Man of Lawlessness   (2 Thess 2:3-4)

These antecedent activities conclusively demand that the Day of the Lord, in its tribulational expression, be limited to the very end of the tribulation.

The Day of the Lord has very often been identified with the Pauline use of the 'Day of Christ' or its several variations. The context of the Day of Christ passages is always blessing expected when believers are held accountable before Christ at the Bema. See the Day of Christ discussion in the notes on 5:4. These two prophetic events are to be distinguished, not equated.

Conclusions

The Day of the Lord is a generic Biblical phrase which was used by God's prophets to describe the immediate historical future or the ultimate eschatological consummation. It is not a technical term in the sense that it always refers to only one event in God's plan.

The Day of the Lord is a multiple fulfillment term which is limited in occurrences only by its mention in Biblical revelation. Each appearance of the Day of the Lord must be interpreted in its context to determine if the prophet expected the immediate act of God in history or the Lord's ultimate eschatological visitation.

The Day of the Lord is not bound to a definite time duration. It could last for hours or it could continue for days, even weeks. Only context can determine its longevity and then only general approximations can be made. Nowhere does Scripture give a Day of the Lord time measurement.

The Day of the Lord exclusively involves judgment either against Israel or upon the rebellious world population, individually and collectively. Where blessing is an attendant feature (and it is not always), it is a chronological sequel not an inherent feature. God's judgment can be either providential (Ezek 30:3, 10) or direct (2 Pet 3:10).

Imminency often characterizes the Day of the Lord. In Joel 1:15; 2:1; Isaiah 13:6; Zephaniah 1:7; and Ezekiel 30:3, near historical fulfillments are prominent. The far event is described as 'near' in Obadiah 15; Joel 3:14; and Zephaniah 1:14. In the prophets' minds, the event was certainly coming and would one day occur in the indeterminate future. Day of the Lord judgments are poured out on individual nations, such as Edom, Egypt and its allies, and Israel. Yet, such judgments will one day be inflicted upon all of the nations according to Obadiah 15 and Zechariah 14:1.

Two times of Divine judgment, called the Day of the Lord by Scripture, yet remain for planet earth – the crescendo judgment which climaxes the tribulation period, i.e. Daniel's seventieth week (Acts 2:20; 1 Thess 5:2; 2 Thess 2:2) and the consummation judgment which closes the annals of earth's fallen history (2 Pet 3:10-13). The Day of the Lord will occur at the end of the tribulation period, not throughout its duration, and the Day of the Lord will occur only at the end of the millennium, not throughout its one thousand years.

Now in 5:2b-3, Paul reminds them of what the Day of the Lord will be like. The general backdrop is God's judgment. They knew at least seven features of the Day of the Lord. First, because the Day of the Lord **so comes as a thief in the night**, it arrives *uninvited* and *unannounced*. Thieves don't receive invitations to rob, neither will God be invited to judge. Just as robbers do not publish a schedule of their activities, so people cannot anticipate their every move, neither does God. Paul reaffirms that they cannot know the times (5:1).

A thief in the night is a frequent New Testament image (5:2, 4; Matt 24:42-43; Luke 12:33, 39; 2 Pet 3:10; Rev 3:3; 16:15). All but one of these texts is associated with the time of the Day of the Lord (Rev 3:3 is the exception where Jesus is using this speech figure in a different context). The context of Matthew 24:42-43 and Revelation 16:15 (the sixth bowl) is at the end of Daniel's seventieth week when Christ returns to defeat Satan and set up His kingdom (Rev 19:11-20:6). See the chart *Futuristic Premillennialism* for a perspective on the event.

5:3 The remaining six features of the Day of the Lord relate to the issue of seasons (5:1) or the character of the time. Second, the Day of the Lord arrives *unexpectedly* **when they say, 'Peace and safety!'** The Day of the Lord is anything but peace and safety; it is tumult and danger at the highest level (cf. Rev 16).

This was not a new phenomenon in the annals of history. Jeremiah cried out to God that false prophets had led the people astray by promises of lasting peace without war or famine (Jer 14:13-14; see also 6:14; 8:11; 23:17). This was during a time which preceded the Day of the Lord manifestation in the Babylonian captivity and is analogous to the time preceding the eschatological Day of the Lord. Ezekiel indicted the pseudo-prophets for misleading God's people when there was no peace. It is significant here that this appears in the immediate context of a primary Day of the Lord text (Ezek 7:25; 13:1-6). The people in Amos' day also foolishly, but sincerely, expected blessing rather than judgment (Amos 5:18-20).

Paul is saying that the basic circumstances which existed and provoked the historical Day of the Lord will also bring about the eschatological Day of the Lord. It will be through the deception of Satan (2 Thess 2:9; Rev 12:9; 13:11-14) and the permitted delusion by God (2 Thess 2:11) that they will, like those of old, believe what is false in spite of enormous amounts of evidence around them to the contrary. It will be just like it was in the days of Noah (Matt 24:37-39; Luke 17:26-27) and Lot (Luke 17:28-30).

There is a major grammatical indicator here that the church will not be present during this time; while this is compatible with a pretribulation rapture (see *Appendix 2*, 'The Time of the Rapture'), it does not irrefutably prove it. There is a pronoun switch from the second person in 5:1-2 (**you**) to the third person in 5:3 (**they, them**) and back again to the first and second person in 5:4-11 (**you, we, us**). This seems to indicate that church believers will not be present during this time as a result of the rapture (4:17).

Third, the Day of the Lord arrives *rapidly*. The destruction will be **sudden**. The cause (**it comes**) and effect (**destruction**) will be quick and swift (cf. Luke 21:34). There will be no time to react against it.

Fourth, the Day of the Lord comes *destructively*. The **destruction** (1 Cor 5:5; 2 Thess 1:9; 1 Tim 6:9) will not end in annihilation but it will destroy in the sense of 'render useless'. It is this writer's opinion that since the Day of the Lord is the climax or crescendo to Daniel's seventieth week, then the destruction comes from the vials or bowls of God's wrath in Revelation 16:1-21.

Fifth, the Day of the Lord arrives *inevitably*. Once a **woman** becomes **pregnant, labor pains** are then predictable at the end of her pregnancy. Jesus used the same analogy in the Olivet Discourse (Matt 24:8) in the same context of judgment. In the Old Testament, Isaiah (13:8), Jeremiah (4:31), and Micah (4:9-10) used this imagery also in a similar context. Labor happens at the end of a period that began a long time before, but with predictable results at the outset. So, the Day of the Lord will be a painful culmination (cf. Jer 30:7-8) to Daniel's seventieth week of seven years.

Sixth, like **labor pains**, the process is *irreversible*. The baby cannot be turned back and neither can God's judgment. Once it reaches this stage, the arrival is only a short time away.

Seventh, the Day of the Lord's results come *unavoidably*, since **they shall not** (an emphatic double negative in the Greek text) **escape** (cf. Rom 2:3; Heb 2:3). There is a definite finality to the Day of the Lord for all of those who turned their backs on God.

This is a brief survey of what the certain quality of life will be like when Jesus comes to the earth to conquer, judge, and reign. But Paul's point here is not primarily the revelation of future prophetic details, but rather the present responsibility of Christians to live godly lives in the face of this catastrophic reality, i.e. coming Divine judgment (cf. Titus 2:12-13; 2 Pet 3:11; Rev 1:3).

The Thessalonians' responsibility (5:4-11)

But you, brethren, are not in darkness, so that this Day should overtake you as a thief. You are all sons of light and sons of the day. We are not of the night nor of darkness. Therefore let us not sleep, as others do, but let us watch and be sober. For those who sleep, sleep at night, and those who get drunk are drunk at night. But let us who are of the day be sober, putting on the breastplate of faith and love, and as a helmet the hope of salvation. For God did not appoint us to wrath, but to obtain salvation through our Lord Jesus Christ, who died for us, that whether we wake or sleep, we should live together with Him. Therefore comfort each other and edify one another, just as you also are doing (5:4-11).

5:4 Paul redirects the discussion in two ways here. He shifts from the third person back to the second person. He also moves from what the Thessalonians knew by Divine revelation to their present spiritual responsibility in light of what they knew. The implication is that, because of their personal relationship with Jesus Christ, they would not experience the terror of 5:2-3.

Paul makes this truth vivid with four striking contrasts which distinguish between a true believer and an unbeliever. These opposites are: darkness (5:4, 5) and light (5:5); night (5:5, 7) and day (5:5, 8); sleep (5:6, 7) and watch (5:6); and drunk (5:7) and sober (5:6, 8). A Christian is of the light and day and thus soberly watches his life to cultivate faith, love, and hope. The non-Christian is of the darkness and night, and thus drunkenly sleeps as the Day of the Lord overtakes him.

The **brethren are not in darkness** (5:5). **Darkness** is a frequent New Testament term to describe spiritual deadness, a lack of a redemptive relationship with God, or the absence of holiness (cf. Matt 4:16; John 3:19; Rom 1:21; 11:10; 2 Cor 6:14; Eph 4:18; Col 1:13; 1 Pet 2:9). This is the first of four characteristics which mark the unbelievers who will be **overtaken as a thief by this Day** (see the notes on 5:2). Because **the brethren are not in darkness**, then neither will they be **overtaken** like the ones in **darkness**, i.e. without the light of Jesus Christ. Jesus Himself taught that to believe in Him would remove a person from spiritual darkness (John 8:12; 12:46).

This Day refers to the Day of the Lord in context (5:2), not to the day of Christ which appears six times in the New Testament in four variations: (1) the day of the Lord Jesus Christ (1 Cor 1:8); (2) the day of the Lord Jesus (1 Cor 5:5; 2 Cor 1:14); (3) the day of Jesus Christ (Phil 1:6); and (4) the day of Christ (Phil 1:10; 2:16). The Day of the Lord has judgment of unbelievers in view, while the Day of Christ speaks of blessing for believers. The Day of Christ anticipates the positive completion of a believer's salvation at the judgment seat of Christ (Rom 14:10; 1 Cor 3:10-15; 2 Cor 5:10). The day of Christ is very similar to, if not to be identified with, Christ's *parousia* at the rapture (2:19; 3:13; 4:15; 5:23; 2 Thess 2:1). It is also called at times 'the revelation of the Lord Jesus Christ' (1 Cor 1:7; 1 Pet 1:7, 13; 4:13). For a more complete discussion of 'revelation', see notes on 2 Thessalonians 1:7.

5:5 In contrast to those who will be overtaken by the Day of the Lord, the Thessalonian believers are **sons of light** (Eph 5:8) and **sons of day**, without exception (**all**). 'Sons of...' is a Hebrew expression describing a characteristic or the source of a characteristic. These would be the opposite of the sons of disobedience (Eph 2:2; 5:6). God is **light** (1 John 1:5; cf. James 1:17) and His spiritual children are **sons of light**, which represent the redeemed (Rom 13:12; 2 Cor 6:14; Eph 5:8; Col 1:12; 1 Pet 2:9). Jesus is the light of the world (John 1:7-9; 9:5). **Sons of day** is just another way of describing genuine believers, since it is Christ who enlightens every believer (John 1:9).

Just the opposite is true of unbelievers for **we are not of the night nor of darkness**. Paul identifies with the Thessalonians as he switches from 'you' to **we**. **The night** describes the time of **darkness** (see notes on 5:4), with which he comes full circle to where he began in 5:4. In 5:4-5, Paul has contrasted the character of the believer as that of **light** and **day** in comparison to the unbeliever who is of **darkness** and the **night**.

5:6 Based on characteristics which determine conduct (**therefore**), Paul negatively and positively describes the proper activity of one who will not be in the Day of the Lord. **Let us not sleep, as others do**. Another word for **sleep**, different from the word in 4:13-15 to describe death, is used metaphorically here to describe inattentiveness to the important spiritual matters at hand. In strong contrast, true Christians are to **watch** (1 Cor 16:13; 1 Pet 5:8) **and be sober** (cf. 5:8; 2 Tim 4:5; 1 Pet 1:13; 4:7; 5:8). The former speaks of the activity; the latter looks to the attitude. Jesus' parable of the Ten Virgins illustrates the point (Matt 25:1-13).

5:7 Paul contrasts the unbeliever in 5:7 with the true believer in 5:8. Two activities characterize those who are of the **night** (5:5) – **sleep** (5:6) and drunkenness. **Those who get drunk** (or are dull minded) describes the spiritual stupor of those who are of the night. They are not looking for, nor are they alert to, the things of God. They epitomize those who continually satisfy self with the activities of the night and reject the things of God.

5:8 By contrast, believers are **sober** (5:6) or alert to spiritual matters. And in so doing, they are prepared for spiritual battle by being attired in **faith**, **love**, and **hope** (see notes on 1:3). Paul takes his imagery from Isaiah 59:17 where righteousness is associated with the breastplate (Eph 6:14), and salvation with the helmet (Eph 6:17). In Psalm 18:35, salvation is associated with the shield. They are to be righteous before God by **faith** and righteous towards men through **love**. Their **hope** in this life is the finality of **salvation** after death. Elsewhere in the New Testament, Paul also used figures of spiritual warfare (Rom 13:12; 2 Cor 6:7; 10:4; see *Overview*, 'True Love', 5:13).

5:9 For God did not appoint us to wrath is reminiscent of a similar statement in 1 Thessalonians 1:10 regarding **wrath**. Paul reminded the Thessalonians that it was **Jesus who delivers us from the wrath to come** (see notes on 1:10). **Wrath** is also spoken of in 1 Thessalonians 2:16. Context is the best indicator to determine what this **wrath** is. Looking back at 5:8 points to the context of **salvation** as does looking ahead to 5:10. It is this writer's opinion that, in light of the immediate context and the larger context of Paul's other uses of **wrath** in this letter, it is certain he refers to God's eternal wrath here. Thus, nothing here helps the interpreter to determine the time of the rapture.

Because the Thessalonians had been elected by God unto salvation (1:4), chosen by God for salvation (2 Thess 2:13), and called by God into His kingdom (2:12) to obtain the glory of the Lord Jesus Christ (2 Thess 2:14), it is most appropriate for Paul to make this negative/positive statement. The good news is that God appointed them **to obtain salvation through our Lord Jesus Christ**. See *Overview*, 'God's Role in Salvation' (1:4). This salvation was bought with Christ's shed blood at Calvary (Acts 20:28), so that the elect could obtain salvation (2 Thess 2:14; Eph 1:14) by God's grace through the elect's faith in **Jesus Christ** as their only **Lord** and Savior according to the gospel. **Salvation** is obtained as a free gift from the gracious hand of God, without any merit or works deserving salvation on the part of the unworthy recipients (Eph 2:8-9; Titus 3:5-7). Christians are justified by faith alone (Rom 3:28; 5:1).

5:10 It was the Lord Jesus Christ **who died for us** (1 Cor 15:3). Christ was the believer's Substitute to provide a vicarious atonement on his behalf (Isa 53:4-12). Christ was made sin on behalf of those who believe (2 Cor 5:21). Christ gave Himself for the believer's sins that He might deliver him out of this present evil age (Gal 1:4). Christ was delivered up for the believer's transgressions (Rom 4:25). Christ gave Himself as a ransom for many (Matt 20:28). Christ delivered Himself up for believers (Gal 2:20; Heb 7:27). Christ appeared in order to take away a believer's sin (1 John 3:5). Christ suffered for believers (1 Pet 2:21). Christ paid it all.

As a result, **whether we wake or sleep**, we **should live together with Him**. **Wake or sleep** are used here in the sense of being alive or being dead physically. Regardless of one's physical state, a believer is always alive unto Him (John 11:25-26) and thus should live together with Him (4:17; John 14:1-3; 2 Cor 5:8).

5:11 In light of these grand truths (**Therefore**), the Thessalonians were to **comfort** (4:18) and **edify** (Eph 4:12, 16, 29) one another (see *Overview*, 'New Testament "One Anothers",' 3:12). These are the true spiritual purposes of knowing prophetic matters, that we might minister effectively now in view of what one knows is certain to come later (cf. Isa 2:5, 12; 2 Pet 3:10-11, 14). As usual, Paul ends with a positive encouragement, **just as you also are doing** (4:1, 10). The Thessalonians were to stay the course.

There are at least ten major points of encouragement: (1) they were of the day and light; (2) they were not of the night and darkness; (3) they were sober and watchful; (4) they were not drunk and sleeping; (5) they would not be overtaken by the Day of the Lord; (6) they were wearing faith, love, and hope; (7) their eternal destiny was God's salvation; (8) Christ died for them; (9) they would live eternally with other believers; and (10) they would live eternally with Christ.

OVERVIEW

Why Study Prophecy? (5:11)

1. About one-third of the Bible was prophetic when penned. To set aside this significant portion is to ignore a large part of what God has revealed. Paul wrote that all Scripture is profitable to equip (2 Tim 3:16-17); therefore, prophecy too is profitable.

2. Prophecy provides answers to life's questions that are found nowhere else. For example, the relationship between the resurrection and the rapture (1 Thess 4:13-18).

3. The study of prophecy follows in the footsteps of the prophets who desired to know the future things about the Lord Jesus Christ (1 Pet 1:10-11).

4. The study of prophecy encourages patient enduring in the midst of suffering and trials (James 5:7-11).

5. Prophetic expectation purifies (1 John 3:2-3).

6. Prophecy gives perspective on holy living today (1 Thess 5:6-8; Titus 2:11-14; 2 Pet 3:11-12).

7. Prophecy is the Christian's source of hope and encouragement (1 Thess 5:11; Titus 2:13).

8. Prophecy assures that persecution of the righteous will be avenged by God (2 Thess 1:5-10).

9. The study of prophecy promotes obedience and is the gateway to God's blessing (Rev 1:3; 22:7).

10. Prophetic study equips the saints to refute those who mock the Christian hope (2 Pet 3:1-9).

11. Fulfilled prophecy proves that the Bible is true and inspires confidence in Scripture (Acts 13:32-35 with 42-43).

12. Prophecy provides a biblical basis for prayer (cf. Dan 9:1-19 with Jer 25:11-12).

---

6. Church harmony (5:12-15)

Right relationships are paramount for the church, both within and without the congregation. Paul deals with four categories of people in this brief section: church leaders (5:12-13a); the flock (5:13b); difficult people (5:14); and evil people (5:15). Practical advice is given in terms of a godly response to each group.

And we urge you, brethren, to recognize those who labour among you, and are over you in the Lord and admonish you, and to esteem them very highly in love for their work's sake. Be at peace among yourselves. Now we exhort you, brethren, warn those who are unruly, comfort the fainthearted, uphold the weak, be patient with all. See that no one renders evil for evil to anyone, but always pursue what is good both for yourselves and for all (5:12-15).

5:12 Paul deals first with how the congregation should respond to their pastors. This is the closest that Paul comes to mentioning church leadership in this letter, but in an unusual way. Rather than speaking about titles or qualifications (listed in 1 Tim 3:1-7; Titus 1:5-9), the apostle indirectly mentions three overarching roles that pastors play, but he does so to directly spell out how the **brethren** in the assembly should respond to their shepherds.

Paul requests (**urge**) this kind of behavior like a supervisor softly commanding a subordinate, i.e. graciously but mandatorily (4:1). He begins with the flock's first response to the shepherds, **recognize** them. This could also be translated 'respect' or 'appreciate'. The basic idea is to cultivate an intimate relationship with knowledge that leads to proper recognition. He urges them **to recognize**, literally, 'to know' the shepherds, even as they had recognized Paul (1:5; 2:1-2, 13; 3:6-8; 4:2). But this is not recognition merely because of the shepherds' role or position in the church; it is earned respect. Hebrews 13:7 and 17 expand on this responsibility.

If someone were now asking, 'Why should I do this?', Paul gives three reasons. In so doing, he also outlines the major responsibilities of the shepherds. First, the recognized pastors were to **labor among** them (**you**). Their ministry was to be validated by diligent, strenuous labor which led to the point of weariness and exhaustion. The Thessalonians had a good example in Paul (2:9; 3:5) who elsewhere illustrates this with the hardworking farmer (2 Tim 2:6).

Those who labor indicates multiple leadership (cf. 'them' and 'their' in 5:13). Titles such as elders (Titus 1:5), overseers (Acts 20:28), or pastors (Eph 4:11) are not used here; rather the functions are described. Paul, Silas, and Timothy had been an example (1:1). **Among you** indicates involved leadership. They were not detached but rather alongside the congregation, like Paul (1:5). Paul told the elders of the Ephesian church, 'I always lived among you' (Acts 20:18).

Second, the recognized pastors were to be **over** them (**you**). This is literally 'to stand before' which means to have charge over like a presiding official (cf. 1 Tim 3:4-5 in regard to one's family).

The shepherds were to lead in the sphere (**in**) of matters that belonged to **the Lord** because they had been appointed by God (Acts 20:28). Theirs was a spiritual leadership (1 Tim 5:17). The general, normal pattern for the flock's organization is outlined in Philippians 1:1 – overseers, deacons, and saints. This seems to have been true from the earliest days of the church (cf. Acts 11:30; 14:23; 15:2; 20:17; James 5:14; 1 Pet 5:1) and can be assumed here, although it is not stated explicitly.

Third, the recognized leaders were those who **admonish you** or, literally, 'set in mind' the Word of God or give instructions. At Ephesus, Paul engaged in this activity day and night (Acts 20:31). Later in this letter, Paul strongly exhorts this to also be a function of the flock (warn those who are unruly, 5:14; 2 Thess 3:15). Pastors were to admonish, confront, and encourage the flock, as did Paul (1:5; 2:13; 4:1).

Interestingly, these three basic functions correspond to the three titles given to the one role of pastoring the flock. Elder, Overseer, and Pastor are terms used interchangeably in Scripture to describe the various functions carried out by the same person (cf. Acts 20:17, 28; Titus 1:5, 7; 1 Pet 5:1-2). The pastors were to work diligently among the flock; the overseers were to stand before the flock in the Lord as examples and leaders; and the elders were to admonish the flock wisely from the Word of God.

5:13 Paul now picks up the second responsibility (cf. 5:12) of the flock towards their pastors: **esteem them very highly**. To esteem the pastors would be to obey them. This is not a forced obedience because of rank, but rather a reasoned obedience based on Scripture. In terms of extent, the obedience or esteem was not to be half-hearted, it was to be done **very highly**, i.e. abundant to the point of being excessive (cf. 3:10; Eph 3:20). In terms of excellence, it was to be **in love**.

OVERVIEW

True Love (5:13)

These qualities characterize authentic, biblical love according to the Apostle Paul as outlined in 1 Corinthians 13:4-7. He then promises, 'Love never fails' (13:8).

1. 'Love suffers long.' Therefore, I will bear with a person's worst behavior, without retaliation, regardless of the circumstances.

2. 'Love is kind.' Therefore, I will diligently seek ways to be actively useful in another person's life.

3. 'Love does not envy.' Therefore, I will delight in the esteem and honor given to someone else.

4. 'Love does not parade itself.' Therefore, I will not draw attention to myself exclusive of others.

5. 'Love is not puffed up.' Therefore, I know I am no more important than others.

6. 'Love does not behave rudely.' Therefore, I will not engage any person in ungodly activity.

7. 'Love does not seek its own.' Therefore, I will be others oriented.

8. 'Love is not provoked.' Therefore, I will not resort to anger as a solution to difficulties between myself and others.

9. 'Love thinks no evil.' Therefore, I will never keep an account due on others.

10. 'Love does not rejoice in iniquity.' Therefore, I will never delight in another's unrighteous behavior, nor will I join its expression.

11. 'Love rejoices in the truth.' Therefore, I will find great joy when truth prevails in another's life.

12. 'Love bears all things.' Therefore, I will be publicly silent about another's faults.

13. 'Love believes all things.' Therefore, I will express unshakeable confidence and trust in others.

14. 'Love hopes all things.' Therefore, I will confidently expect future victory in another's life, regardless of the present imperfections.

15. 'Love endures all things.' Therefore, I will outlast every assault of Satan to break up relationships.

Both the recognition and the esteem of the flock were to be rendered to the pastors **for their work**, i.e. their work of laboring, their work of leading, and their work of feeding (5:12). It was not because of their personality, reputation, education, or prominence. It was because they carried out their God-ordained responsibilities in the church.

The end result envisioned by Paul would be **peace among yourselves**. If pastors carry out their Divinely appointed roles with diligence in the church and if the congregation responds as commanded by Scripture, then there will be **peace**, stability, and tranquility. There is every reason to believe that Paul is here admonishing the Thessalonians to continue doing what they have already done (cf. 5:23; Ps 133:1; 2 Thess 3:16).

5:14 Paul changes the subject from the shepherds and the flock to the flock's responsibility towards difficult people. He emphasizes the importance of this by using the word **exhort** (cf. 4:1, 10). All four categories have been dealt with previously: the **unruly** (4:11-12); **the fainthearted** (4:13-18); **the weak** (4:3-8); and **all** (3:12). Here, Paul gives a one-word response summary for each which would be the individual and corporate responsibility of the church (**brethren**).

First, **warn** (cf. 5:12; 2 Thess 3:15) **those who are unruly**. The unruly were those who lived literally 'out of step' with the rest and in rebellious disregard for God's instructions on living. They were to be warned in an admonishing way with the word of God to change their behavior. Paul did just this very thing in 2 Thessalonians 3:6-15 with those who refused to work.

Second, **comfort the fainthearted**, or, literally, 'the small souled'. They were to give encouragement to those who were anxious or timid in their faith, like Paul recalls that he did when he was among them (2:12) and as he did earlier in the letter to those who were distressed over the future of their deceased loved ones (4:13-18).

Third, **uphold the weak**, literally, 'hold on to and don't let go' of those who do not have the spiritual strength to obey or function spiritually on their own. Paul did this for those who might be tempted sexually (4:3-8) and he frequently heeded his own counsel with the Corinthians. He taught this truth to the Ephesian elders (Acts 20:35).

Fourth, **be patient with all**, literally, 'be long tempered' or 'long-suffering'. This is self-restraint without anger in the face of provocation (cf. 1 Cor 13:4). As God has been patient with the redeemed (2 Pet 3:9), so they are to be with others. Patience is a Christian virtue frequently mentioned in the New Testament (Gal 5:22; Eph 4:2; Col 3:12; 2 Tim 3:10). **With all** seems to mean 'all in the assembly' in this context, but it could extend to all men, both within and without the church (cf. 3:12; 2 Thess 3:2).

5:15 Paul now turns to what would be the most difficult kind of situation, i.e. when someone does evil to another person. The natural response is to strike back with retaliation. But Paul wrote, **see that no one renders** (pays back) **evil for evil to anyone** (cf. Rom 12:17-21). This was also taught by Jesus (Matt 5:38-39), Peter (1 Pet 3:9), and John (3 John 11). This is an absolute statement with no loopholes as Paul says **no one ... to anyone**. Revenge is strictly forbidden behavior for any Christian towards anyone else for anything done. Paul could easily have had Proverbs 20:22 in mind as he wrote this. Paul draws the ultimate conclusion on righteous vindication in 2 Thessalonians 1:5-10.

Just the opposite response should prevail at all times – **always pursue what is good**. This end is to be sought after with all diligence (Phil 3:14). God will benefit both self and others (**yourselves, all**). Paul again refuses to accept any exception to this principle with **always...all**. For an extended discussion on 'good' and 'evil', see notes on 5:22.

7. The Christian life (5:16-22)

Writing like the author of Proverbs, Paul finishes off the instructions in his letter with eight short, penetrating statements which strike at the very heart of the Christian life. Each is a command that expects obedience. These imperatives could be viewed as the ABCs of Christian living.

Rejoice always, pray without ceasing, in everything give thanks; for this is the will of God in Christ Jesus for you. Do not quench the Spirit. Do not despise prophecies. Test all things; hold fast what is good. Abstain from every form of evil (5:16-22).

5:16 Rejoice always should be a regular, predictable pattern of one's Christian life (1:2; 3:6; 5:15; 2 Thess 1:3, 11; 2:13). See *Overview*, 'The Joy of the Lord' (1:6). Joy in the Lord should be the centerpiece of a Christian's outlook (Phil 3:1; 4:4). It is an acceptable response to life on both the mountain top and in the valley (Job 6:10; Pss 31:7; 35:9; 40:16; Col 1:24; 1 Pet 4:13).

5:17 Pray without ceasing should also be a regular staple in every Christian's life (Rom 12:12; Eph 6:18). See notes on 1:2 which describe Paul's prayer life in these two letters. Paul's own prayers were without ceasing (1:3; 2:13). Daniel's prayer life stands out as a noteworthy example (Dan 6:10; 9:2-21).

5:18 In everything give thanks should also characterize the Christian life as it did Paul's life (1:2; 2:13; 2 Thess 1:3; 2:13) and writings (Eph 5:20). Thanklessness marks the unbeliever (Rom 1:21; 2 Tim 3:2). Remember the example of Christ who anticipated the worst – crucifixion by man and being forsaken by God – but still gave thanks in the upper room (Mark 14:22-23; Luke 22:19-20). Why should a Christian so live? Because **this is the will of God in Christ Jesus for you**. See *Overview*, 'The Will of God' (4:3). All three injunctions regarding rejoicing, praying, and giving thanks come under the banner of God's will, regardless of whether Paul intended the explicit statement here to extend back to 5:16-17 or not.

5:19 Do not quench the Spirit. Since the Spirit (1:5-6; 4:8; 2 Thess 2:13) is pictured as a flaming fire in Matthew 3:11 and Acts 2:3, then the imagery is appropriate in prohibiting the extinguishing of the Spirit's work in a believer's life (cf. 2 Tim 1:6). This is similar to the command in Ephesians 4:30: 'Do not grieve the Holy Spirit of God' (cf. Isa 63:10). Rather, the believer is to be filled (controlled) by the Spirit (Eph 5:18-20), to walk by the Spirit (Gal 5:16), and to be led by the Spirit (Gal 5:18). What would put the Spirit's fire out? Unquestionably, deeds of the flesh (Gal 5:17). See *Overview*, 'Ministries of the Holy Spirit' (2 Thess 2:13).

5:20 Do not despise prophecies. Prophecy in the New Testament can mean the spoken word (1 Cor 14:6; 1 Tim 1:18; 4:14; Rev 11:6). But more often it refers to the written words of Scripture (Matt 13:14; 2 Pet 1:20-21; Rev 1:3; 22:7, 10, 18-19). Paul probably had in mind God's written Word and thus it could be rendered, 'Despise not Scripture!' **Despise** might involve: looking down on; mocking; denying; finding contemptible; and/or disbelieving (cf. Jer 8:8-9; 42:1–43:4; 1 Tim 6:1; Titus 2:5). God's Word is not to be treated lightly, but rather taken seriously.

There is also a possibility that Paul is referring to the spoken prophetic ministry like that in Antioch (Acts 13:1), like Judas and Silas (Acts 15:32), or like those who were the gifted men mentioned in Ephesians 4:11. But regardless of what it immediately referred to in Paul's day, by application, it now applies only to the finalized, written word of God. Although many commentators read a form of the Corinthian problem into this text (1 Cor 12, 14), there seems to be no actual warrant to do so.

5:21 It has been suggested by some that **test** and **hold fast** refer to **prophecies** in 5:20. They appeal to the general context and a doubtful textual variant which would be translated 'and'. In my opinion, 5:21-22 stand alone with a broader meaning than just 5:20, although the application to 5:20 would be appropriate. If the **test** was limited to **prophecies** alone, the standard would be truth and error, but this is not the language used here. The reference for the **test** (2:4) is certainly God's word and will (Deut 13:1-5; 18:20-22; Isa 8:20; 1 John 4:1-3). The results would be categorized as to their nature, either **good** or bad. That which is deemed **good** is something to which one should **hold fast** (1 Cor 11:2; Heb 10:23) and never let go (Phil 1:10; 4:8).

5:22 Paul continues the discussion of 5:21 with **abstain from every form of evil** or, put another way, 'that which is bad should never be embraced.' Abstention applied to sexual immorality earlier in the letter (4:3); now he expands the idea to **every form** (sexual or non-sexual) **of evil**. In Greek, there are two sets of words used for good and evil (*kalos, kakos, agathos, poneros*). At times, the first pair can refer to the intrinsic value and the second to the experiential value. However, Paul seems to use them interchangeably in 5:15 (*kakos, agathos*) and 5:21-22 (*kalos, poneros*) with an emphasis on the experiential side of life. *Agathos* is also used elsewhere in these letters (1 Thess 3:6; 2 Thess 2:16-17) as is *poneros* (2 Thess 3:2-3). That which is associated with God is good (John 10:11, *kalos*) and that which is connected with Satan is evil (2 Thess 3:3; *poneros*). The Thessalonians were to **abstain** from not just that which was viewed as or appeared **evil** (to which all would agree), but rather **every** kind of **evil**, even if it was only internalized in a nonvisible way. Ultimately, the practiced ability to obey this command evidences whether a professing believer is an actual Christian. 'Beloved, do not imitate what is evil, but what is good. He who does good is of God, but he who does evil has not seen God' (3 John 11; cf. Isa 1:16-17). Paul might have had Job in mind here as a positive example (Job 1:1, 8; 2:3).

B. Paul's Closing Words (5:23-27)

Paul concludes this first letter with a prayer (5:23), a doctrinal word of encouragement (5:24), a personal request for prayer (5:25), and two seemingly unrelated commands (5:26-27). It appears that Paul has responded to all that Timothy reported (3:6) and now closes with a short list of thoughts that immediately come to mind.

Now may the God of peace Himself sanctify you completely; and may your whole spirit, soul, and body be preserved blameless at the coming of our Lord Jesus Christ. He who calls you is faithful, who also will do it. Brethren, pray for us. Greet all the brethren with a holy kiss. I charge you by the Lord that this epistle be read to all the holy brethren (5:23-27).

5:23 Paul begins his prayer with an appeal to the **God of peace** (2 Thess 3:16). This is one of at least seven communicable attributes of God which Paul mentions in his two letters. The other six are:

righteousness (2 Thess 1:5); faithfulness (5:24; 2 Thess 3:3); love (2 Thess 2:16; 3:5); patience (2 Thess 3:5); goodness (2 Thess 1:11); and grace (5:28; 2 Thess 1:12; 3:18).

OVERVIEW

Knowing God (5:23)

What is God like? Can we really know? Is it all that important to know? On one hand, the knowledge of God is shrouded in mystery (Col 2:2), locked up to human understanding (Rom 11:33). On the other hand, believers are admonished to glory in the knowledge and understanding of God (Jer 9:24). Yet for us to comprehend God without divine instruction would be like a person, blind and deaf from birth, trying to describe accurately the surrounding world. As mere mortals, we require God's help even to know Him.

Let's be thankful God has chosen to reveal Himself in various ways to those whom He created (Heb 1:1-2). Therefore, even though He is invisible, we can dimly gaze upon His divine beauty. In spite of the fact that God is incomprehensible, we can begin to understand Him. We can actually express the indescribable, even if in limited ways, because He chose to reveal Himself. By His great grace, true believers in Jesus Christ can approach the otherwise inaccessible God through our heavenly High Priest (Heb 4:14-16). A person's eternal future actually depends on knowing God.

The Mystery of God
Theophilus of Antioch in the late second century AD wrote: 'For in glory He is incomprehensible, in greatness unfathomable, in height inconceivable, in power incomparable, in wisdom unrivaled, in goodness inimitable, in kindness unutterable.' This church father echoed what had been confessed by the writers of Scripture, that God is unknowable unless He chooses to reveal Himself.

King David marveled at how perfectly God knew him, but how little he knew of God (Ps 139:1-6). David later wrote of the Lord, 'His greatness no one can fathom' (Ps 145:3). Zophar tested Job, 'Can you fathom the mysteries of God?' (Job 11:7). Paul lamented, 'Now I know in part; then I shall know fully' (1 Cor 13:12). All of these men travailed in their valiant but exhausting efforts to know Him.

God eternally exists before time, through time, and beyond time. But fully comprehending such lofty thoughts of Him is exceedingly more challenging than attempting to ascend Mount Everest. God's fullness can never be completely scaled by our human mind. Writers of Scripture use the following 'out-of-reach' concepts in trying to portray our indescribable God. He is *unfathomable* (Isa 40:28), *unreachable* (Isa 55:8-9), *unsearchable* (Rom 11:33), *invisible* (1 Tim 1:17); and *unapproachable* (1 Tim 6:16). The fullness of God remains immeasurably beyond human understanding.

God's Attributes

Irenaeus (about AD 175) clearly admitted, 'Without God, God cannot be known.' So God's condescending love graciously stooped down from the heavenly summits so that we might knowingly glimpse, in an elementary way, something of His greatness.

God has given us an especially detailed revelation about Himself in the Bible, including many of His attributes. An attribute or 'characteristic' helps describe the nature of something or someone. In the case of God, His attributes tell us who He is, in terms we can understand.

Theologians categorize God's attributes in various ways; but I will use the phrases *non-communicable* and *communicable*. God's non-communicable qualities are unique to His deity. In contrast, communicable attributes are those He shares, at least in part, with us human beings.

Non-communicable attributes are those major characteristics of God that no one else will ever experience. They include His *omnipotence* (Jer 32:17), *omniscience* (Ps 139:1-6), *omnipresence* (139:7-10), *immutability* (Ps 102:27), *sovereignty* (1 Chron 29:11-12), *eternality* (Ps 90:2), *immortality* (1 Tim 1:17), *greatness* (Ps 135:5), and *self-existence* (Isa 44:6).

While we can never aspire to these qualities, they tell us something significant about God in His relationship with us. For example, because God is all-powerful or omnipotent, nothing and no one in life will defeat Him. No problem is too hard for God to solve.

Because God is omniscient or all-knowing and is omnipresent or everywhere, nothing surprises Him, and He misses nothing in our lives. He will be with us in both good times and bad.

His immutability or unchanging character, sovereignty, eternality, immortality, greatness, and self-existence all point to the exclusive nature of His deity, which is shared by no one else. We worship the one true God who is ever consistent with Himself from eternity to eternity, is dependent on nothing, will be victorious over all, and whose eternal purposes will be completely accomplished.

Communicable attributes find their complete expression in God, while humans can only experience them in limited form. They include *wisdom* (Rom 16:27), *faithfulness* (1 Cor 10:13), *truthfulness* (Exod 34:6), *love* (1 John 4:8), *goodness* (Ps 100:5), *righteousness* (Ps 92:15), *mercy* (Ps 86:15), *compassion* (Lam 3:22), *holiness* (Ps 99:9), *graciousness* (Ps 116:5), *patience* (2 Pet 3:15), *peace* (Heb 13:20), *kindness* (Ps 117:2), *gentleness* (2 Cor 10:1), *joy* (John 17:13), *forgiveness* (Exod 34:7), and *justice* (Deut 10:18).

Several Christmases ago, my wife introduced me to a hobby that I now dearly enjoy – model railroading. My planned N-gauge layout represents the actual Pennsylvania Railroad on which my Grandfather Mayhue served 40 years. N-gauge trains (about half the size of HO) are scaled at 1/160th the size of the real thing. As you might guess, replica models do not contain every detail of a full-size engine or rail car, but no one would mistake the fact that they have been scale-modeled after the originals.

These electric trains illustrate godliness. God is the prototype after whom Christians are fashioned to be scale models. We will never be identical in size to God – only miniatures; we will never possess all the characteristics of God, only those that are communicable.

Or put another way, we will never become or even approach deity, but we are exhorted by Scripture to be like God. He intends Christians to be representative copies of Himself.

Pictures of God

God is the Creator, nevertheless, Scripture figuratively describes Him in created-being terms. God condescendingly reveals the greater truth about Himself using the lesser characteristics of His created world. He uses human forms of Himself such as mouth (Deut 8:3), hand (1 Sam 5:11), eyes (2 Chron 16:9), and heart (Hosea 11:8) to describe divine speaking, doing, knowing, and loving.

Human passions such as jealousy (Exod 20:5) and anger (2 Kings 13:3) figuratively characterize God's demand of exclusive worship and His righteous wrath. At other times, Scripture uses figures of speech that compare God to parts of His creation. For example, 'The LORD is my rock' (Ps 18:2), or 'He rushes at me like a warrior' (Job 16:14).

God also is pictured, in human terms, as a nurturing father to a son (Ps 89:26), a loving husband to a wife (Jer 31:32), a caring shepherd to the sheep (Ps 23:1), a sovereign king to his subjects (Ps 10:16), a compassionate savior to the perishing (Isa 45:15), a protective soldier to the embattled (Exod 15:3), a true friend to the outcast (Jer 30:17), a merciful deliverer to the oppressed (Ps 18:2), a benevolent master to a slave (Ps 123:2), and a righteous judge to the lawless (James 4:12).

God is described by theologians as *transcendent* or *remote* in the sense that He is beyond our universe and time; this helps to define the divine *otherness* of His character. God is pictured in Psalms 113:4-6, 123:1, and Isaiah 6:1-4 as independent of and separate from the created order.

In contrast, God is also portrayed as intimately operating in the confines of time and space in the world and among people. This *immanent* relationship of God with His creation is illustrated in Psalms 104:27-30, 139:7-12, Amos 9:2-4, and Acts 17:27-28. Scripture speaks of God as being both transcendent and immanent at the same time; He is removed and up close simultaneously.

A few individuals have experienced God nearby and lived to write about their close encounters. Job learned of God's sovereign greatness (Job 42:1-5). Moses experienced God's grace and glory (Exod 3:4-6; 24:15-18; 33:18-23). God's holiness was on display to Isaiah (6:1-10), as was God's glory to Ezekiel (1:4-28). Paul encountered God's redeeming love on the road to Damascus (Acts 9:3-6; 22:6-10; 26:13-18) and later visited God's throne room in the third heaven (2 Cor 12:2-4) to see the unspeakable spectacle of God's glory. The apostle John was caught up in spirit to experience worship at the heavenly throne (Rev 4:1-5:14).

A Tantalizing Wait

Will we ever satisfy our curiosity to know more of God? The unknowable qualities of God will have to await our arrival in heaven. Still, while here on earth, we can know something of what God is like from what He has shown us.

Yet the highest knowing of God is not in an academic sense, but in a relationship with Him that moves us from the intellectual level to the intimate. The supreme knowledge of God is described in 1 John 5:20 as knowing 'that the Son of God has come and has given us an understanding, that we may know Him who is true; and we are in Him who is true, in His Son Jesus Christ. This is the true God and eternal life' (see John 17:3; Gal 4:9; Phil 3:10; 1 John 2:3).

To really know God is to believe in Him by faith for salvation, to be adopted into His family, and to be called 'a child of God' (Rom 8:14-17). The ultimate knowledge of God is not just to know what God is like, but also to be like Him.

The remainder of the prayer is quite similar to the prayer of 3:13 (see notes). Paul speaks of **God...Himself** because no one else could **sanctify...completely**, which looks to the ultimate (future and final) sanctification that will be total in the most complete fashion. What God began as initial sanctification, i.e. salvation (2 Thess 2:13), what progressed by God's hand during one's life on earth (4:3-4, 7), will finally be finished by God to perfection (3:13). This is also known as glorification (see notes on 4:3). See *Overview*, 'God's Role in Salvation' (1:4).

Paul expands his thought with **and** (it could be translated 'even'). **Your whole spirit, soul, and body** refers to the complete person. Basically, humans are made up of a material portion (the body) and an immaterial (invisible) portion. Death occurs when there is a separation of the material (body) from the immaterial, i.e. spirit (2 Cor 5:8; James 2:26). So what does Paul mean by **spirit, soul, and body**? The Bible is neither clinical nor scientifically detailed in speaking of the human make-up in such passages as Deuteronomy 6:5, Matthew 10:28, Mark 12:30, and Luke 10:27. Therefore, it would be the opinion of this writer that humans are basically comprised of two parts (dichotomous), not three parts (trichotomous). For a more complete discussion see Hendrickson, 146-50, and Augustus H. Strong, *Systematic Theology* (Old Tappan, NJ: Fleming H. Revell, 1907) 483-88. **Blameless** (cf. Phil 2:15) describes the condition of having no grounds for accusation (3:13).

At the coming of our Lord Jesus Christ describes the time which Paul has in mind. See *Overview*, 'Christ's Coming' (2:19) and notes on 2:19, 3:13, and 4:15. This passage refers to the same time and event mentioned three times previously, i.e. Christ's coming at His rapture and the subsequent judgment seat of Christ (Rom 14:10; 1 Cor 3:10-15; 2 Cor 5:10).

5:24 Because God is **faithful** (cf. 2 Thess 3:3 notes), He will accomplish (Phil 1:6) what Paul prayed for, i.e. final sanctification or glorification (cf. Num 23:19). God **calls** believers to salvation (see notes on 2:12) as the first step to the final destination of glorification. Salvation is assured because it begins and ends with

God (Rom 8:28-39). See the discussion regarding God's faithfulness in the notes on 2 Thessalonians 3:3.

5:25 It seems that as Paul prayed for the Thessalonians (**brethren**) so Paul would also have them pray for him, Silas, and Timothy (**us**, 2 Thess 3:1). It was not unusual for Paul to request prayer on his behalf from those to whom he wrote (Rom 15:30-32; 2 Cor 1:11; Eph 6:19-20; Phil 1:19; Col 4:3, 18; Phile 22). See notes about Paul's prayer life on 1:2. Some ancient manuscripts end with 'also'.

5:26 The **holy kiss** is commanded four other times in the New Testament (Rom 16:16; 1 Cor 16:20; 2 Cor 13:12; 1 Pet 5:14). First century Christians (**all the brethren**) were to greet one another righteously with the cultural hug and kiss in recognition that they were brothers and sisters in the family of God. See *Overview,* 'New Testament "One Anothers" ' (3:12). First Peter 5:14 refers to this as a 'kiss of love'. In this context, most believe that Paul is asking the leaders of the church to greet the flock on his, Silas', and Timothy's behalf since 'one another' is not included. It is possible to also take Paul's command as a general imperative to be carried out by the whole congregation, as he writes elsewhere.

5:27 I charge you by the Lord indicates the seriousness with which Paul writes this **epistle**. He is saying in effect, 'I obligate you with an oath before the Lord.' Presumably, the **you** refers to the leadership (5:12-13) who will be responsible to **read** Paul's letter **to all the holy brethren**. It appears from New Testament manuscript evidence that **holy** was a later addition. Reading the Scripture publicly had been done by the Jews (Neh 8:8; Luke 4:16; Acts 13:27) and now also in the church (Col 4:16; 1 Tim 4:13; Rev 1:3). Paul undoubtedly believed that it was imperative for all the Thessalonians to hear what he had written because it had come from the Lord.

C. Paul's Benediction (5:28)

The grace of our Lord Jesus Christ be with you. Amen.

5:28 It was standard fare, without exception, for Paul to conclude each letter with the mention of **grace**, much as he began all thirteen of his epistles. He, above all things spiritually, would have **the grace of our Lord Jesus Christ** continually **be with you**. By this, he means that they should live in both a state of and in the actual experience of Christ's benevolent, unmerited favor which was provided by His death on the cross and appropriated by faith. Older manuscripts do not have **Amen** (cf. 2 Thess 3:18). This prayer, without question, came from a pastor's heart with the wish for God's highest spiritual blessing to be the experience of those whom he loved so dearly.

2 THESSALONIANS

A
Concerned Letter
to a
Consecrated Church

Several months, at least, have transpired since Paul wrote First Thessalonians and he remains under duress in Corinth, c. late AD 50 or early AD 51. Reports have come back to him from Thessalonica, most likely either by letter and/or messenger (cf. 'we hear,' 3:11), that several severe problems have newly arisen or escalated in seriousness. Still unable to return (Acts 17:9-10), Paul writes again. This time his correspondence is shorter and sharper. It is not nearly as autobiographical, but far more issue oriented. This epistle carries a much higher level of concern than the first one and a greater sense of urgency for obedience to his instructions. He insistently exercises his pastoral responsibility for the spiritual welfare of his disciples in Thessalonica.

Paul writes to bolster a church which continues to grow, even in the midst of painful trials. From a distance, he comforts a persecuted church (1:3-12), instructs a frightened and falsely taught church about the future (2:1-12), and confronts a disobedient and undisciplined church (3:6-15).

1. PAUL'S GREETING (1:1-2)

Paul, Silvanus, and Timothy, to the church of the Thessalonians in God our Father and the Lord Jesus Christ: Grace to you and peace from God our Father and the Lord Jesus Christ (1:1-2).

1:1-2 Paul's greeting in this second letter is virtually identical to that of the first epistle with two slight variations. First, Paul uses **our Father** here, whereas he employed **the Father** in 1 Thessalonians. There is no interpretive significance since Paul elsewhere affirms God the Father in a personal way (1 Thess 3:11). Second, in the first letter there is strong evidence that **from God our Father and the Lord Jesus Christ** was not a part of the original text, while here its inclusion is uncontested. Since both greetings are so close in wording, the reader is directed to see the notes on 1 Thessalonians 1:1 as the commentary for 1:1-2.

2. PAUL'S ENCOURAGEMENT IN TROUBLED TIMES (1:3-12)

Apparently, the persecution mentioned in 1 Thessalonians (1:6; 2:14) had escalated since then (1:4). The exact circumstances are unknown, but the trouble probably was instigated by the Jews in the synagogue (Acts 17:5, 13). This first section of 2 Thessalonians is intended by Paul to bolster their faith and serve as an encouragement in the midst of trial. The apostle begins with thanksgiving and affirmation (1:3-4), followed by significant truth about God's righteous judgment on those who trouble them (1:5-10), i.e. the Thessalonians would be vindicated by God in the future and justice would prevail. He closes off this portion of the letter with prayer (1:11-12). His focus is always on the purposes of God and eternal issues, never on the earthly and temporal. Paul built the Thessalonians up, while the enemy attempted to tear and wear them down.

A. With Thanksgiving and Affirmation (1:3-4)

We are bound to thank God always for you, brethren, as it is fitting, because your faith grows exceedingly, and the love of every one of you all abounds toward each other, so that we ourselves boast of you among the churches of God for your patience and faith in all your persecutions and tribulations that you endure (1:3-4).

1:3 Paul's acknowledgment of their pastoral prayers (**We**), including Silas and Timothy, is quite similar to 1 Thessalonians 1:2-3 (see notes). He speaks of their rejoicing as a spiritual obligation (**bound**, cf. 2:13) which was **fitting** or appropriate (cf. 1 Thess 3:9 notes). It was not unusual for Paul to remind his flock that he and his friends prayed for them (2:13; 1 Thess 3:9-10). His thanksgiving (1:3; 1 Thess 1:2; 2:13) was a regular pattern (**always**) of his prayer life (1:11; 2:13; 1 Thess 1:2) and characterized all of Paul's epistles to churches, except 2 Corinthians and Galatians.

He outlines two key reasons why they wanted **to thank God always for you, brethren** (cf. Eph 1:15-16). First, **your faith**

grows exceedingly or luxuriantly. Paul had been concerned about their **faith** after he had to leave (1 Thess 3:2, 5), even though it had begun well (2:13; 1 Thess 1:3, 8). They had been overjoyed when Timothy returned with a good report about their **faith** (1 Thess 3:7) but knew their **faith** needed to grow still more (1 Thess 3:10; 4:1). He urged them to put on the breastplate of **faith** (1 Thess 5:8). Here, he thanks the Lord for their **faith** that **grows exceedingly** and later prays for their **faith** that produces works (1:11; cf. 1 Thess 1:3).

Second, he commends their **love**. He had commented on their initial labor of love in 1 Thessalonians 1:3, and Timothy reported back about the good news of their subsequent love (1 Thess 3:6). He prayed that the Lord would cause them to abound in love (1 Thess 3:12; cf. 4:1) and urged them to put on the breastplate of love (1 Thess 5:8). God answered Paul's prayer and the Thessalonians fulfilled their responsibility because **the love of every one of you all abounds toward each other**. See *Overview*, 'True Love' (1 Thess 5:13) and *Overview*, 'New Testament "One Anothers" '(1 Thess 3:12). Before the letter is over, he will once again pray for their **love** towards God (3:5).

1:4 As a result (**so that**) of the Thessalonians' growing faith and abounding love (1:3), Paul and his friends (**we ourselves**) **boast** (translated 'rejoice' in 1 Thess 2:19, see notes) **of you among the churches of God** (cf. 1 Thess 2:14). Since Paul is writing from Corinth, these would be the assemblies of Achaia and Macedonia. Whereas, other Christians were telling Paul about the Thessalonians earlier (1 Thess 1:8-9), now Paul is reporting their progress to other churches. Their boasting focused (**for**) on the Thessalonians' godly response to increased hostilities because of their faith. They reacted with **patience**, i.e. a willingness to remain under the burden (cf. 'perseverance', NASB). Paul had already commended them for the patience that produced hope (1 Thess 1:3) and will pray later on for their patience (3:5). Also, they did not abandon or retreat from their **faith** (see notes on 1:3). Put another way, Paul commends the way they **endure** or forbear in the face of **persecution** and **tribulations,** unlike the person in

Matthew 13:21 where these same two words are used together. Aggressive opposition characterized the **persecutions** (cf. Acts 8:1; 13:50; 2 Cor 12:10; 2 Tim 3:11) which would never separate them from the love of God (Rom 8:35), regardless of intensity or outcome. **Tribulations** refers to the pressure on all sides produced by their spiritual enemies (cf. 1:6; 1 Thess 1:6; 3:3, 7). They were in the midst of the battle and standing firm with victory in sight (cf. 2 Cor 4:8-9).

B. With Revealed Truth (1:5-10)

Paul is not writing a detailed, precise, or even chronological prophetic treatise here but rather is wanting to give the Thessalonians hope that, in the end, God's righteousness would prevail for them and for their tormentors. It is the writer's opinion that this section, like many in the Old Testament (Isa 61:1-2; cf. 2 Pet 1:10-11), is somewhat compressed so that the range of time is not always obviously apparent, nor are all the details. These truths will particularly be true for those who are alive at Christ's second coming and more universally true at the end of the Millennium. Paul states the case for the righteous judgment of God (1:5) in three parts: the two realities of (1:5-7a); the general time of (1:7b); and the consequences of (1:8-10). This applies to both the saved and the unsaved (cf. Dan 12:2; John 5:28-29).

which is manifest evidence of the righteous judgment of God, that you may be counted worthy of the kingdom of God, for which you also suffer; since it is a righteous thing with God to repay with tribulation those who trouble you, and to give you who are troubled rest with us when the Lord Jesus is revealed from heaven with His mighty angels, in flaming fire taking vengeance on those who do not know God, and on those who do not obey the gospel of our Lord Jesus Christ. These shall be punished with everlasting destruction from the presence of the Lord and from the glory of His power, when He comes, in that Day, to be glorified in His saints and to be admired among all those who believe, because our testimony among you was believed (1:5-10).

1:5 Paul draws a conclusion here, based on his factual observations in 1:3-4. The faith and love of the Thessalonians anchored them immoveably and when the storms of persecution and tribulations came, they endured, not drifting in their faith. This then is

manifest evidence, not circumstantial or even subject to doubt, that **the righteous judgment of God** would ultimately prevail on their behalf. Just as God had elected them (2:13; 1 Thess 1:4), He would complete the work (2:14; 1 Thess 5:23-24). Their patience and faith (1:4) proved beyond a reasonable doubt that their conversion was authentic (cf. 1 Thess 1:9-10).

God is righteous (Rev 15:3; 16:5; see *Overview*, 'Knowing God', 1 Thess 5:23). His judgments are **righteous** (Acts 17:31; Rev 16:7; 19:2, 11). Therefore, **God** is the righteous judge of all (2 Tim 4:1, 8; Heb 12:23). It is sometimes difficult to determine from individual passages whether God the Father or God the Son (the Lord Jesus Christ) is the judge unless one realizes that the Father will judge through the Son (John 5:22, 27; Acts 10:42; 17:31; Rom 2:16), who will judge both the just (Rom 14:10; 2 Cor 5:10) and the unjust (Rev 20:11-15).

Because the Thessalonians are unquestionably genuine converts to Christ and because Christ always does what is right, they will be **counted worthy of the kingdom of God** (cf. 1:11; 1 Thess 2:12). Their relationship and behavior is befitting the nature of the judge (Luke 20:35; Acts 5:41). See *Overview*, 'The Kingdom of God' (1 Thess 2:12). Here, **the kingdom of God** refers to the realm of salvation and the cause of the King.

Now they **suffer**[1], but in the end they will be given rest (1:7) and their tormentors Divine retribution (1:6). Suffering for Christ in one's life was the standard, not the exception, in Paul's day. Paul suffered (2 Tim 1:12); the Philippians suffered (Phil 1:29); the church at Smyrna suffered (Rev 2:10); and the dispersed church suffered (1 Pet 2:21). Why not the Thessalonians, too? Suffering was not without benefits, however, such as: teaching obedience (Heb 5:8); making one dependent on God (2 Cor 12:9); and developing Christian character (Rom 5:3-4). Peter writes the most helpful material for those who suffer for Christ's sake (1 Pet 2:19-25; 3:13-18; 4:1-2). It was, and still is, a message of delayed gratification or reward (James 5:7-11).

---

1. See John MacArthur, 'Scripture on God's Purposes in Suffering' in Joni Eareckson Tada and Steve Estes, *When God Weeps* (Grand Rapids: Zondervan, 1997) 232-40 for an excellent treatment.

1:6 It would have been unrighteous for the Thessalonians to retaliate against their persecutors (see notes on 1 Thess 5:15). But, **it is a righteous thing with God** (see notes on God's righteousness in 1:5). Both the Old Testament and New Testament clearly declare that it is God's **righteous** responsibility **to repay** (cf. 1 Thess 3:9) or avenge the unrighteous who make the righteous suffer (Deut 32:35; Prov 20:22; Rom 12:19; Heb 10:30). **God** will return **tribulation** to **those who trouble you** (literally, 'tribulation for tribulation,' e.g. see Exod 23:22). Although there is a time coming on earth (Daniel's seventieth week – see the chart *Futuristic Premillennialism*) known as the 'great tribulation' (Matt 24:21; Rev 7:14), this is not what Paul had in mind. Rather, it is eternal tribulation in hell (cf. 1:9).

1:7 Retribution will be the destiny of their tormentors, while those **who are troubled** will be given **rest** (Rev 14:13) **with us**, i.e. Paul, Silas and Timothy. Paul is not speaking of peace and ease in this life but in eternity, which is the rest (but with a different Greek word) that is spoken of by the writer of Hebrews (3:18–4:11). In other words, those who lived with unrest (tribulation and persecution) for Christ's sake, in this life, will have eternal rest with Christ forever.

   Having detailed the two results of God's righteous judgment – rest for the righteous and retribution for the unrighteous (1:5-7a) – Paul now turns to **when** that will be: when **the Lord Jesus Christ is revealed from heaven with His mighty angels**.

OVERVIEW

First Century BC Messianic Expectations[1] (1:7)

Based on what they knew of Old Testament prophetic material, the first century BC Jewish community was not looking for the first advent of Christ as presented in the Gospels. Rather, they believed that Messiah's second coming was near and would end Jewish tribulation at the hands of

---

1. Summarized from Emil Schürer, *A History of the Jewish People in the Time of Jesus Christ*, rev.ed. (Edinburgh: T & T Clark, 1979) 2:514-47.

other nations, plus establish the Davidic kingdom (2 Sam 7:12-17) on earth.

The following features summarize their biblical expectations concerning Messiah.

1. A season of extreme tribulation would prevail prior to Messiah's arrival.
2. In the midst of this upheaval, Elijah would arrive as the forerunner and announcer of Messiah.
3. Messiah would then come to earth.
4. The nations would rise up against Messiah.
5. A coalition of nations would be defeated and destroyed.
6. Jerusalem would be reoccupied and rebuilt.
7. The Jewish Diaspora would return to Jerusalem.
8. Israel would become the capital of the world.
9. A time of peace and prosperity would be inaugurated.

Interestingly, this is what Futuristic Premillennialism is expecting at the time of Messiah's second arrival. Writing with broad, sweeping statements, without regard to particular features, nor intending to mention every detail, Paul refers to this in 2 Thessalonians 1:6-10.

Christ's revelation or the time when He **is revealed** is a term used of two different events, each determined by context. Christ's revelation can be at the *parousia* in the sense of the rapture and subsequent Bema judgment (see *Overview*, 'Christ's Coming' [1 Thess 2:19] which is also called the Day of Christ [see notes on 1 Thess 5:4]) as found in 1 Corinthians 1:7 and 1 Peter 1:7, 13; 4:13. Christ's revelation can also refer to, and does in this text, to the end of Daniel's seventieth week when Christ comes (Matt 24:27, 37, 39) and is revealed (Luke 17:30) in judgment. Neither *parousia* nor *revelation* are technical terms reserved for just one event. See notes on 1 Thessalonians 4:17 which distinguish between the two events in terms of their dramatically different contexts.

There are four indicators that **Jesus** being **revealed from heaven** here refers to the end of Daniel's seventieth week (see *Appendix 1*, 'Various Millennial Views'). First, this is in the context of judgment (1:5). Second, Christ is **revealed** with **His**

mighty angels. This is a chief characteristic of this moment (Zech 14:5; Matt 13:39-42, 49-50; 25:31; Mark 8:38; Rev 20:1). This is the only place in the New Testament where angels are termed 'mighty' (*dunamis*), although three times they are termed 'mighty' or 'strong' (*ischuros*) in Revelation (5:2; 10:1; 18:21). This would indicate strength and power for judgment.

OVERVIEW

Titles of Angels (1:7)

1. Men (Gen 18:2; Acts 1:10)
2. Sons of God (Job 1:6; 38:7)
3. Morning stars (Job 38:7)
4. Literally, 'gods' (Ps 8:5)
5. Mighty ones (Pss 29:1; 78:25)
6. Chariots (Ps 68:17; cf. 2 Kng 2:11; 6:17)
7. Sons of the mighty (Ps 89:6)
8. Holy one(s), literally, 'saints' (Ps 89:7; Dan 4:13, 17, 23; Zech 14:5)
9. His Hosts (Ps 103:21); cf. 'hosts of heaven' (Neh 9:6) and 'heavenly host' (Luke 2:13)
10. Watcher(s) (Dan 4:13, 17, 23)
11. Archangel (1 Thess 4:16; Jude 9)
12. Angel (2 Thess 1:7)
13. Ministering spirits (Heb 1:14; cf. Ps 103:20-21)

1:8 Third, **flaming fire** is associated with angels (Ps 104:4; Heb 1:7) and with divine judgment (Matt 3:10-12; 13:40, 42, 50; John 15:6; Heb 12:29). When Christ comes in judgment, His eyes will be like a flame of fire (Rev 19:12). Fourth, Christ will be **taking vengeance** (Luke 18:7-8; Rom 12:19; Heb 10:30).

The objects of His retribution will be **those who do not know God** (see notes on 1 Thess 4:5). To **not know God** is to lack a personal relationship with Jesus Christ. They are further defined as

those who do not obey the gospel. They will be judged on their rejection of Christ and His gospel. See notes about 'the gospel' at 1 Thessalonians 1:5; 2:2, 8. Their momentary opposition to the gospel, by persecuting the Thessalonians, only indicated outwardly that they were an enemy of the gospel inwardly. Paul has begun with this striking picture to describe the eternal consequences of both unbelief (1:8-9) and belief (1:10) in **our Lord Jesus** and the gospel. **'Christ'** does not appear in the oldest manuscripts.

1:9 Those who do not know God nor obey the gospel (**These**) **shall be punished** or, literally, 'pay the penalty', NASB (cf. Prov 27:12 [LXX]), as Paul has already noted (1:6, 8). However, he goes on to describe with unmistakable details what this punishment involves. First, it is **everlasting**. While it is true that the Greek adjective for eternal or everlasting (*aiōnios*) can mean a very long time, but not forever (cf. Phile 15), the overwhelming use in the New Testament refers to the eternal nature of God (Rom 16:26), the eternal nature of salvation (Rom 6:23), or the eternal penalty of unbelievers (Matt 18:8). In Matthew 25:46, this same adjective is used twice to describe both 'everlasting punishment' and 'eternal life'.

Second, it involves **destruction**[1] or a dramatic, ruinous decline in or loss of quality of life (cf. Phil 3:19). It can be used in a temporal (1 Cor 5:5; 10:10; 1 Thess 5:3; Heb 11:28) or an eternal sense (Acts 3:23; 1 Tim 6:9) and is never translated 'annihilation' in the New Testament. The idea of annihilation is certainly not attached in the temporal use and therefore should not be applicable in eternal matters either.

OVERVIEW

Conditional Immortality and Annihilationism (1:9)

Outside of liberal and cult theology, not until recently have conservatives seriously considered the possibilities that believers are granted immortality only at the final judgment and that unbelievers are then

---

1. See NIDNTT discussion of the various New Testament words (1:462-71).

annihilated or put out of existence. It has been the generally accepted testimony of the church that all humans will live forever – believers blissfully in the presence of God and unbelievers in conscious torment in a real place called Gehenna or Hell.

Universalists have always been considered to be outside the boundaries of orthodoxy. Some universalists believe that all who die are immediately transported into a new blissful life forever. Others believe in a postponed universalism wherein, after the resurrection, all are placed in the presence of God.

There are at least three forms of annihilationism. First, the atheistic view proposes that at death all humans go out of existence. Second, some believe that at the resurrection unbelievers will be given a second chance to believe and those who do not are then annihilated. Third, the majority of annihilationists believe that, after the final judgment, all unbelievers are annihilated.

The almost unanimously held view by the church through the centuries has been that after the final resurrection and judgment, believers will live forever blissfully in the presence of God and unbelievers will live in conscious torment in the fires of hell away from the presence of God forever. Numerous biblical texts and theological concepts point decidedly to this conclusion as the truth about the final judgment and life after death.

Key Biblical Texts

Matthew 25:46: This writer asserts that "eternal life" shares a common idea with 'eternal punishment', i.e. they both imply a forever conscious existence. The contrast is obviously in a differing quality of existence that is endless in both cases.

Mark 9:43, 48 (cf. Isa 66:24): The 'unquenchable fire' of 9:43 must have an endless supply of fuel otherwise it would be quenchable, which would be impossible if one took the annihilation view. Since the worm does not die, the illustration implies an endless supply of food which could not be with the annihilation view.

John 3:36: With parallelism much like that in Matthew 25:46, the verse declares that the true believer has eternal life and the unbeliever has God's wrath abiding, with the sense of continuation, on him. The concept of annihilationism would contradict the biblical sense of 'continued abiding'.

2 Thessalonians 1:9 (cf. Matt 10:28): This text is seemingly meaningless if 'eternal destruction' meant annihilation. Rather the vocabulary and the implied contrast to believers in the presence of God point to eternal existence in a ruinous state.

Revelation 14:10-11: There are at least four major contextual/exegetical indicators that a conscious, continual experience is in view here, not annihilation: (1) the torment is done in the presence of the holy angels and the Lamb; (2) the smoke of torment is an eternal phenomenon. Where there is smoke, there must be fire; and where there is fire, there must be fuel. So, eternal smoke demands eternal fuel, i.e. the lost; (3) those being tormented have no rest or, in other words, they are in torment. This would not be true if this referred to annihilation; and (4) the torment goes on 'day and night', which would be incompatible with annihilationism.

Revelation 19:20 and 20:10 (cf. Matt 25:41): In Revelation 19:20, the beast and the false prophet are thrown alive into the lake of fire. One thousand years later they are still alive (20:10). The phrase in 20:10, 'tormented day and night forever', indicates that what their previous tormented experience had been for a millennium would continue throughout eternity. This also describes the experience provided by the 'eternal fire' of Matthew 25:41. Since this is true of them, would it not also be true of others who eventually reside in the lake of fire?

Revelation 22:15: The focus of attention here is the New Jerusalem whose occupants have washed their robes (22:14). Those who have not and are unclean dwell outside, implying a continuing existence, not a non-existence.

Key Theological Concepts

Intermediate Torment
Luke 16:24, 25 points to lasting, conscious torment on the part of unbelievers immediately after death, just as Revelation 20:10 (cf. Matt 25:41; Rev 19:20) indicates one thousand years of torment during the millennium. Now, it would seem that philosophical arguments used by annihilationists against eternal conscious torment would be equally applicable here, but the facts of the texts contradict them. Since the annihilationists' thinking is not true here in the temporal sense, nothing would necessarily make them valid in the eternal sense.

Degrees of Eternal Punishment
Matthew 10:15; 11:22, 24 and Luke 10:12, 14; 20:47 point to the decided idea that there will be degrees of punishment in Gehenna for unbelievers appropriate to the evil deeds done during one's life. This would strongly argue against annihilationism which basically calls for a 'one size fits all' approach in that all are annihilated without variation.

Resurrection and the Second Death
Both Daniel 12:2 and John 5:29 point to the ultimate resurrection of the lost. Then, Revelation 20:11-15 describes their judgment by God with the outcome of a 'second death' in the lake of fire (cf. 21:8). Just as the first death did not result in annihilation, as evidenced by resurrection, neither will the second death.

Suffering in This Life
Annihilationists argue that it would be unloving and unmerciful for God to allow a person to experience eternal torment. They also reason that the punishment of eternal torment does not fit the nature of a temporal crime. Such logic seemingly fails to take into account that, from a human perspective, the sufferings of Job (Job 1–2) were not deserved, but God allowed them or that the sin of Achan (Josh 7) did not seem to deserve death as the consequence, but God demanded it of both him and his family. Remember also the death penalty imposed on the one caught gathering wood on the Sabbath (Num 15:32-36). None of these situations, apart from divine revelation, seem to square with the character of God as humanly defined, yet Scripture authenticates them all as true and consistent with God's perfect being. Thus annihilationists, who rest a large part of their case on this kind of thinking, should be extremely cautious in practicing theodicy.

Third, had Paul intended to convey the idea of extinction, he would not have added these next two descriptions prefaced by **from**. The concept of banishment, not being blotted out, is intended. The unbelievers are banned **from the presence of the Lord**. The idea of presence is literally 'before the face of ' (Heb 9:24; Rev 6:16; 20:11; 22:4). Believers are looking forward to being at home with the Lord (2 Cor 5:8), to always being with the Lord (1 Thess 4:17), to living together with Christ (1 Thess 5:10), to being like Him and seeing Him just as He is (1 John 3:2), and are eagerly waiting for the Savior to return (Phil 3:20). Just the opposite is true of unbelievers.

Fourth, Paul heightens his description of this absence from the Lord as away **from the glory of His power**. Power or strength (omnipotence) is one aspect of God's **glory** (Eph 1:19; 6:10). See *Overview*, 'The Glory of God' (1 Thess 2:12) and *Overview*, ¦Knowing God' (1 Thess 5:23). Power is attributed to God the Father (Rev 7:12) and God the Son (Rev 5:12) by the heavenly choir. Believers will dwell forever in the presence and glory of His power.

Hell does not involve annihilation but, rather, a new state of conscious existence which is dramatically worse than the first (cf. Rev 20:14-15). The absence of God's presence and the lack of Divine glory are elsewhere in the Bible spoken of as: a lake of fire (Rev 20:10); a furnace of fire (Matt 13:42); unquenchable fire (Matt 3:12); fire and brimstone (Luke 17:29); outer darkness (Matt 22:13; 25:30); the second death (Rev 2:11; 20:6, 14; 21:8); a place of no rest (Rev 14:11); a place of torment day and night forever and ever (Rev 14:11; 20:10); a place of weeping and gnashing of teeth (Matt 8:12); and eternal fire (Matt 25:41).

This picture of hell has as its backdrop the Valley of Hinnom immediately south of Jerusalem. Because it was regularly used as a garbage dump, fires continually smoldered and smoke from the burning debris ascended night and day. The Hebrew 'Valley of Hinnom' is translated into Greek as 'Gehenna' which in turn is translated into English as 'Hell'. It provides a startling, graphic symbol of the unimaginable horrors of life after death without Christ.

1:10 The thought of **when He comes** is picked up again from 1:7, where Paul spoke of Christ's provision of rest for those who persevered through the persecution on account of their faith (Rev 14:13). This is in distinct contrast to the plight of the unsaved in 1:9.

In that Day refers to the general time **when He comes** and is not used in a technical sense. One part of this time period will be the Day of the Lord (2:2; 1 Thess 5:2) when punishment and judgment prevail (1:6, 8-9; 2:8, 12; 1 Thess 5:2-3). As a result of and subsequent to God's judgment, vindication and blessing will come for believers which is spoken of here. See *Overview*, 'The Day of the Lord' (1 Thess 5:2). **His saints** (see notes on 1 Thess 3:13) and **those who believe** are referring to the redeemed who will glorify Christ at His coming (1:12) and will admire or marvel at Christ in His presence (see *Overview*, 'The Glory of God' [1 Thess 2:12]). The particular time Paul has in mind with this description seems to be at the end of Daniel's seventieth week (judgment) and the beginning of the Millennium (blessing) such as in Zechariah 14 and Matthew 24–25. See the chart *Futuristic Premillennialism* and *Appendix 1*, 'Various Millennial Views.'

The apostle concludes his teaching with a cause and effect statement, **because our testimony among you was believed**. Rather than focus on God's sovereignty in salvation, as he has elsewhere (1 Thess 1:4; 3:13; 5:23-24) and will continue to do (2:13-14), Paul looks at their salvation, which results in eternal blessing, from the human responsibility side. First, he refers to **our testimony** among you, i.e. the preaching of the gospel (1 Thess 2:2, 8-9) by Paul, Silas, and Timothy. The gospel message was then believed by the Thessalonians (1 Thess 2:10, 13) and they were saved (1 Thess 1:9-10). If Paul had not preached and/or the Thessalonians had not believed, this would not be their eternal hope.

C. With Prayer (1:11-12)

Therefore we also pray always for you that our God would count you worthy of this calling, and fulfill all the good pleasure of His goodness and the work of faith with power, that the name of our Lord Jesus Christ may be glorified in you, and you in Him, according to the grace of our God and the Lord Jesus Christ (1:11-12).

1:11 Paul's prayers were offered both in light of (1:6-10) and in spite of (rising above) their persecution. He did not pray for a cessation of their suffering, but rather that, through it and because of it, they would accomplish God's spiritual purposes in their lives.

He picks up here where he left off in 1:5. Because the eternal outcome was certain, as he just taught (**Therefore**), Paul prayed regularly (**always**) for them (see notes on Paul's prayers in 1 Thess 1:2). This is the first of several prayers in this letter (2:16-17; 3:5, 16, 18; cf. 1 Thess 3:11-13; 5:23, 28).

The apostle has been concerned that the life they lived would be counted **worthy** of God's **calling** in salvation (see notes on God's call in 1 Thess 2:12) and had exhorted them to walk worthy of God (1 Thess 2:12), to which they had responded positively (1:5). Now, he prays that **God would count** them **worthy** or affirm that they had lived up to the purpose of their salvation. He further elaborates by defining this as when **God would...fulfill the good pleasure of His goodness** in their lives. See *Overview*, 'Pleasing God' (1 Thess 2:4) and *Overview*, 'Knowing God' (1 Thess 5:23). **The work of faith** (1:3; 1 Thess 1:3) **with power** would refer to their salvation at its inception (1 Thess 1:5) and its continuation (Eph 2:10; 3:20).

1:12 The ultimate spiritual result would be **that the name of our Lord Jesus Christ may be glorified** (cf. 1:10). See *Overview*, 'The Names of God' (1 Thess 3:9) and *Overview*, 'The Glory of God' (1 Thess 2:12). Christ can be glorified (1:10) **in** the lives of obedient Christians (**you**) because Christians are first **in Him** redemptively. All of this salvation is founded on the basis of **the grace of our God and the Lord Jesus Christ** (Eph 2:5, 8-9; Titus 3:7).

3. PAUL'S RESPONSE TO DOCTRINAL ERROR (2:1-17)

The apostle now turns to an eschatological problem that has rocked the congregation. What might have been a hint of confusion about the Day of the Lord in 1 Thessalonians 5:1-11, has erupted into a major issue. Somehow (2:2), the Thessalonians have been misled into thinking that their current persecution is a part of the Day of the Lord. Because this seemed so real experientially, but did not intellectually square with what Paul had taught (2:5), they were unsettled in their faith. So, their father-in-the faith writes a tightly reasoned polemic to convince them that his original teaching was correct and that they are not actually in the the Day of the Lord. For this writer's prophetic preferences, see *Appendix 1*, 'Various Millennial Views' and the chart, *Futuristic Premillennialism*.

A. By Affectionate Exhortation (2:1-2)

Now, brethren, concerning the coming of our Lord Jesus Christ and our gathering together to Him, we ask you, not to be soon shaken in mind or troubled, either by spirit or by word or by letter, as if from us, as though the day of Christ had come (2:1-2).

2:1 Now...we ask you actually begins 2:1 in the Greek text as a point of emphasis where Paul appeals gently, but with authority, as one brother (**brethren**) to another (cf. 1 Thess 4:1; 5:12). He writes **concerning the coming of our Lord Jesus Christ and our gathering together to Him**. Grammatically and contextually, **the coming** and **our gathering together** refer to the same prophetic event which is the rapture of the church and the subsequent Bema judgment of believers by Christ (Rom 14:10; 1 Cor 3:10-15; 2 Cor 5:10). See *Overview*, 'Christ's Coming' (1 Thess 2:19) and *Appendix 2*, 'The Time of the Rapture'.

   2:2 With regard to the relative time of the rapture in respect to the time of the **Day of** the Lord, a major error has been introduced into the Thessalonian assembly since Timothy had been there (1 Thess 3:6), which has **shaken** and **troubled** the flock (cf. 2 Tim 2:16-18). A major textual variant in this verse provides the options of either **the day of Christ** or the 'Day of the Lord'. Because there is better and older manuscript evidence, because the context involves Divine judgment, and because Paul argues that they cannot be in the Day of the Lord (2:3-12), then the Day of the Lord rather than the Day of Christ is the best alternative as recognized in both the NASB and NIV. See *Overview*, 'The Day of the Lord' (1 Thess 5:2) and Day of Christ notes on 1 Thessalonians 5:4.

   The error or false teaching which alarmed them was that **the day of** the Lord **had come** and they were caught unawares, which did not square with what Paul had previously taught them in 1 Thessalonians 5:4. It also had to do with the relative times of the rapture (2:1) and the Day of the Lord. It seems certain from what follows that they incorrectly thought that their present tribulation (1:4-10) was that the Day of the Lord (**had come**). They believed that they were in the the Day of the Lord, i.e. the Day of the Lord was present.

Paul does not seem to be certain as to how this heresy came to Thessalonica. Possibly it came **by a spirit** which the apostle John elsewhere equates with false prophets (1 John 4:1-3). The implication is that heretics get their message from a false spirit (Satan, demons, other false teachers, or even their own false thinking) while a teacher of the truth gets his message from the true Spirit, i.e. the Holy Spirit. This false teacher would have claimed that Paul sent him. If it was not a false prophet in person, then possibly it was **by word**, i.e. someone brought a message (hearsay) allegedly from Paul. Or possibly, it came **by letter** which claimed to have been written by Paul (cf. 3:17). However the alarming teaching had come, it was **as if from us**, i.e. Paul, Silas, and Timothy.

The error had debilitating effects on the Thessalonians, who were **soon shaken in mind** and **troubled**. While Paul graphically uses **shaken** in a metaphorical sense here, of the **mind**, the term is understood elsewhere in Scripture physically of the wind which shakes a reed (Matt 11:7) or an earthquake which shakes a building (Acts 16:26). False teaching, like a gale wind, has caused the Thessalonians to slip their mental anchor in the midst of a doctrinal storm, i.e. they were no longer thinking clearly as Paul had taught them earlier (cf. 2:5), at least on this issue. As a result, they were troubled, i.e. alarmed and disturbed. For the Thessalonians, this was no minor matter nor some obscure bit of prophetic trivia. If Paul had been wrong, their Christian hopes were now fading fast. However, if he was right, they needed to quickly readjust their thinking with the truth which he had previously taught them.

OVERVIEW

A Paradigm to Understand 2 Thessalonians 2:1-12 (2:2)

Paul has shifted from a very generalized view of the future in 1:5-10, where he developed the theme of reward for believers and retribution for unbelievers without specific regard for exact chronology. He spoke there with the same compressed prophetic perspective expressed by the Lord Jesus Christ in John 5:29 when He contrasted the resurrection of life with the resurrection of judgment.

Second Thessalonians 2 begins by referring to the rapture in 2:1 and then the Day of the Lord in 2:2. The Thessalonians were confused and frightened about their relationship to those two prophetic events in light of the present circumstances of severe persecution (1:4-10) and the recent false teaching (2:2). They believed that the Day of the Lord was currently present (2:2) and thus they were alarmingly shaken.

How is all of this to be understood in terms of: (1) What had Paul taught them in the past?; (2) What was the false teaching?; and (3) Why were the Thessalonians upset?

The Evidence

Four pieces of information must be correlated and harmonized to ensure that a correct re-creation of the Thessalonian dilemma has been achieved. They are:

1. Paul's original teaching on the rapture's time;
2. The false teaching that disturbed the Thessalonians;
3. The Thessalonians' response to the false teaching;
4. Paul's answer to the Thessalonians to correct the false teaching.

Three of the four pieces of data are contained in 2 Thessalonians. The false teaching that disturbed the Thessalonians was to the effect that the Day of the Lord was present (2:2). The Thessalonians' response was one of alarm and disturbance (2:2). Paul's answer to correct the false teaching (2:3-12) can easily be outlined this way:

A. Certain future events precede the Day of the Lord, therefore, you cannot be in the Day of the Lord because these events have not yet occurred (2:3-4). These events are:

1. The mid-tribulational apostasy known as the abomination of desolation (2:3a).
2. The man of lawlessness revealed (2:3b-4).

B. Certain immediate factors preclude the precursors to the Day of the Lord from occurring yet (2:6-8).

1. The present hindrance of lawlessness (2:6-7).
2. The man of lawlessness is not yet revealed (2:8).

C. Certain explainable reasons, which are not yet present, account for the precursors to the Day of the Lord (2:9-12).

1. Diabolical deception (2:9-10).
2. Divine delusion (2:11-12).

The unknown (at least in 2:1-12) of what Paul originally taught with regard to the time of the rapture must be deduced from the other three pieces of given data. The final question to be answered becomes, 'What original teaching about the rapture would account for the Thessalonian panic over the false thought that the Day of the Lord was present and also accounts for the way Paul responded in correcting the error?'

The Possibilities
First, it is possible that the errorists taught that the Thessalonians were in the Day of the Lord knowing that Paul had taught posttribulationism. But, if that were the case, one would expect the Thessalonians to rejoice because the rapture would be imminent. But, in fact, the Thessalonians panicked and thus it is concluded that this is not the correct reconstruction.

Second, it is possible that the errorists taught that the Thessalonians were in the Day of the Lord knowing that Paul had taught pretribulationism. The conclusion would be that the Thessalonians had missed the rapture. But this seems unlikely because the Thessalonians would know that the errorists themselves and certainly many others, including Paul, had missed the rapture also.

A third possibility does exist. The false teachers taught the Thessalonians that they were in the Day of the Lord and additionally that Paul was wrong altogether in that there would be no rapture. Regardless of what Paul taught about the time of the rapture, they insisted that Paul was wrong about the fact of the rapture, i.e. there would be none. If there was no rapture, then the Day of the Lord had overcome them, also contrary to what Paul had previously taught them. The following reasons make this possibility the most compelling.

1. This third possibility explains why Paul does not appeal directly to the rapture. To do so would have opened Paul to the charge of circular reasoning and there were no Old Testament passages to which he could point. Therefore, he appealed to Daniel to show that the Thessalonians could not be in the Day of the Lord. Paul's strategy was to demonstrate that the errorists were wrong on one major point and, therefore, were unreliable in other major areas such as the fact of the rapture.

2. It explains why he showed them that they were not in the great tribulation of the last 3½ years of Daniel's seventieth week. He wanted to teach them how misleading it was to develop or interpret their theology based on current events.

3. It explains why the Thessalonians were shaken. They tested the errorists' theology against the times in which they lived and concluded that they were right and the apostle was wrong. If Paul was wrong on this point, he could have been wrong anywhere.

4. It explains why Paul appealed to his previous messages. His theology had not changed and it was in perfect harmony with Daniel. Paul supported revelatory authentication of theology and discredited experiential verification.

5. It explains why Paul did not assertively appeal to his apostolic authority. The Thessalonians were already under intense pressure from unbelievers in the community and from the disappointment that Paul might be wrong. Paul turns them back to the Scriptures for their sense of immediate and eternal hope.

Conclusions

If this third alternative is true, then it is impossible to determine conclusively whether Paul originally taught pre- or posttribulationism from 2 Thessalonians 2. With a correct interpretation of the components here, either position could be potentially understood.

Therefore, 2 Thessalonians 2 is not a primary determinative passage with which to decide the rapture timing issue. To this writer, the Thessalonian epistles could be possibly understood in light of either position. There are no 'watershed' passages on the time of the rapture in Paul's correspondence to the Thessalonian church. See *Overview*, 'The Time of the Rapture' (1 Thess 4:17), for a biblical determination of the relative time of the rapture.

B. By Doctrinal Instruction (2:3-12)

Paul writes a very carefully reasoned correction, in three parts, to the false teaching that has so greatly troubled the Thessalonians. He builds on the Old Testament and on what he had previously taught them (2:5) with new prophetic revelation.

1. Certain events yet future precede the Day of the Lord (2:3-5)

Let no one deceive you by any means; for that Day will not come unless the falling away comes first, and the man of sin is revealed, the son of perdition, who opposes and exalts himself above all that is called God or that is worshiped, so that he sits as God in the temple of God, showing himself that he is God. Do you not remember that when I was still with you I told you these things? (2:3-5).

2:3 Let no one deceive you by any means not only serves as a warning, but also as an indictment of what actually happened (2:2). They were purposely misled in much the same manner as Satan deceived Eve in the garden (2 Cor 11:3). They allowed an experiential approach to biblical interpretation to overshadow what they knew to be true (2:5). So, Paul reminds them that they could not possibly be in the Day of the Lord because two events which precede the Day of the Lord had not yet occurred. The phrase *that Day will not come* was not a part of the original text (NKJV, NASB, NIV); it has been added because it makes the best sense in the context, since Paul has just referred to the Day of the Lord in 2:2 (see notes).

First, **the falling away comes first** or 'before the Day'. The Greek word *apostasia*, or apostasy, refers to a deliberate abandonment of a formerly professed position, allegiance, or commitment. It could have domestic, military, political, or religious overtones (cf. Josh 22:22 [LXX]; 2 Chron 29:19 [LXX]; Acts 21:21; 1 Tim 4:1; Heb 3:12). The word literally means 'departure' and another form of the word refers to a 'bill of divorcement' (Matt 5:31; 19:7). Some have erroneously suggested, based on remote linguistic evidence, that Paul means spatial departure in the sense of rapturing the church. However, the context decidedly points to a religious departure.

Paul refers to **the falling away** in the sense of a well known or prominent religious rebellion. What did he have in mind? The event is strongly indicated by that which follows, i.e. the apostasy occurs when **the man of sin is revealed**, which is the second event that must precede the Day of the Lord. Older and better manuscript evidence prefers 'man of lawlessness' (cf. 1 John 3:4 where 'sin' and 'lawlessness' are equated).

This man of lawlessness is also called **the son of perdition**, which was a title used of Judas Iscariot (John 17:12). **The son of** is a Hebrew way of pointing to a characteristic of the person in mind. In this case, the quality is literally 'destruction' or 'the son of one who destroys' (cf. Ps 89:22). In this writer's opinion, **perdition** points to Satan who is known as Abaddon (literally, 'destruction' in Job 26:6; 28:22; 31:12; Ps 88:11; Prov 15:11; 27:20) and Apollyon (literally, 'destroyer' in Rev 9:11). Satan was directly involved in Judas' life (John 6:70; 13:2, 27) and it is also true here (cf. 2:9).

Who is this person? Through the centuries, many suggestions have been offered such as: the personification of the abstract principle of evil; the Roman Emperor Gaius (Caligula) who attempted unsuccessfully to set up his statue in the temple at Jerusalem; the Roman Emperor Nero who severely persecuted Christians; Judas Iscariot reincarnated; or one of the Roman Catholic popes. Here is a brief summary of what the Bible says about this person.

OVERVIEW

The Antichrist (2:3)

The New Testament warns against false brethren (Gal 2:4), false teachers (2 Pet 2:1), false prophets (Matt 24:11), false apostles (2 Cor 11:13), and even false christs (Matt 24:24). Each of these categories begins with the prefix *pseudo* in Greek, which is easily understood in English as someone who is actually false or counterfeit, but wanting people to believe that he is the genuine article.

John refers to another kind of false christ as antichrist (1 John 2:18; 22; 4:3; 2 John 7). The prefix *anti* in Greek means 'in place of' and therefore carries the resulting connotation of 'being against' or 'in opposition to'. The antichrists of John's day did not confess the incarnation of Christ (1 John 2:22; 4:3; 2 John 7) and thus denied the Father who testified to Christ's sonship several different times (Matt 3:17; 17:5). Those antichrists who were in the world at John's time (1 John 2:18b, 22; 4:3b; 2 John 7) prefigured or anticipated the ultimate Antichrist (1 John 2:18a; 4:3a) who actually would put himself in the place of Christ as an object of worship (Dan 9:27; 12:11; Matt 24:15), which 2 Thessalonians 2:4 describes in detail. This usurper doesn't portray himself falsely as Christ, but rather presents himself as another god in opposition to Christ.

Daniel (7:7-8, 19-21, 24-26; 8:9, 23-26; 9:26-27; 11:36-45) and Ezekiel (38:1-23) anticipated such a person who would lead the last and most insidious rebellion against Christ before He would come to destroy all opposition and set up His kingdom on earth. Paul (2 Thess 2:1-12) and John (Rev 13:1-18; 17:7-17; 19:19-20; 20:10) build on the Old

Testament revelation (primarily from Daniel) with more details about this person and his endtime activities. He is an agent of Satan (Rev 13:2, 4) and embodies the ultimate in spiritual deceit (Dan 8:25; Rev 13:5-8).

The Antichrist possesses extraordinary intellectual and rhetorical skills (Dan 7:20). He combines political (Dan 9:26, 'the prince'), economic (Rev 13:16-17; Rev 18), diplomatic (Dan 9:27, 'confirm a covenant'), military (Dan 11:40-45), and spiritual (2 Thess 2:4) abilities which allow him to ultimately rule the world for a short time (Rev 13: 5-8; 19:19) before his final demise (Rev 19:20; 20:10).

2:4 Not only is this person lawless and Satanically destructive, but he **opposes and exalts himself above all that is called God or that is worshiped**. This person fulfills the desire of Satan to usurp God's rightful role over creation (Isa 14:13-14; cf. 2:9-10). His opposition to God is chronicled by Daniel (7:25; 8:25; 9:27; 11:36-37). This is the 'revealing' spoken of in 2:3 when this person's true identity and actual character are uncovered and exposed for all to see in horror.

The ultimate act of lawlessness occurs when **he sits as God in the temple of God showing himself that he is God**. The best Greek manuscripts do not use the phrase **as God**. Figurative meanings for temple are impossible since the lawless one actually enthrones himself. In Scripture, this is called 'the abomination of desolation' (Dan 9:27; 11:31; Matt 24:15), which is the ultimate 'falling away' or apostasy spoken of in 2:3 and which occurs at the Jewish temple in Jerusalem. The historical preview occurred c. 167 BC when Antiochus Epiphanes, claiming to be the earthly manifestation of his patron deity, the Olympian Zeus, erected the altar of Zeus on top of the Lord's altar in the Holy of holies in the Jerusalem temple (cf. Dan 11:31). The prophetic fulfillment of 2:4 was written about first in Daniel 9:27, then referred to by Christ (Matt 24:15), and now by Paul. It is this writer's opinion that these two events, i.e. the apostasy and the revelation of the Antichrist, are yet future to the present day. The exact identity of this person remains unknown.

By way of summary, Paul is attempting to convince the Thessalonians that the Day of the Lord could not be present. In 2:3-

4, he does so by affirming that two events previously revealed in Daniel must occur before the Day of the Lord, i.e. the well known apostasy called the 'abomination of desolation' and the revelation of the Antichrist must come first. They had not come in Paul's day; therefore, the Thessalonians could not be in the Day of the Lord.

When does this 'falling away' and 'revelation' occur? According to Daniel 9:27, it commences at the mid-point of Daniel's seventieth week (see chart, *Futuristic Premillennialism*). Matthew 24:15 indicates that this event will trigger a great tribulation, the likes of which will surpass anything ever seen in human history (Matt 24:21). Revelation 13:5-7 indicates that Antichrist's open opposition to God will continue through the last half of Daniel's seventieth week. The world will worship him during this time (Rev 13:4, 8).

In addition to these two precursors of the Day of the Lord, there were three more that Paul could have given them: (1) an Elijah-like forerunner will precede Christ in the Day of the Lord (Mal 4:5); (2) the nations will be assembled in the valley of decision as the Day of the Lord draws near (Joel 3:14); and (3) there will be remarkable signs from the sun, moon, and stars that will unmistakably signal the Day of the Lord (Joel 2:30-31; Matt 24:29).

2:5 While this material might be new to the reader of this commentary, Paul expected the Thessalonians to know it already. **Do you not remember that when I was still with you I told you these things?** (cf. 3:10; 1 Thess 3:4; 4:2). Paul implies that he had repeatedly taught them these truths which they really should not have forgotten. If they had only used what they knew to be true to evaluate this teaching, they would have judged it to be false and, thus, would not have been shaken and troubled (2:2). Paul appealed to previously revealed Scripture (Daniel) so that he could not be accused by the heretics of making this material up under the guise of being an apostle. They would have labeled him as one who resorts to circular reasoning if he had done so.

2. Certain immediate factors preclude the Day of the Lord from being present (2:6-8)

And now you know what is restraining, that he may be revealed in his own time. For the mystery of lawlessness is already at work; only He who now restrains will do so until He is taken out of the way. And then the lawless one will be revealed, whom the Lord will consume with the breath of His mouth and destroy with the brightness of His coming (2:6-8).

2:6 The Thessalonians knew the truths in 2:3-4 (cf. 2:5) and, additionally, knew what is **now...restraining** (literally, 'holding down'). For them, this was a review. For the modern reader, this is information not revealed in this manner elsewhere in Scripture. The first factor precluding the Day of the Lord from being present is a restraining ministry. Who or what is the **restraining** one and what is being restrained? And for how long will the **restraining** activity go on? **Lawlessness** (2:7) is being restrained until the **lawless one** (see notes on 2:3-4) is revealed (2:8). This **restraining** ministry will continue until the restrainer moves aside (2:7). That much is rather clear in context, but who or what restrains?

Numerous suggestions have been made as to the identity of the restrainer: (1) the Roman Empire; (2) human government; (3) the Jewish state; (4) gospel preaching; (5) the binding of Satan; (6) angels; (7) the providence of God; (8) some prophetic person like Elijah or Paul; (9) the church; or (10) the Holy Spirit. Which one is correct and why?

The lawless one is empowered by Satan (2:9; cf. Rev 13:2, 4), so who or what is powerful enough to severely restrain (not eliminate) Satan's influence over thousands of years? In reviewing the alternatives, the Holy Spirit seems most likely. See *Overview*, 'Ministries of the Holy Spirit' (2:13). Early in Scripture, the Holy Spirit exercised that kind of ministry (Gen 6:3) and there is no reason to believe that He has relinquished it (cf. John 16:8-11; Acts 7:51). Only God has the power to effectively control Satan and his delegated evil (cf. Michael the archangel who deferred to God in a conflict with Satan in Jude 9). Only the Holy Spirit is referred to in the New Testament with both the neuter gender (2:6) and the masculine gender (2:7), much like in John 16:13-14. How the Holy

Spirit restrains is not mentioned, although it could possibly be through a combination of means such as human government (Rom 13:1-7) and true believers, i.e. the church.

The purpose of the present (**now**) **restraining** is so **that he** (the lawless one of 2:3, 8) **may be revealed in his own time** (literally, 'season'). Put another way, God ultimately controls the lawless one and will determine when a period of unhindered lawlessness will be permitted (**revealed**; 2:3, 6, 8) on earth.

2:7 However, it is not like lawlessness has not been present, **for the mystery of lawlessness** (1 John 3:4; 5:17) **is already at work**. It has been active in the world and the human race since the fall of Adam and Eve (Gen 3:1-7), but lawlessness remains a mystery in the sense that it has not yet been fully revealed or manifested in its worst, unchecked form. As sinful as the world has seemed to be in the past or as lawless as it appears currently, sin has been tempered in its spread and intensity by the restraining ministry of the Holy Spirit.

This restraint will continue **until He who now restrains...is taken out of the way**. This does not mean that the Holy Spirit is removed or departs because believers have been raptured. The Holy Spirit will maintain His presence in the world after the Rapture. The phrase **taken out of the way** means 'moved to one side'. It is like the closed doors of a dam, which hold back the waters of a lake or river, being opened, or pulled aside, to let the torrent of formerly restrained water freely cascade forward. The restraining doors are still present, but they no longer restrain. In similar fashion, this is what Paul refers to here.

2:8 The second factor that precludes the Day of the Lord from being present is that the lawless one had not yet been revealed. When will that be? Paul has already written in 2:3 that it will be at the 'falling away' or 'the apostasy' which I suggest is the time of the abomination of desolation in the middle of Daniel's seventieth week. The lawless one **will be revealed** in the sense that he is then known and seen for what he actually is, i.e. the chief agent of Satan on earth (see notes on 2:3).

Rather than go into any detail about what happens after the revealing of the lawless one, Paul moves immediately to the end. There is a violent and decisive confrontation with the **Lord** (older Greek manuscripts add 'Jesus') which is given in much more detail by John in Revelation 19:11-21 (cf. Dan 2:44; 7:26; 8:25; 9:27; 11:45). The actual outcome is specifically chronicled in Rev 19:20: 'Then the beast was captured, and with him the false prophet.... These two were cast alive into the lake of fire burning with brimstone' (cf. Rev 20:10).

The Lord will consume the lawless one. There is a major textual variant here and a better way is to understand the verb as meaning 'do away with' or 'overthrow' rather than 'consume'. Although the verb (literally, 'to take up') can be translated 'slay' (see NASB: Matt 2:16; Luke 22:2), it is better understood in a more general sense, as in Acts 7:21 and Hebrews 10:9, because the lawless one, the beast of Revelation 19, does not die (cf. Rev 19:20). However, he will be removed in a decisive fashion **with the breath of His mouth**. This figure of speech is used in the Old Testament in the sense of creation (Ps 33:6) or the expression of God's wrath (Job 4:9; Isa 11:4; 30:28). This same idea is pictured in Revelation by a sword coming forth from Christ's mouth (1:16; 2:16; 19:15, 21).

The final statement in verse 8 adds to the detail. **The Lord...will destroy** the lawless one **with the brightness of His coming**. The word translated **destroy** could better be rendered 'set aside' or 'bring to an end' (NASB) in light of the known outcome of the beast being thrown alive into the lake of fire (Rev 19:20) and still being alive one thousand years later (Rev 20:10). The authority of the beast is definitely abolished and he is banished to the lake of fire **with the brightness of His coming**. Rather than **brightness**, *epiphaneia* would better be translated 'startling appearance' (1 Tim 6:14; 2 Tim 1:10; 4:1, 8; Titus 2:13). It is used in conjunction with **coming** (*parousia*) which appears here for the sixth time in these letters (2:1; 1 Thess 2:19; 3:13; 4:15; 5:23). Each of the previous occasions (in context) referred to a time of blessing which occurred at the rapture. Here, it is a time of judgment which will occur at the end of Daniel's seventieth week.

See notes on 2 Thessalonians 1:7 which detail the different usages, determined by context, of Christ's 'coming' and 'revelation'. The very fact of Christ's arrival spells doom for the cause of the lawless one and victory for the King of kings.

A good and literal translation of 2 Thessalonians 2:8 which takes into account the theological context of the verse would be: 'And then the lawless one will be revealed whom the Lord Jesus will do away with by the breath of His mouth and will set aside with the startling appearance of His coming.' In the end, the pure light of Christ dispels the utter darkness of Satan and the lawless one.

3. Certain factors which account for the Day of the Lord precursors are not yet operative (2:9-12)

The coming of the lawless one is according to the working of Satan, with all power, signs, and lying wonders, and with all unrighteous deception among those who perish, because they did not receive the love of the truth, that they might be saved. And for this reason God will send them strong delusion, that they should believe the lie, that they all may be condemned who did not believe the truth but had pleasure in unrighteousness (2:9-12).

Diabolical deception (2:9-10)

2:9 The coming of the lawless one refers to his presence as a result of his 'revelation' (2:8). See *Overview*, 'Christ's Coming' (1 Thess 2:19) for a discussion of the various aspects of *parousia* which here refers to the Antichrist. This lawless one will be authorized and energized (**working**) by **Satan** (see *Overview*, 'Satan' [1 Thess 2:18]) who is at his very core a liar (John 8:44).

Deception (*plane*) will characterize this period of time. A lesser form has been operative in the world up to this point (1 Tim 4:1; 2 John 7). But deception will generally mark Daniel's seventieth week (Matt 24:4-5, 11; Rev 18:23) and will be promoted by Satan, the master deceiver (Rev 12:9; 20:3, 8, 10). Specifically, by means of **all power, signs, and lying wonders**, the lawless one will deceive the world into following his lead and rendering unto him the worship which is exclusively due Christ (Matt 24:24; Rev 13:13-14; 19:20). This most likely means **power** and **signs** which produce false (**lying**) **wonders** or amazement in

OVERVIEW

Christ and Antichrist Compared (2:9)

Antichrist will attempt to deceptively convince the world that he is
Messiah by imitating Christ in a powerful, but failed, effort to usurp
His rightful kingdom authority to rule on earth. Here are some
significant parallels:

	Christ	*Antichrist*
1. revelation	2 Thess 1:7	2 Thess 2:3, 6, 8
2. coming	2 Thess 2:1, 8	2 Thess 2:9
3. message	2 Thess 2:10 (the truth)	2 Thess 2:11 (the lie)
4. deity	John 1:1 (real)	2 Thess 2:4 (claimed)
5. authenticating signs	Acts 2:22	2 Thess 2:9
6. empowerment	Acts 2:22 (God)	2 Thess 2:9 (Satan)
7. death	Mark 15:37	Rev 13:3, 12, 14
8. resurrection	Mark 16:6	Rev 13:3, 12, 14

support of the lie (2:11). They will be like the works of Pharaoh's
magicians, which for a time matched those from God through
Moses and Aaron (Exod 7:9-13, 19, 22; 8:1-7), but in the end fell
far short of the real thing (cf. Exod 8:18-19; 2 Tim 3:8-9). It will
also be like the Babylonian conjurers versus Daniel (Dan 2:1-12;
25-49). These false means (**all**) of authentication will stand in stark
contrast to the genuine signs, miracles, and wonders by which God
the Father attested Christ as God the Son (Acts 2:22) and those
which were the true signs of an apostle (2 Cor 12:12).[1]

---

1. See Richard Mayhue, *The Healing Promise* (Ross-shire, Scotland: Mentor, 1997)
175-85 for a discussion on why God-given signs, wonders, and miracles ceased with
the Apostles.

2:10 In addition to pseudo-miracles, there will be **all unrighteous deception** (*apatē*). **All** sorts of avenues to promote deceitfulness will prevail such as riches (Matt 13:22), lusts of the flesh (Eph 4:22; 2 Pet 2:12-14), self (James 1:26), false teaching (Eph 5:6; Col 2:8; 1 Tim 2:14), and sin in general (Heb 3:13). Deception will pointedly be used to promote general unrighteousness in the world. Those who embrace this deception will be those who perish as a result, i.e. those whose eternal outcome Paul generically referred to in 1:9.

These people are just the opposite of the Thessalonians in at least four ways: they do not **love...the truth**; they did not **receive** or embrace the word of God; they are not **saved**; and they will **perish**. Satan's lies thus lead to the spiritual death of everyone who embraces them, just like Adam and Eve (Gen 2:17; Rom 5:12). So, Satan is a murderer without equal. The world of that time will be led away from God's truth and love by diabolical deception to an eternity of conscious torment in hell, which is decidedly marked by God's absence (1:9).

Divine delusion (2:11-12)

2:11 Periodically, God gives incorrigible people over to their own sin (Rom 1:24, 26, 28) and no longer strives against their iniquity (Gen 6:3; John 16:8-11; Acts 7:51). Further still, in rare moments, God actually aids them in their **delusion**. He permitted Satan (the deceiving spirit) to have his way by a demon invasion of Ahab's prophets with the end result of delivering deceitful messages to the wicked king Ahab, who died as a result (1 Kings 22:19-23, 34-40).

How does God do this without contradicting His holy character by being unrighteous Himself? It seems to this writer, that in context here, **God will send them strong delusion** (literally 'a working of deceit') by having the restrainer step aside (2:6-7) and by letting Satan's undiluted and unchecked lying have its sway over all the earth. God does this by His permissive will, not His determinative will. In other words, Satan will be, for a time, totally free to give the people exactly what they want to **believe**, i.e. **the lie** (cf. John 8:44; Rom 1:25; 1 John 2:21). The populace will not be restrained (cf. 2:7) from believing Satan's ultimate deception – the lie that Antichrist is God and salvation is through him.

2:12 Paul repeats here what he first wrote in 2:10. The results of diabolical deception and divine delusion are identically the same. Satan actively pursues this goal for a time, which God passively (but sovereignly) allows.

This kind of life is described in three ways. First, **they did not believe the truth**, rather they believed the lie (2:11). They rejected the truth of God's word and the truth of God's redemptive love in Christ's salvation work on the cross. They embraced the lie that Satan was God and the Antichrist was their Savior.

Second, **they had pleasure in unrighteousness** (cf. 2:10, they embraced 'all unrighteous deception'). Having rejected the truth of God's word and the truth of salvation in Christ alone, they engaged in unrighteous deeds. Most likely, they blasphemously labeled their unrighteousness as righteous in nature.

Third, **they all** are **condemned** (cf. 2:10, 'those who perish'). They will be righteously judged in the end by their rejection of truth and their unrighteous deeds (cf. 1:5). This is spoken of in Revelation 20:11-15 as the Great White Throne judgment (see chart, *Futuristic Premillennialism*). Their eternal outcome will be as Paul taught earlier in 1:9.

C. By Wise Counsel (2:13-17)

Paul puts his doctrinal correction (2:1-12) in proper perspective with a pastoral confession (2:13-14), a personal exhortation (2:15), and a promising supplication (2:16-17). The best of theological and pastoral style is displayed here by the apostle.

But we are bound to give thanks to God always for you, brethren beloved by the Lord, because God from the beginning chose you for salvation through sanctification by the Spirit and belief in the truth, to which He called you by our gospel, for the obtaining of the glory of our Lord Jesus Christ. Therefore, brethren, stand fast and hold the traditions which you were taught, whether by word or our epistle. Now may our Lord Jesus Christ Himself, and our God and Father, who has loved us and given us everlasting consolation and good hope by grace, comfort your hearts and establish you in every good word and work (2:13-17).

2:13 But we are bound (obligated) **to give thanks to God always for you** is an almost exact duplication of Paul's statement in 1:3 (see notes; cf. 1 Thess 1:2; 2:13). Paul is here taking his own preaching to heart (1 Thess 5:18). Perpetual thanksgiving was true in spite of the doctrinal dullness with which Paul has just had to deal.

The Thessalonians are referred to as **brethren beloved by the Lord**, an almost identical phrase to that found in 1 Thessalonians 1:4 (see notes; cf. 2:16). They are the **beloved...because God from the beginning chose you** (the Thessalonians) **for salvation** which repeats the same idea, as in 1 Thessalonians 1:4, of God's election, but with a different word for chose (*aireomai*; cf. Phil 1:22; Heb 11:25). See notes on 1 Thessalonians 1:4 and *Overview*, 'God's Role in Salvation' (1 Thess 1:4). Paul deals again with election in 1 Thessalonians 5:9 with a third different word for chose (*tithēmi*; see notes). All three members of the triune Godhead participate in the salvation process: God the Father (2:13); God the Son (2:14); and God the Holy Spirit (2:13).

In the Thessalonian epistles, there are either strong hints of or direct affirmations of all five elements of what have been called the doctrines of grace: (1) complete and inherent depravity (1 Thess 1:9); (2) unmerited and sovereign election (2:13; 1 Thess 1:4; 5:9); (3) believer's atonement (1 Thess 5:10); (4) utterly compelling grace (1:12; 2:16); and (5) steadfastness of true Christians (1:4-5; 3:5). These precious truths are not the outcome of historical church councils; they were actually taught by Paul in the New Testament.

From the beginning or 'firstfruits' are the two textual options here. They are very similar to one another in appearance. However, **from the beginning** seems best, both textually and contextually (the choice of NASB, NIV, NKJV). Paul uses this phrase, in this manner, only here. The sense of it would be 'from the beginning of time' (cf. Gen 1:1; John 1:1). It would reflect God's electing choices made before time began (Eph 1:11; 3:11; 2 Tim 1:9; Titus 1:2).

God selected the Thessalonians for salvation (cf. 1 Thess 5:8-9), which is described with three different time aspects used in Scripture: declared (Rom 10:9, 13); progressing (1 Cor 1:18); and future (Rom 13:11). All three are true perspectives. Here, it would seem that Paul is using the declared aspect at the initial time of salvation spoken of in 1 Thessalonians 1:6-10.

Paul speaks of their salvation from the Divine side – **sanctification by the Spirit** (1 Thess 1:5-6; 4:8; 5:19) and the

human side – **belief in the truth**. Christians are saved by the sanct-
ifying (setting apart) work of the Holy Spirit (Acts 26:18; Titus
3:5-7; 1 Pet 1:2) employing the power of God's word (Rom 1:16-17;
1 Cor 1:18) as Paul described in 1 Thessalonians 1:5. See notes on 1
Thessalonians 4:3 for a more detailed discussion of sanctification.

OVERVIEW

Ministries of the Holy Spirit (2:13)

Baptismal Medium	1 Cor 12:13
Calls to Ministry	Acts 13:2-4
Channel of Divine Revelation	2 Sam 23:2; Neh 9:30; Zech 7:12; John 14:17
Empowers	Exod 31:3; Judg 13:25; Acts 1:8
Fills	Luke 4:1; Acts 2:4; Eph 5:18
Guarantees	2 Cor 1:22; 5:5; Eph 1:14
Guards	2 Tim 1:14
Helps	John 14:16, 26; 15:26; 16:7
Illuminates	1 Cor 2:10-13
Indwells	Rom 8:9-11; 1 Cor 3:16; 6:19
Intercedes	Rom 8:26, 27
Produces fruit	Gal 5:22, 23
Provides Spiritual Character	Gal 5:16, 18, 25
Regenerates	John 3:5, 6, 8
Restrains/Convicts of Sin	Gen 6:3; John 16:8-10; Acts 7:51
Sanctifies	Rom 15:16; 1 Cor 6:11; 2 Thess 2:13
Seals	2 Cor 1:22; Eph 1:13; 4:30
Selects Overseers	Acts 20:28
Source of Fellowship	2 Cor 13:14; Phil 2:1
Source of Liberty	2 Cor 3:17, 18
Source of Power	Eph 3:16
Source of Spiritual Gifts	1 Cor 12:4-11
Source of Unity	Eph 4:3, 4
Teacher	John 14:26; Acts 15:28; 1 John 2:20, 27

2:14 Paul continues looking at salvation from the Divine and human perspectives with the phrases **He called you** (see notes on 1 Thess 2:12) and **by our gospel** (see notes on 1 Thess 1:5; 2:2, 8) respectively. The ultimate end of salvation is **for the obtaining** (cf. 1 Thess 5:9) **of the glory of our Lord Jesus Christ** (see notes on 1:10, 12; 1 Thess 2:12; see *Overview*, The Glory of God' [1 Thess 2:12]). One obtains **the glory of...Christ** by the work of God's salvation, not one's own efforts. This is the hope of every believer (2 Cor 3:18; Col 3:4).

2:15 Moving from his pastoral confession to a personal exhortation, the apostle gives two commands whose outcome should be a direct result or fruit of their salvation (**Therefore, brethren**). First, **stand fast** (see notes on 1 Thess 3:8; cf. 1 Cor 16:13). Second, **hold,** which means to 'hold onto strongly' or 'firmly grasp' (cf. Heb 4:14; Rev 2:13; 3:11). The idea is that of having such a secure grip, one never lets go. Paul has in mind their tenacious handle on **the traditions which you were taught. Tradition** can be the fallible teachings of men (Matt 15:2; Gal 1:14; Col 2:8) or the dependable truth of God (3:6; 1 Cor 11:2), as here. This would include the teachings (**by word**) of Paul, Silas, and Timothy in person (2:5; cf. 1 Thess 1:5) or in **our epistle,** i.e. 1 Thessalonians.

2:16 Paul ends with a promising supplication in 2:16-17 (see notes regarding Paul's prayer life on 1 Thess 1:2). This is the seventh and last time that Paul appeals to **our Lord Jesus Christ Himself, and our God and Father** (cf. 1:1-2; 1 Thess 1:1, 3; 3:11, 13; see notes on 1 Thess 1:1). The combination of persons strongly points to Christ's deity and the triune arrangement of the Godhead (cf. Holy Spirit in 2:13). 'God our Father' is the preferred textual variant.

The apostle notes two features about Divine favor. First, He **loved us,** i.e. the Thessalonians when they were yet in their sin (Rom 5:5, 8) because He had already elected them unto salvation (2:13; 1 Thess 1:4) with a love that cannot be broken (Rom 8:35, 39). See notes regarding love on 1 Thessalonians 4:9. Second, He has **given us everlasting consolation and good hope by grace**.

Both of these gifts refer to the assurance of salvation's eternal outcome.

2:17 Having described the Ones to whom he prayed, Paul now asks the Lord to **comfort your hearts**, referring to the inner life of the believer which would include both the intellectual and emotional aspects (cf. 3:5; 1 Thess 2:4; 3:13). Next, he asks the Lord to **establish** or strengthen the Thessalonians. This is both a work to be done by the pastor (1 Thess 3:2) and God (3:3; 1 Thess 3:13). When Paul sent Timothy back to Thessalonica, it was to **comfort** and **establish** them (1 Thess 3:2). Answered prayer would manifest itself in all that they did (**work**) and said (**word**), and which should characteristically show the Divine quality of **good** (see notes regarding 'good' on 1 Thess 5:21-22) in one who has been redeemed.

4. PAUL'S PRAYER FOR STEADFASTNESS (3:1-5)

Paul ended the previous section with prayer and immediately begins the final portion of this letter, again, with prayer. First, he requests prayer for himself and his colleagues (3:1-2). Then, after expressing faith in the Lord (3:3) and the Thessalonians (3:4), he prays for the flock (3:5). Paul's intent is to spiritually prepare them in a positive way for the most direct and harsh words to be found in either epistle. This is a classic example of spiritual confrontation over sin, by authority, in love, and with the expectation of total obedience.

A. Regarding Himself (3:1-2)

It was not unusual for Paul to seek prayer support on behalf of himself, his pastoral colleagues, and their ministry (1 Thess 5:25; Rom 15:30-32; 2 Cor 1:11; Eph 6:19-20; Phil 1:19; Col 4:3; Phile 22). He prays for freedom here in two aspects of ministry: freedom for the word of the Lord to be effective (success) and freedom for Paul and his friends from persecution by those who would willingly disrupt their ministry (safety). He realized that, ultimately, any ministry advance through enemy territory would come from the hand of Almighty God. See notes about Paul's prayer life on 1 Thessalonians 1:2.

Finally, brethren, pray for us, that the word of the Lord may run swiftly and be glorified, just as it is with you, and that we may be delivered from unreasonable and wicked men; for not all have faith (3:1-2).

3:1 Finally, brethren signifies that Paul is going to change subjects, although he will here preface his concluding remarks (3:6-15) with words regarding prayer and encouragement (see notes on 1 Thess 4:1). Paul had asked the Thessalonians to **pray for us** earlier (see notes on 1 Thess 5:25 and notes about prayer on 1 Thess 1:2). Read Acts 18:5-17 to get a sense of what Paul and his companions were experiencing and why they sought prayer. They desired intercession for two specific areas of ministry as an expression of their self-acknowledged inadequacy for their task (see 2 Cor 3:5-6).

First, **that the word of the Lord may run swiftly and be glorified** (cf. Eph 6:19-20; Col 4:3-4). See notes on 1 Thessalonians 2:13 and *Overview*, 'The Word of God' (1 Thess 2:13). Paul would specifically have the gospel in mind here, which he has previously mentioned eight times (1:8; 2:14; 1 Thess 1:5; 2:2, 4, 8-9; 3:2; see notes on 1 Thess 1:5; 2:2, 8).

Paul desires that the preaching of the gospel be unhindered or, in other words, **run swiftly** (cf. Acts 6:7; 12:24; 19:20). Literally, Paul asks for prayer that the gospel may 'sprint freely' (Ps 147:15). This same word (*trechō*) is also used of: (1) running instead of walking (Matt 28:8); (2) running a race (1 Cor 9:24); (3) the Christian life (1 Cor 9:24; Gal 5:7; Heb 12:1); and (4) Christian ministry (1 Cor 9:26; Gal 2:2; Phil 2:16). Here, it is applied to preaching Christ.

Also, he asks that the preaching of the gospel **be glorified** or honored, much like it was in Pisidian Antioch on the first missionary journey when the Gentiles began to rejoice and glorify the word of God by believing (Acts 13:14, 48). Here, Paul recalls and uses the earlier Thessalonian experience as an example, i.e. **just as it is with you**, which would be better translated **just as it was with you**. The apostle remembered back to their great response when the gospel was freely preached (see notes on 1 Thess 1:5-10). He intensely wanted to avoid another sluggish ministry like he had at Athens (Acts 17:16-34).

3:2 Second, Paul prays **that we may be delivered from unreasonable and wicked men** (cf. Rom 15:31; Phil 1:19). Paul has had a consistent history of being opposed in his preaching of the gospel (see notes on 1 Thess 2:14-19; 3:3, 7), so he anticipates that this kind of hostility will continue apart from God's intervention and deliverance (*rhuomai*). It would appear that Paul and his party (**we**), at the time of this writing, are not actually in the hands of the opposition but just in potential danger of being opposed (see notes on 1 Thess 1:10). His gospel enemies are described as **unreasonable** and **wicked** (cf. Phil 3:18-19). **Unreasonable** literally means 'out of place' in an improper or perverse way (cf. Job 11:11; 34:12 [LXX]). **Wicked** could also be translated 'evil' and speaks of the ungodly activities in which they had been engaged (cf. 3:3) and which they still continued (see notes on 1 Thess 5:22). He would be referring directly to his opposition at Corinth (Acts 18:6, 12-17). Paul is a realist as he explains that **not all have faith** when referring to these men. This is certainly a clear Scriptural declaration that Universalism (all will be saved) is not true. **Faith** is used here in the sense of salvation (see notes on 1:3; 1 Thess 3:2). Paul knew of what he wrote, because the apostle himself had been just such a man less than two decades earlier (1 Tim 1:12-17).

B. Regarding the Thessalonians (3:3-5)

But the Lord is faithful, who will establish you and guard you from the evil one. And we have confidence in the Lord concerning you, both that you do and will do the things we command you. Now may the Lord direct your hearts into the love of God and into the patience of Christ (3:3-5).

3:3 Paul revisits a previous theme (1 Thess 5:24) and transitions with a wonderful affirmation of God which looks back to 3:1-2 and ahead to 3:3b-5. **But the Lord is faithful** (cf. Deut 7:9; Isa 49:7; Hosea 11:12; 2 Tim 2:13). Christ is called faithful elsewhere (Rev 1:5; 3:14; 19:11). God is faithful in regard to: (1) completing His salvation (1 Cor 1:9); (2) aiding Christians to resist temptation (1 Cor 10:13); (3) fulfilling His promises (2 Cor 1:18; Heb 10:23; 11:11); (4) vindicating believers who suffer (1 Pet 4:19); and (5) cleansing Christians from sin (1 John 1:9). His faithfulness is a major theme in the Psalms (36:5; 88:11; 89: 1-2, 5, 8, 24, 33, 49; 92:2; 119:90). So magnificent is this particular attribute of God, that Jeremiah wrote a most memorable line with tears as he watched the temple being destroyed and Jerusalem burned: 'Great is Your faithfulness' (Lam 3:23). God's faithfulness stands in monumental contrast to the faithless men in 3:2. See *Overview*, 'Knowing God' (1 Thess 5:23) and notes on 1 Thessalonians 5:23.

In this context, God **is faithful** to **establish** and **guard from the evil one**. To **establish** or strengthen, i.e. buttress and reinforce, is both a ministry of God (2:17; 1 Thess 3:2, 13) and of pastors (Rom 1:11; see notes on 1 Thess 3:2). God (like a spiritual sentinel) is also faithful to **guard** or protect the believer (2 Tim 1:12; Jude 24), just as the Christian is also responsible, humanly speaking (1 John 5:21). The Thessalonians needed protection from **the evil one**, i.e. Satan, who is the embodiment of evil (cf. Matt 13:19, 38; John 17:15; Eph 6:16; 1 John 2:13-14; 5:18-19). See *Overview*, 'Satan' (1 Thess 2:18) and *Overview*, 'Defeating Satan' (1 Thess 3:5). **The evil one** undoubtedly worked through the evil men of 3:2. So, Paul prays that the Lord would **guard** the Thessalonians like He protected Noah through the flood (2 Pet 2:5) and like Christ kept the disciples (John 17:12).

3:4 Because the Lord is faithful (3:3), these pastors (**we**) can **have confidence in the Lord concerning you** whom He has chosen and called to salvation (cf. Gal 5:10; Phil 1:6). Paul has elsewhere expressed this same kind of unreserved persuasion (cf. Rom 8:38-39; 2 Tim 1:12). With respect to the Thessalonians, Paul is focused on both the present (**that you do**) and the future (**will do**), particularly in regard to **the things we command you**. Paul had demanded obedience of them with full Divine authority in the past (1 Thess 4:2, 11) and is here preparing the way for his immediate commands in 3:4, 6, 10, 12, as though he were dispensing the will of the Lawgiver (James 4:12) for those who possess citizenship in His kingdom.

3:5 Paul now directly prays for the Thessalonians with this third (1:11-12; 2:16-17) of four prayers (3:16, 18) which he renders on their behalf in this letter (cf. also 1 Thess 3:11-13; 5:23, 28; see notes regarding Paul's prayers on 1 Thess 1:2).

Love has been a consistent theme throughout each epistle regarding both human love (1:3; 1 Thess 1:3; 3:6, 12; 5:8, 13) and God's love (2:13, 16; 1 Thess 1:4). See *Overview*, 'True Love' (1 Thess 5:13) and notes on 1 Thessalonians 3:12. This undoubtedly refers to both the Thessalonians' **love** for **God** by obeying His commandments and God's **love** through them towards the brethren and those outside the faith.

Patience (cf. 'steadfastness,' NASB) refers to a willingness to remain under and bear an unusually heavy load (cf. 1:4; 1 Thess 1:3). This seems to refer to Christ's example of enduring the cross (Heb 12:2) which Christians are to follow (cf. Heb 12:1). The Ephesian church (Rev 2:2-7) and the martyrs in Daniel's seventieth week (Rev 14:12) are commended as examples of patience, although Job (James 5:11) seems to be the most outstanding individual human model. Trials are designed by God to develop just this kind of **patience** (James 1:2-4) which is expected of all Christians (Rom 12:12; Col 1:11; 1 Tim 6:11; 2 Tim 3:10; Titus 2:2). It is actually one of the expressions of love (1 Cor 13:7). Perseverance to the end is a mark of genuine Christian behavior (Matt 10:22; 24:13) which validates one's true salvation.

Neither **love** nor **patience** is a constant, natural attribute, so Paul prays that **the Lord** would **direct your hearts into** these godly qualities. See notes on 1 Thessalonians 3:11. This involves both an intellectual and emotional assent (**your hearts**) to obey the Lord's absolute direction (cf. 2:17; 1 Thess 3:13).

5. PAUL'S REBUKE OF UNDISCIPLINED BROTHERS (3:6-15)

What began as no more than a minor problem has now escalated into public sin. What Paul could deal with in a few words earlier (1 Thess 4:11-12), now requires a major confrontation. However, there does not seem to be any obvious connection between the false doctrine dealt with in 2:1-12 and the pattern of undisciplined living mentioned here. Of all that Paul has written in either letter, this is by far the most stern as he deals with the issue of unruly living habits on the part of some in the Thessalonian congregation. Paul issues the command of 3:6 based on the model of his own lifestyle while among them (3:7-9), the instructions he gave while in their midst (3:10), and his present intervention over their sin (3:11-15). He actually deals more with how the church is to deal with the disorderly ones than he does with the disorderly themselves.

A. Through Present Exhortation (3:6)

But we command you, brethren, in the name of our Lord Jesus Christ, that you withdraw from every brother who walks disorderly and not according to the tradition which he received from us (3:6).

3:6 As if possessing a lawful order (with judicial or military overtones) from heaven, **we command you brethren**, writes Paul (cf. 3:4, 10, 12; see notes on 1 Thess 4:11). Obedience is not optional for the Thessalonians because the Apostle orders them **in the name of our Lord Jesus Christ** (cf. 1 Cor 5:4) or, in other words, by Christ's authority (see *Overview*, 'Knowing God' [1 Thess 5:13]). It is mandated by Divine sanction, so **we command...that you withdraw from** (cf. 2 Cor 8:20; Gal 2:12). The idea is to distance one's self and keep away from the sinning brethren (cf. 3:14; Matt 18:17; 1 Cor 5:9, 11). The same is true regarding those who teach false doctrine (Rom 16:17-18). Here, Paul is speaking of the final step of church discipline which would be administered to **every brother** who continues to knowingly, willfully, and habitually engage in sin. This kind of person contemptuously disregards the will of God as reported by Paul and his friends.

OVERVIEW

Church Discipline[1](3:6)

In 2 Thessalonians 3:6-15, Paul commands the church to exercise church discipline because of a pattern of unrepentant sin, i.e. undisciplined living which has taken hold of some Christians. During his ministry among them, he had taught against this kind of lifestyle (cf. 3:10). In his first letter, the apostle had instructed them against being a sluggard (1 Thess 4:11-12). Now, for those who ignored his previous, gracious promptings, a more visible and personal level of admonition is introduced, hopefully to turn the offenders back to a biblical lifestyle.

These instructions need to be understood in the context of other New Testament passages which also deal with church discipline. Unbiblical beliefs (Gal 1:8; 1 Tim 6:3-5, 20-21; 2 Tim 2:24-26; Titus 1:9; 3:10-11) and/or unbiblical behavior (1 Cor 5:1-13; Gal 6:1-5; 1 Tim 5:19-20) are the grounds for which this process was designed by God. Jesus, in Matthew 18:15-17, laid out a basic four-step procedure whose design was to call a believer back to holy living. All other church discipline texts in the New Testament need to be understood in light of this core teaching by Christ.

The four steps include: (1) privately confronting the brother (Matt 18:15); (2) if unsuccessful in step one, taking witnesses (people with first hand knowledge of the sin) to rebuke the offender (Matt 18:16); (3) if rebuffed again, then telling it to the church so that they can go to the brother and urge his repentance (Matt 18:17a); and (4) if steps 1–3 fail to turn back the sinning believer, then putting him out of the church and not affording him the privilege of Christian fellowship (Matt 18:17b).

Church discipline is not a 'witch hunt', nor a way to be vindictive, nor even a means to justify rumors in the church. Rather, it is an orderly and honorable way to deal with alleged or well known patterns of sin. It is to be practiced with gentleness (Gal 6:1), humility (2 Tim 2:25), and a view towards restoration (Matt 18:15-17; Gal 6:1).

The major purposes of church discipline are: (1) to deal with sin in the church before Christ has to step in and deal with it personally (Rev 2-3); (2) to restore offending believers to a place of unhindered fellowship

---

1. Daniel E. Wray has written a helpful booklet, *Biblical Church Discipline* (Edinburgh: Banner of Truth, 1978).

(Matt 18:15-17; Gal 6:1); (3) to warn and deter others from sin (1 Tim 5:20); (4) to prevent desecrating the Lord's Table (1 Cor 11:27-32); (5) to purify the church (1 Cor 5:6-8); and (6) to glorify God (1 Cor 10:31).

Paul's direct purpose in writing 2 Thessalonians 3:6-15 was not to instruct the church in the steps of discipline from Matthew 18:15-17, but rather to encourage them to confront the obvious sin in their midst. However, all the steps which Jesus outlined are either implied or explicitly mentioned in Paul's admonition here. Preliminarily, the missionaries had taught the people the truth about disciplined living (3:10; 1 Thess 4:11-12). It is then implied and thus assumed that private consultation has already taken place (cf. 1 Thess 5:14) and witness testimonies have been verified (3:11). Public mention to the church has then been accomplished in 3:12. Paul, therefore, reaffirms that, if these previous three steps continue to be rebuffed, the person is to be put outside of the church (3:6, 14). Yet, there is always the hope that the sinning person will repent and be restored as a brother in Christ (3:15).

Paul particularly directs this confrontational response to any Christian **who walks disorderly** (see notes on 1 Thess 4:11-12; 5:14). **Walk** represents the pattern of one's life (cf. 3:11; see notes on 1 Thess 2:12; 4:1, 12). **Disorderly** refers to, in this context, an idle, lazy person who is defiantly, insubordinately, and rebelliously out of line with a lawful order for disciplined living (cf. 3:7, 11). The apostle immediately explains that he means a disobedient **walk** which is **not according to the tradition which he received from us** (cf. 3:10). **The tradition** (see notes on 2:15) would refer in general to Paul's past teaching on this subject (cf. 1 Thess 4:11) and in particular to 1 Thessalonians 4:11-12 which had been **received** (1 Thess 2:13; 4:1) **from** the apostle and his colleagues (**us**). They were not ignorant of God's direction and, therefore, were personally responsible for their own obedience.

A major textual issue arises in regard to who **received...the traditions**. There are three variants from which to choose: (1) **he**; (2) you; and (3) they. **He** is attested with weak evidence and is the least likely choice. Either 'they' or 'you' is a strong possibility, but 'you' (NASB, NIV) is more likely since Paul most often employs 'you' when speaking to the Thessalonians in general, as he does here.

B. Through Personal Example (3:7-9)

Earlier, Paul appealed back to his consistent pastoral behavior in
order to quiet his critics (1 Thess 2:1-12). Here, he once again
looks back to his ministry in Thessalonica (cf. 1 Thess 2:9), this
time in order to reinforce his rebuke of those who rebelliously lived
in idleness and disorder. The missionaries actually lived out what
they preached in order to effectively reinforce their message.

For you yourselves know how you ought to follow us, for we were not
disorderly among you; nor did we eat anyone's bread free of charge, but
worked with labour and toil night and day, that we might not be a burden to
any of you, not because we do not have authority, but to make ourselves an
example of how you should follow us (3:7-9).

3:7 Paul begins with a *mandate* for the Thessalonians. **For you
yourselves know** is a familiar appeal from Paul (cf. 1 Thess 1:5;
2:1-2, 5, 11; 3:3-4) as a reminder of his godly lifestyle, ministry
pattern, or previous teaching. Here, their (**us**) spiritual example
provided a model which the Thessalonians were obligated (**how
you ought**; cf. 1 Thess 4:1) **to follow** (cf. 3:9; see notes on 1 Thess
1:6). The writer of Hebrews wrote: 'Remember those who rule
over you, who have spoken the word of God to you, whose faith
follow, considering the outcome of their conduct' (13:7).

Paul continues by reviewing their *manner* of life (see notes on
3:6; 1 Thess 4:11-12; 5:14), first negatively and then positively.
Since **we were not disorderly among you**, therefore, the
Thessalonians were not to be that way (cf. 3:11) among themselves
or in the community. This is the first of two disclaimers concerning
the kind of negative behavior which they avoided.

3:8 The second disclaimer is **nor did we eat anyone's bread free
of charge**. This does not mean that the ministry team was never
legitimately an invited guest to someone's house for a meal
(**bread**) as would be normal. However, it does indicate that they
did not go back to that home or any other home repeatedly, looking
for never-ending handouts or free meals. **Free of charge** is
elsewhere used in the New Testament of the abundant water of life
in the New Jerusalem (Rev 21:6; 22:17) and the free grace of
justification (Rom 3:24).

In strong contrast (**but**), Paul and his men positively led an active, productive life in the midst of intensive ministry. Here, he resorts back to the language of 1 Thessalonians 2:9 (see notes). They **worked** (cf. 3:10-12; 1 Thess 4:11) **with** exhausting **labor** (cf. 1 Thess 1:3; 3:5) **and toil night and day** (cf. 1 Thess 2:9). Paul uses this phrase, **night and day**, indicating a consistent pattern in regards to: (1) prayer (1 Thess 3:10; 1 Tim 5:5; 2 Tim 1:3); (2) working (1 Thess 2:9); (3) teaching (Acts 20:31); and (4) serving God (Acts 26:7).

Paul's *motives* were pure in this as indicated by the two reasons he provides for why they adopted this kind of ministry lifestyle. First, **that we might not be a burden** (see notes on 1 Thess 2:9) **to any of you**. Paul never wanted the gospel to be a secondary issue or for the gospel ministry to be discredited.

3:9 They lived this way **not because we do not have authority**. They did have Divine authority as apostles (see notes on 1 Thess 2:6; cf. 2 Cor 13:10). However, they often exercised their liberty not to impose their rights and authority when they believed that this way would serve the gospel in a more fruitful manner (cf. 1 Cor 9:4-6, 12, 19-23). Under normal conditions, men in the ministry should be taken care of by those to whom they minister (Gal 6:6; 1 Tim 5:17-18).

Second, **but, to make ourselves an example**. Literally, 'But that ourselves an example we might give.' Paul viewed their lifestyle as a gift imprint (*tupos*) on the Thessalonians. This is to be true of all men in ministry (cf. Phil 3:17; 1 Tim 4:12; Titus 2:7; 1 Pet 5:3) as it had been of Paul and his friends (see notes on 1 Thess 1:7). The apostle ends here, where he began in 3:7, by urging the Thessalonians (**you**) to **follow us** (see notes on 3:7; 1 Thess 1:6).

C. Through Previous Teaching (3:10)

For even when we were with you, we commanded you this: If anyone will not work, neither shall he eat (3:10)

3:10 Paul now draws their attention to why they (**we**) **had commanded** (see notes on 3:6) them (**you**) **when we were with**

you (see *Introduction*, 'At Thessalonica' [Acts 17:1-9]). He has, on occasion, previously recalled for them his repeated teaching during those early months when he was still with them (cf. 2:5; 1 Thess 3:4; 4:2), as he does here. The intent is to remind the Thessalonians that they had repeatedly been taught this truth (cf. 2:5).

Paul literally speaks of **anyone** who **wills** (*thelō*) **not** to **work**. The issue is that they won't work, even though they could; it is a volitional choice not to work that Paul condemns as sinfully disobedient. If someone wills to work, but is unable for any legitimate reason (due to the unavailability of work or an inability to work), then Christian compassion is to be shown to those kind of people, such as orphans, widows, or the disabled (James 1:27). But that is not the case here in Thessalonica.

It is a generally accepted biblical principle that a person will reap the fruit of his labor (Gal 6:7). This can be in a positive sense (Ps 126:5; 2 Cor 9:6; Gal 6:8) or a negative one (Prov 22:8; Hosea 8:7; 10:13; 2 Cor 9:6; Gal 6:8). Here, the outcome is a painful one, i.e. the one who plants nothing (refuses to work), reaps nothing (has no food to eat). He is like the sluggard in Proverbs (13:4; 20:4; 24:30-34). His laziness is not to be indulged with handouts because to coddle the loafer would nullify a part of God's curse on Adam's race (Gen 3:19).

D. Through Pointed Confrontation (3:11-15)

Paul writes for two categories of people in the congregation: (1) those who walk in a disorderly manner (3:11-12) and (2) those who walk in an orderly fashion (3:13-15). He confronts those who are disorderly with how to re-order their lives and counsels the orderly on how to spiritually respond to the disorderly, if they refuse to revitalize their lives.

For we hear that there are some who walk among you in a disorderly manner, not working at all, but are busybodies. Now those who are such we command and exhort through our Lord Jesus Christ that they work in quietness and eat their own bread. But as for you, brethren, do not grow weary in doing good. And if anyone does not obey our word in this epistle, note that person and do not keep company with him, that he may be ashamed. Yet do not count him as an enemy, but admonish him as a brother (3:11-15).

3:11 For we hear, i.e. repeatedly, indicates that multiple reports have come to Paul in Corinth from Thessalonica. The messages were, in effect, **that there are some who walk** (cf. 3:6; see notes on 1 Thess 2:12; 4:1, 12) **among you in a disorderly manner** (cf. 3:6-7; see notes on 1 Thess 4:11-12; 5:14). He goes on to explain that the disorderly are **not working** (cf. 3:8, 10, 12; see notes on 1 Thess 2:9; 4:11) **at all, but are busybodies**. Paul uses a play on words here in that the disorderly are **not working at all** but, at the same time, they are literally 'working round about' in everybody else's business but their own, i.e. they are **busybodies** (cf. 1 Tim 5:13). Whoever brought the reports must have had credibility in Paul's estimation because he assumes that the accusations are true.

3:12 Having established the problem in 3:11, Paul now turns to the solution. He writes tactfully to **those who are such**, i.e. those who walk in a disorderly manner and are busybodies, by the authority (**through**) of **our Lord Jesus Christ** (see notes on 3:6). With a **command** (cf. 3:4, 6, 10; see notes on 1 Thess 4:11) and an **exhortation** (cf. 1 Thess 4:1; 5:14), Paul orders, by virtue of his relationship to the **Lord Jesus Christ**, the unruly to amend their lives in two ways. First, **they** are to **work in quietness** (cf. Eph 4:28; see notes on 1 Thess 4:11). Second, as a result, **they** are able to **eat their own bread**, i.e. provide for their own way in life by earning a living wage through productive labor.

3:13 Paul turns now to the obedient **brethren** with a reminder and word of encouragement. **Do not grow weary** (cf. Gen 27:46 [LXX]; Num 21:4 [LXX]; Luke 18:1) **in doing good** (cf. 2 Cor 13:7). Paul does not want them to react with extremism and shut off all the nobleness of benevolence and compassion to those who truly need and deserve help (cf. 1 Tim 5:3-16 concerning widows). Nor does he want the Thessalonians to become so cynical toward the unruly that they give up on them. Rather, they are to be proactively good (cf. 1 Thess 5:21-22) towards those who need help as outlined in 1 Thessalonians 5:14 (see notes; cf. similar instructions in Gal 6:9-10). At the same time, they are not to indulge the incorrigible.

3:14 If Paul's instructions, commands, and exhortations (**our word**) **in this epistle** are not **obeyed**, then the Thessalonians had no other alternative than to take the last steps in church discipline (see *Overview*, 'Church Discipline' [3:6]). The practical process would be that they are to first note that person, i.e. literally to mark that person out for special notice, which would be the equivalent of making a public announcement to the church (cf. Matt 18:17). Second, **do not keep company with** (literally, 'do not mix it up socially') that person (**him**). This is the same language used in 1 Corinthians 5:9, 11 and seems to parallel treating the person as a Gentile and tax collector in Matthew 18:17. However, it is this writer's opinion that the person dealt with in 1 Corinthians 5 was clearly an unbeliever.

What does this accomplish? How will it help the erring brother? By shaming (cf. Ps 35:26 [LXX]; Isa 44:11 [LXX]; 1 Cor 4:14; Titus 2:8) him into repentance so that he can ultimately be returned to the fellowship. To **be ashamed** is the first step towards acknowledging that a behavior pattern is sinful and needs to change. While these instructions seem to be addressed to the church in general, the leaders would certainly take special notice in order to carry out their pastoral responsibilities.

3:15 Paul concludes with a very important qualifying statement, **Yet do not count him as an enemy**. This erring Christian is not to be counted as or considered to be the enemy. Why? Church discipline is designed for repentance that leads to restoration, not to irreversible removal from the assembly (Gal 6:1-5). In marked contrast (**but**), the Thessalonians were to **admonish him as a brother** (see notes on 1 Thess 5:14). Admonish represents a Greek word from which the idea of 'nouthetic counseling' is derived. It literally means 'to set in one's mind'. In this context, it means to admonish with God's word towards the goal of obedience. This is: (1) encouraged behavior among Christians (Rom 15:14; Col 3:16; see *Overview*, 'New Testament "One Anothers" ' [1 Thess 3:12]); (2) the pattern of Paul (1 Cor 4:14; Col 1:28); (3) the role of pastors (1 Thess 5:12); and (4) the proper Christian behavior toward the disorderly, as in this passage (see notes on 1 Thess 5:14). Taken in this sense, then 3:15 is an overarching principle of administering church discipline.

There is another possible way of understanding this final instruction. It could be understood as the proper response to the shamed brother who has now repented. If taken in this manner, then Paul is reminding the Thessalonians to forgive and restore the formerly errant one (cf. Paul's instructions on this very topic to the Corinthians in 2:1-11 of the second letter). To do otherwise would be to be a pawn of Satan.

6. PAUL'S CLOSING WORDS AND BENEDICTION (3:16-18)

Paul's fourth prayer (3:16, 18) for the Thessalonians (1:11-12; 2:16-17; 3:5) concludes his second letter to the church (see notes about Paul's prayers on 1 Thess 1:2). Although short in length, it is long in compassion and spiritual influence.

Now may the Lord of peace Himself give you peace always in every way. The Lord be with you all. The salutation of Paul with my own hand, which is a sign in every epistle; so I write. The grace of our Lord Jesus Christ be with you all. Amen (3:16-18).

3:16 Paul begins each of his thirteen epistles with the mention of **peace** (see notes on 1 Thess 1:1; 5:23). In no letter would it be more appropriate at the close to appeal to **the Lord of peace Himself** (cf. John 14:27; 16:33) than this one, which was written to a persecuted congregation who had endured a major doctrinal disruption and was dealing publicly with the first serious (and possibly widespread) sin issue in the history of the church. The antidote for their turmoil would be God's peace. For unknown reasons, Paul did not end all of his epistles with a mention of peace (cf. 1 Corinthians, Philippians, Colossians, 1, 2 Timothy, Titus, and Philemon) as he does here.

Paul prays that God's peace would be pervasive, i.e. **always** (at all times) and **in every way** ('every circumstance,' NASB). Several older manuscripts have 'in every place', but this appears to be a later scribal error. **The Lord be with you all** is Paul's prayer for their constant sense of the Lord's superintending presence in the midst of the Thessalonian church, which would portend spiritual blessing and peace.

3:17 The salutation of Paul with my own hand indicates that the apostle had dictated this letter to a secretary (amanuensis), but now takes the pen in hand to personally greet, i.e. salute (cf. Matt 23:7; Luke 1:29) the Thessalonians and conclude the letter. This practice was not unusual in the ancient world, nor was it foreign to Paul (cf. Rom 16:22; 1 Cor 16:21; Col 4:18). This was true of **every** letter, even though Paul did not always mention it.

By doing so with the **sign** of his unique handwriting (cf. Gal 6:11), **Paul** authenticated **every epistle** he wrote. This would be especially meaningful to the Thessalonians who, perhaps, had been deceived and greatly disturbed by a forged letter as if from Paul (see notes on 2:1-2). Since Paul had been so authoritative with his instructions in this letter (2:15; 3:14), it was imperative for the Thessalonians to be confident that they possessed a genuine piece of correspondence from the apostle (**my own hand**; cf. Phile 19). **So I write** was simply to say that this was the official indicator for which to look. Anything else was to be rejected outright as bogus.

3:18 As he does in every letter, Paul closes with a benediction of grace (see notes on 1 Thess 1:1; 5:28). **The grace of our Lord Jesus Christ be with you all. Amen**. This is identical to the close of 1 Thessalonians 5:28, except **all** has been added here by Paul. **Amen** is most likely a later scribal addition (cf. 1 Thess 5:28 also). Even though there are some in the congregation who have grievously sinned and to whom Paul has written hard words, he stills extends Christ's grace to **all** the believers. Pastor Paul well understood that the peace, blessed presence, and grace of God the Father and God the Son would be most beneficial to his beloved flock in light of the intense spiritual conflicts which raged all around them (cf. Num 6:24-26).

Appendix 1: Various Millennial Views

Four basic views of prophecy prevail today: Postmillennialism, Amillennialism, Historic Premillennialism, and Futuristic Pre-millennialism.[1]

Because of the significant amount of prophetic material in 1 and 2 Thessalonians (30%; see *Overview*, 'What Does the Future Hold?' [1:3]) and the limited amount of space to discuss these complex issues, I intend to define each of the four perspectives, and then explain which one this writer prefers and why. This will identify the theological basis that emerges from the exegetical treatment of the text in these two 'forward looking' epistles.

The terms 'millennium' and 'millennialism' come from the Latin word *mille*, meaning 'one thousand'. Biblically, they refer to the Greek phrase *chilia etē*, 'one thousand years', which appears six times in Revelation (20:2, 3, 4, 5, 6, 7). The prefix 'post' refers to Christ's second coming after the millennium, i.e. intermediate kingdom of the church age; while 'a' indicates that there is no millennium on earth before or after Christ's second coming. Both of the 'pre' positions believe that there is a millennial period on earth which is preceded by Christ's second coming.

Postmillennialism teaches that the kingdom of God is currently being advanced, with increasing triumph in the world through gospel preaching and the ministry of the church. Christ now rules over this 'golden age' of undetermined length from heaven and will return to earth at the end, thus being a postmillennial return. The church is considered to be spiritual Israel, having inherited the promises made to Abraham and David, which were abrogated for Israel by their national disobedience. Therefore, there is no future for a national Israel with any biblical significance. When Christ returns at the end of the millennium, the rapture, second advent, general resurrection, and judgment all take place in rapid

---

1. Darrell L. Bock, gen. ed., *Three Views on the Millennium and Beyond* (Grand Rapids: Zondervan, 1999) for the most recent discussion of millennial views.

sequence, and then comes the eternal state.

Amillennialism teaches that the church is now spiritual Israel, having inherited God's promises to Abraham and David which were forfeited by Israel because of continued disobedience. Christ rules over this spiritual kingdom from heaven, and the redemptive work of Christ continues on earth, but without the optimism of postmillennialism. There is no expectation of a restored national Israel which will have prophetic significance. The affairs of earth will deteriorate until Christ intervenes at His second coming. All of the end-time events – e.g. the rapture, general resurrection, and the judgment – happen in a short span of time as the immediate prelude to eternity future.

Historic Premillennialism teaches that Christ will return to rapture the church, judge living unbelievers, and set up an earthly kingdom (some say it will be one thousand years in length, while others believe '1000' is a symbolic number meaning 'a long time'). Christ now rules over the earth from heaven and in the future will rule over a millennium where little distinction is made between the church and restored national Israel. At the end of the millennium, there is the resurrection of unbelievers and the final judgment, which is followed by the eternal state. This category of premillennialism generally interprets Revelation chapters 6–18 in a 'historic' sense rather than looking to the future, thus the name 'historic premillennialism'.

Advocates of *Futuristic Premillennialism*[2] use a consistent grammatical-historical approach to both the Old and New Testament Scriptures, by which the Bible is interpreted normally throughout, regardless of whether it is non-eschatological or eschatological. Therefore, God's promises to Abraham and David are viewed in a futuristic sense as anticipating a restored nation of Israel. In this pattern, the rapture comes first (it can be pre-tribulational, mid-tribulational, or post-tribulational), followed by Christ's second coming at the end of the seven-year tribulation period, biblically spoken of as Daniel's seventieth week. See *Appendix 2*, 'The Time of the Rapture'. After judging the earth and its inhabitants, Christ rules over the earth for one thousand years

---

2. See the chart on *Futuristic Premillennialism*.

(the millennium) from His Davidic throne in Jerusalem. At the end of the millennium, Satan rebels for one final time but is instantly defeated. Then comes the resurrection and judgment of all unbelievers at the Great White Throne of judgment, which is followed by the New Jerusalem and the eternal state.

The Preferred View[3]

Obviously, one cannot be a 'fence sitter' on an issue of such immense proportion and be only promillennial, i.e. 'Whatever God wills, I am all for it.' So after twenty-five years of study, this writer has come to prefer Futuristic Premillennialism for six major reasons.

1. Consistent Approach to Interpretation

Futuristic Premillennialism does not require new special rules of interpretation when it comes to prophetic texts. The biblical text is taken at normal face-value, in its context, recognizing symbolic language and speech figures, plus the reality that they represent. It allows the interpreter to take the same general approach to the unvarnished history of Joshua, or the highly figurative images of Solomon's Song, or the prophetic books.

Normal interpretation produces the correct understanding of Old Testament prophecies that have already been fulfilled in history. For example, Genesis 17:6 predicts that from Abraham would come real kings, and they did. Daniel prophesied of coming Persian, Greek, and Roman nations, and they came to be.

Most convincing to this writer is the manner in which Christ's first advent prophecies are correctly interpreted, i.e. by consistently using the normal or grammatical-historical approach. Christ was born in the tribe of Judah (Gen 49:10); He was born in Bethlehem (Micah 5:2); He died by crucifixion (Ps 22) and rose from the grave (cf. Ps 2:7 with Acts 13:33; 16:10; Isa 55:3).

Therefore, unless there is some clear uncontested mandate from Scripture to change how one interprets second coming prophecies (and there is not), then prophetic Scripture should be interpreted

---

3. See David Larsen, *Jews, Gentiles, and the Church* (Grand Rapids: Discovery House, 1995) for an excellent treatment of Futuristic Premillennialism.

consistently throughout Scripture. Even the amillennialist O.T. Allis[4] and the postmillennialist Loraine Boettner[5] admitted that if a consistent, normal approach is followed, then Futuristic Premillennialism will be the outcome.

2. Unconfused Identities of Israel and the Church

The book of Acts speaks frequently of the 'church' (nineteen times) and 'Israel' (twenty times). However, 'church' refers to those believing at Pentecost and beyond; while 'Israel' refers to the nation – historically and ethnically. The terms are never used synonymously or interchangeably. The church is never called 'spiritual Israel' or 'new Israel' in the New Testament; furthermore Israel is never called 'the church' in the Old Testament.

There are really only three texts that might even remotely be considered to equate Israel with the church.

1. Romans 9:6 distinguishes between physical birth and the new birth.

2. Romans 11:26 promises that all elect Jews will be saved.

3. Galatians 6:16 refers to the believing Jews in the Galatian congregations.

'Church' is mentioned at least eighteen times in Revelation chapters 1–3. It is not later confused with 'Israel' in Revelation chapters 6–19. Between Revelation 3:22 and Revelation 22:16, there is no mention of the church. Only Futuristic Premillennialism accounts for this clear Biblical distinction.

3. Preservation of the Jewish Race and Israel

The Jewish race is the most persecuted ethnic group in world history. The ten northern tribes of Israel have been extremely obscure since the Assyrian captivity in 722 BC. The nation of Israel never regained any degree of its former sovereign rule after the Babylonian captivity in 586 BC until the nation was restored in

---

4. O.T. Allis, *Prophecy and the Church* (Nutley, NJ: Presbyterian and Reformed, 1945) 238.

5. Loraine Boettner, 'Postmillennialism,' in *The Meaning of the Millennium*: *Four Views* ed. by Robert Clouse (Downers Grove, IL: InterVarsity, 1977) 95.

AD 1948. Yet, today the Jewish race and the nation of Israel are a recognized people residing in the ancient land of their ancestors who trace their roots back to Abraham in Genesis 12 (c. 2165-1990 BC).

The Old Testament promised that Israel would again regain international prominence in spite of their ancient exiles, Ezekiel 37:15-28 being the most prominent text. Both Jeremiah 31:35-37 and 33:19-26 guarantee that this promise is as sure as the laws of nature. At least five Old Testament texts promise that once Israel is fully restored, she will not ever be overthrown or shamed again (Jer 31:40; Ezek 37:25; Amos 9:15; Joel 2:26-27; Zeph 3:20). Only with Futuristic Premillennialism is this expected.

very good

4. Unconditional Covenants

Both the Abrahamic and Davidic Covenants were intended to be unconditional in their ultimate effect. Nowhere does Scripture suggest that Israel forsook their blessings forever, which have now allegedly been made spiritual and inherited by the church. To say otherwise, in effect, is to make God a liar.

The Abrahamic Covenant is called an everlasting covenant in which God gave Abraham and his descendants the land of Israel as an everlasting possession (Gen 17:7-8). God's promise to Abraham is corroborated in 1 Chronicles 16:15-17 and Psalm 105:8-15. By this covenant, a people and a land are promised for Israel.

The Davidic Covenant of 2 Samuel 7:8-16 is called an everlasting covenant in 2 Samuel 23:5, 2 Chronicles 21:7, and Psalm 89:3-4, 19-29, 36. By this covenant, a throne is promised for Israel. Of the four eschatological options, only Futuristic Premillennialism takes these features into consideration.

5. Order of Christ's Returning and Reigning

In prophetic Scripture, Christ is portrayed as first returning to earth for His kingdom and then reigning over it. In Daniel 2:34-35, He returns and then reigns in Daniel 2:44-45. He first returns in Zechariah 14:5 and then reigns in 14:9. Christ's coming first appears in Matthew 24:27, 30, 37, 42, 44, followed by His reign in

Matthew 25:31. In Revelation 19:11, He returns to reign as described in Revelation 20:4. Only Futuristic Millennialism holds to this pattern. In the other three prophetic profiles, Christ first reigns before coming to earth.

6. Revelation 20:1-10

Revelation 20:1-10 might well be considered the *summum bonum* of millennial studies. For in this section one encounters a unique historical period which is designated as 'one thousand years' (vv. 2, 3, 4, 5, 6, and 7).

There are several preliminary inquiries that logically precede determining a correct eschatological understanding of Revelation 20. First, it needs to be asked if this period of time is yet future or has it already been fulfilled? Next, is this period actually one thousand years in length or does the term represent another length of time, e.g. 5000 years? Finally, how has the 'one thousand' of Revelation 20:1-10 normally been interpreted in the past?

(a) The Time of Fulfillment

Several peculiar events occur during this special segment of time. An angel binds Satan with a great chain (20:1-2). Satan is then incarcerated in the abyss which is shut and sealed (20:3). Thus, Satan no longer deceives the nations until the one thousand years transpire. The Tribulation martyrs are resurrected to reign with Christ (20:4, 6). When the one thousand years end, Satan is released for a short time to once again deceive the nations (20:3, 7-8).

Now, has this already been fulfilled? Most who hold to a form of covenant theology respond affirmatively and point to Christ's victory over Satan at the cross as the starting point. Such texts as Matthew 12:22-29 are employed to bolster the position that Satan is *now* bound in fulfillment of Revelation 20.

While it is true that Christ won the victory at Calvary and Satan's doom was eternally settled, it is not true that Satan has been incapacitated in the manner demanded by this text. Satan still entices men to lie (Acts 5:3). He is blinding the minds of unbelievers to the gospel of the glory of Christ in God (2 Cor 4:4). Satan currently disguises himself as an angel of light to deceive the church (2 Cor 11:2-3, 13-15). The devil hinders ministers of God (1 Thess 2:18) and roams about the earth to devour its population (1 Pet 5:8). Revelation 20 could never refer to the present time in light of these abundant testimonies of Satan's present, frenetic pace (cf. 2 Cor 2:11; Eph 6:11-12). Therefore, it can be concluded that Revelation 20 looks to some future time of special magnitude. Since it is yet ahead, it is asked next, 'How long will this time last?'

(b) The Period of Time
The bottom line in this discussion asks, 'Does *chilia etē* in Revelation 20 really mean a literal one thousand years?' The discussion begins by looking at Biblical numbers in general and then narrowing the focus to Revelation and 'one thousand' in particular.

It is commonly understood as a basic rule of hermeneutics that numbers should be accepted at face value, i.e. conveying a mathematical quantity, unless there is substantial evidence to warrant otherwise. This dictum for interpreting Biblical numbers is generally accepted by all as the proper starting point.

This rule holds true throughout the Bible, including Revelation. A survey of numbers in the Apocalypse supports this. For instance, seven churches and seven angels in Revelation 1 refer to seven literal churches and their messengers. Twelve tribes and twelve apostles refer to actual, historical numbers (21:12, 14). Seven lampstands (1:12), five months (9:5), two witnesses (11:3), twelve hundred and sixty days (11:3), twelve stars (12:1), ten horns (13:1), sixteen hundred stadia (14:20), three demons (16:13), and five fallen kings (17:9-10) all use numbers in their normal sense. Out of the scores of numbers in Revelation, only two (seven spirits in 1:4 and 666 in 13:18) are conclusively used in a symbolic fashion. While this line of reasoning does not prove that 'one thousand' in Revelation 20 should be taken normally, it does put the burden of proof on those who disagree with accepting 'one thousand' as one thousand to prove otherwise.

Not only are numbers in general to be taken normally in Revelation but, more specifically, this is also true with numbers referring to time. In Revelation chapters 4–20 there are at least twenty-five references to measurements of time. Only two of these demand to be understood in something other than a literal sense and, with these instances, numbers are not employed. The 'day of His wrath' (6:17) would likely exceed twenty-four hours and 'the hour of His judgment' (14:7) seemingly extends beyond sixty minutes. There is nothing, however, in the phrase 'one thousand years' that suggests a symbolic interpretation.

This next point is very important. Never in the Bible is 'year' used with a numerical adjective when it does not refer to the actual period of time that it mathematically represents. Unless evidence to the contrary can be provided, Revelation 20 is not the one exception in the entire Scripture.

Also, the number 'one thousand' is not used elsewhere in the Bible with a symbolic sense. Job 9:3; 33:23; Psalms 50:10; 90:4; Ecclesiastes 6:6; 7:28; and 2 Peter 3:8 have been used in support of the idea that 'one thousand' in this text is used symbolically. However, these attempts fail because in each of these texts 'one thousand' is used in its normal sense to make a vivid point.

One thousand and its varied combinations are used frequently in both Testaments. No one questions the response to five thousand believers (Acts 4:4), twenty-three thousand men killed (1 Cor 10:8), or seven thousand killed (Rev 11:13). Likewise, there is no exegetical reason to question the normality of one thousand years in Revelation 20.

(c) The Testimony of History

From the earliest post-apostolic era, the church understood the 'millennium' of Revelation 20 as a literal, one thousand years. Papias, Barnabas, Justin Martyr, Irenaeus and Tertullian all gave evidence of this fact in their writings. The church taught nothing else until the fourth century.

When ancient theologians began to go beyond what the Bible taught about the millennium, when they began to make it a period of time that would be more for the enjoyment of man than for the glory of God, some reacted to correct this excess by interpreting this time as something less than an actual historical period.

Augustine (c.354-430) popularized the approach which

reasoned that the church inherited the blessings promised to Israel and that they are spiritual, not earthly. He taught that Revelation 20 referred to this time.

However, even Augustine understood from Revelation 20 that this period lasted one thousand literal years. So Augustine, called by many the father of Amillennialism, took the one thousand years normally. Even to this day some non-premillennialists interpret Revelation 20 to be actually one thousand years in length. To do less does injustice to the text.

Conclusions

It can be concluded that the one thousand years of Revelation 20 look to the future for fulfillment since an honest appraisal of the text and history determines that it has not yet occurred. Further, a survey of numbers in the Bible and Revelation pointedly demands that the 'one thousand' years be understood in a normal sense. This position received further substantiation through a brief review of how the church has historically interpreted this text.

Although it is not within the scope of this discussion to prove Futuristic Premillennialism from Revelation 20 alone, certainly the next sequentially logical question would be, 'Is there an unmistakable bridge that links the Old Testament promises of a restored earthly kingdom to Israel with the distinctive statements of Revelation 20?' In closing, let it be suggested that there is – the rule and reign of our Lord Jesus Christ on the throne of David in the city of God. Consider 2 Samuel 7:12-16; Psalm 2:1-12; Isaiah 2:2-4; 9:7; Jeremiah 33:14-18; Ezekiel 34:23-24; Daniel 2:44-45; Hosea 3:5; Joel 3:9-21; Zephaniah 3:14-20; and Zechariah 14:1-11 with Revelation 20:4, 6.

APPENDIX 2: The Time of the Rapture[1]

Regardless of one's prophetic preferences, the rapture will be part of any endtimes scenario because the fact of the rapture is so clearly stated in Scripture (1 Cor 15:51-52; 1 Thess 4:15-17). What is not so clear is the time of the rapture in relationship to other prophetic events.

There are three basic time possibilities for the rapture. The *posttribulation* rapture occurs as just one of many events at the end, just prior to eternity future, according to the amillennial or postmillennial scenario. To some premillennialists, the posttribulation rapture occurs at the conclusion of Daniel's seventieth week. To other premillennialists, it occurs at the midpoint of the seven year period of Daniel's seventieth week and is called the *midtribulation* rapture. Others, like this writer, believe that the rapture occurs before this seven year period and is called the *pretribulation* rapture. What follows is a summary of the evidence that makes the pretribulation rapture the preferred view for this writer.

Arguments from silence

While arguments from silence do have their limitations and are never conclusive, they are worthy of consideration. So the question is asked, 'If posttribulationism best describes the biblical data concerning the resurrection and rapture of Church Age saints, what conclusions would we logically expect from this scheme?' This would also be germane to midtribulationism.

First, if the Church does endure this time of tribulation in Daniel's seventieth week, one would naturally expect Revelation, the most detailed account of the tribulation in the Scriptures, to describe the Church's existence during this time.

---

1. This material is adapted from Richard Mayhue, *Snatched Before the Storm* (Winona Lake, IN: BMH, 1980). See Thomas Ice and Timothy Demy, eds., *When the Trumpet Sounds* (Eugene, OR: Harvest House, 1995) for the most convincing case presented on behalf of the pretribulation rapture.

II.) Second, if the Church indeed will experience the unprecedented intensity of wrath predestined for the tribulation, one would expect the epistles to contain preparatory warnings for Church Age saints.

III.) Third, if the Church is to survive the tribulation, one would expect this fact to figure prominently in the need for a rapture.

However, not one of these basic corollaries to an alleged posttribulation or midtribulation rapture is taught in the Scriptures.

The Church is not mentioned in Revelation 4–18

If the Church will experience the tribulation of Daniel's seventieth week, then surely the most detailed study of tribulation events would include an account of the Church's role in Revelation.

It is remarkable and totally unexpected that John would shift from detailed instructions for the Church to absolute silence about the Church for the subsequent fifteen chapters if, in fact, the Church continued into the tribulation.

Looking at this observation from another point, it is also true that nowhere in Scripture is it taught that the Church and Israel would coexist as the mutually exclusive centers for God's redemptive message.

Today, the Church universal is God's human channel of redemptive truth. In the tribulation, Revelation gives certain indications that the Jewish remnant will be God's human instrument. The unbiased reader would certainly be impressed by the abrupt shift from the Church in Revelation chapters 2–3 to the 144,000 from the twelve tribes in Revelation chapters 7 and 14. He would certainly ask, 'Why?'

Further, if Revelation chapter 12 is a mini-synopsis of the tribulation period and if the woman who gave birth to the male child (Rev 12:13) is Israel, then logically the time focuses on the nation of Israel and not the Church.

The epistles do not contain preparatory warnings of an impending Tribulation for Church Age believers

God's instructions to the Church in the epistles contain a variety of warnings, but never are believers warned to prepare for entering and enduring the tribulation.

They warn vigorously about coming error and false prophets

I. Peter 1:3, "all thing pertaining to life and godliness."
II Tim 3:16-17

(Acts 20:29-30; 2 Pet 2:1; 1 John 4:1-3; Jude 4). They warn against ungodly living (Eph 4:25-5:7; 1 Thess 4:3-8; all of 1 Peter).

It is incongruous, then, that the Scriptures would be silent on such a traumatic change for the Church. If posttribulationism were true, one would expect the epistles to teach the fact of the Church in the tribulation, the purpose of the Church in the tribulation, and the conduct of the Church in the tribulation.

The Rapture is rendered inconsequential if it is Posttribulational
First, if God miraculously preserves the Church through the tribulation, why have a rapture? If it is to avoid the wrath of God at Armageddon, why would not God continue to protect the saints on earth (as postulated by posttribulationism), just as He protected Israel (Exod 8:22; 9:4, 26; 10:23; 11:7) from His wrath poured out upon Pharaoh and Egypt? Further, if the purpose of the rapture is to avoid Armageddon, why resurrect the saints who are already immune?

Secondly, if the rapture took place in connection with our Lord's posttribulational coming, the subsequent separation of the sheep from the goats (Matt 25:31ff.) would be redundant. Separation would have taken place in the very act of translation.

Thirdly, if all believers are raptured and glorified just prior to the inauguration of the Millennial Kingdom, who will propagate the human race and thus populate the Kingdom?

The Scriptures indicate that the living unbelievers will be removed from the earth and be judged at the end of the tribulation (Matt 13:41-42; 25:41). Yet, they also teach that children will be born during the Millennium and that people will be capable of sin (Isa 65:20; Rev 20:7-10). Neither of these truths would be possible if all unbelievers had been judged and all believers had been glorified.

Superlative arguments

Revelation 3:10
Victory is claimed by both Pretribulationists and Posttribulationists because of the exegetical support this passage lends to their

interpretation. It is true that Revelation 3:10 is *the* crucial verse. It is the veritable watershed of the tribulation tension. If one side can demonstrate incontrovertibly that it supports their position, then the tribulation controversy should be over. The key phrase is *tēreō ek*.

The meaning of *ek*

It is true that *ek* has the basic idea of emergence, but this is not always the case. Two notable examples are 2 Corinthians 1:10 and 1 Thessalonians 1:10. In the Corinthian passage, Paul rehearses his rescue from death by God. Now Paul did not emerge from a state of death, but rather was rescued from that potential danger.

Even more convincing is 1 Thessalonians 1:10. Here Paul states that Jesus is rescuing us out of the wrath to come. Although *orgē* can be understood in several ways, it is best to interpret it as God's eternal wrath (cf. Rom 5:9; Eph 5:6; 1 Thess 5:9). The idea is not emergence out of, but rather protection from entrance.

Therefore, it is concluded that *ek* can be understood to mean 'a continuing state outside of' rather than 'emergence from within'. Thus, neither pretribulationism nor posttribulationism can be dogmatic at this point. At best, both positions concerning *ek* remain possible.

The meaning of *tēreō ek*

It is argued that if John had meant 'to keep from', he would have used *tēreō apo* (cf. James 1:27). But it is more than equally true that if John had meant 'protection within', he would have used *tēreō* with *en*, *eis*, or *dia*. It is submitted that the greater burden of proof lies with posttribulationism since their position of immunity within the tribulation does not explain the use of *ek*. They do not argue for evacuation in Revelation 3:10, but rather protection.

First, *ek* is much closer to *apo* in meaning than it is to *en*, *eis*, or *dia*. The two frequently overlap, and in modern Greek *apo* is absorbing *ek*. When combined with *tēreō*, *ek* much more closely approximates *apo* than it does *en*, *eis*, or *dia*. The burden is upon the posttribulationists to prove otherwise.

Second, the phrase *tēreō en* is used four times in the New

Testament (Acts 12:5; 25:4; 1 Pet 1:4; Jude 21). In each instance, it implies previous existence within with a view to its continuation within. Now if *tēreō en* means continued existence within, what does *tēreō ek* mean? Since they are anything but synonymous, it quite logically means to maintain an existence outside.

tēreō ek in John 17:15

John 17:15 is the only other passage in the New Testament where *tēreō ek* occurs. This combination of words does not occur in the Septuagint. It is assumed that whatever the phrase means here, it will also have the same meaning in Revelation 3:10.

If *tēreō ek* in John 17:15 means 'previous existence within', then it contradicts 1 John 5:19. Here, the statement is made that believers are of God, and unbelievers are in the evil one. Now if 1 John 5:19 implies that believers are not in the power of the evil one, John 17:15 could not possibly imply that they are in the power of Satan and needing protection. John 17:15 records our Lord's petition to keep them outside of the evil one.

Since John 17:15 means to keep outside of the evil one, then the parallel thought in Revelation 3:10 is to keep the Church outside of the hour of testing. Therefore, a pretribulation rapture is necessitated to fulfill the promise.

[margin note: Same author, consistant in vocabulary.]

The martyrs in Revelation 6:9-11 and 7:14

If Revelation 3:10 means immunity or protection within as posttribulationists posit, then several contradictions result.

First, if protection in Revelation 3:10 is limited to protection from God's wrath only and not Satan's, then Revelation 3:10 denies our Lord's request in John 17:15.

Second, if it is argued that Revelation 3:10 means total immunity, then of what worth is the promise in light of Revelation 6:9-11 and 7:14 where martyrs abound? The wholesale martyrdom of saints during the tribulation demands that the promise be interpreted as 'keeping from' the hour of testing, not 'keeping within'.

Summary

1. *Ek* can mean 'emergence from within', or it can mean 'a continued state outside'.

2. *Tēreō en* is used in Acts 12:5, Acts 25:4, 1 Peter 1:4, and Jude 21 and implies 'previous and continued existence within'. Therefore *tēreō ek* logically demands to be understood as 'continued existence outside'.

3. If a posttribulation rapture was intended to be taught by the immunity of saints to wrath through the tribulation, then John would have used *tēreō en, eis*, or *dia* in Revelation 3:10.

4. Consistent with the previous observations, *tēreō ek* in John 17:15 would contradict 1 John 5:19 if, in fact, it implied 'previous existence within'.

5. If *tēreō* in Revelation 3:10 implies 'previous existence within', it contradicts the prayer in John 17:15, if immunity is limited to God's wrath. Or its alleged promise of total immunity is rendered null and void by the slaughter of saints in Revelation 6:9-11 and 7:14.

6. Only the interpretation of *tēreō ek* in Revelation 3:10 which understands that the church will not enter the tribulation, that is, they will be kept out or guarded from entering, satisfies a thorough exegesis of the phrase. This finding is in perfect harmony with a pretribulational understanding of the rapture.

John 14:1-3

John 14:1-3 refers to Christ's coming again. It is not a promise to all believers that they shall go to Him at death. It does refer to the rapture of the Church. Note the close parallel between the promises of John 14:1-3 and 1 Thessalonians 4:13-18.

Jesus instructed the disciples that He was going to His Father's house (heaven) to prepare a place for them. He promised them that He would return and receive them so that they could be with Him wherever He was. *He returns to recieve us to heaven, that we may be their with Him.*

The phrase 'wherever I am', while implying continued presence in general, here means presence in heaven in particular. Our Lord told the Pharisees in John 7:34, 'Where I am you cannot come.' He was not talking about His present abode on earth but rather His resurrected presence at the right hand of the Father. In John 14:1-3, 'where I am' must be 'in heaven' or the intent of 14:1-3 would be wasted and worthless.

A posttribulation rapture demands that the saints meet Christ in the air and immediately descend to earth without experiencing what our Lord promised in John 14. Since John 14 refers to the rapture, then only a pretribulation rapture satisfies the language of John 14:1-3 and allows raptured saints to dwell with Christ in His Father's house.

The sequence of events at Christ's posttribulational coming demands a pretribulation Rapture

Matthew 24:31
At the rapture, Christ himself will gather the saints (1 Thess 4:16-17). At the posttribulational coming of Christ, the angels will gather together the elect (Matt 24:31). This difference is irreconcilable, if understood in the posttribulation sequence of events.

Matthew 13:41-42
The rapture will first separate believers out from among unbelievers. However, at Christ's posttribulational coming, angels will first gather out unbelievers from believers. Again, only a pretribulation rapture can harmonize these two historical events. See also Matthew 13:49-50 and Matthew 24:37-41 where unbelievers are removed from among believers at the tribulation's termination.

1 Thessalonians 4:13-18
For argument's sake, let us suppose that posttribulationism is true. What would we *expect* to find in 1 Thessalonians 4? How does this compare with what we *do* observe?

First, we would expect the Thessalonians to be joyous over the fact that loved ones are home with the Lord and will not have to endure the horrors of the tribulation. *But*, we discover the Thessalonians are grieving because they fear their loved ones will miss the rapture. Only a pretribulation rapture accounts for this grief.

Second, we would expect the Thessalonians to be grieving over their own impending trial rather than grieving over loved ones. Furthermore, we would expect them to be inquisitive about their future doom. But the Thessalonians have no fear or question about the coming tribulation.

Third, we would expect Paul, even in the absence of interest or questions by the Thessalonians, to have provided instruction and exhortation for such a supreme test which would make their present tribulation seem microscopic in comparison. *But* there is not one indication of any impending tribulation.

First Thessalonians 4 fits the model of a pretribulation rapture. It is incompatible with midtribulationism or posttribulationism.

Peri de in 1 Thessalonians 5:1

Peri de is used eighteen times in the New Testament.[7] In all but four cases, an obvious change in time or topic is implied (Matt 22:31; 24:36; Mark 12:26; 13:32). This prepositional phrase is used by Paul eight times. Every other Pauline use of *peri de* indicates a change in topic. Therefore, it is concluded that Paul's use of *peri de* in 1 Thessalonians 5:1 indicates a change in topic and time. This is consistent with his earlier use in this epistle (cf. 4:9).

In 1 Thessalonians 4:13-18, Paul has answered the question concerning the experience of dead loved ones when the rapture comes. But in 5:1 and following, Paul shifts to the Day of the Lord and the subsequent judgment upon unbelievers. This is a totally different topic than the rapture and an event that will occur at a totally different time than the rapture.

If 1 Thessalonians 4:13–5:11 is to be taken as one unit of thought, then Paul's use of *peri de* means nothing. However, if it is to be explained, it is best interpreted as a major shift in thought within the prophetic context. Only a pretribulation rapture would account for this.

---

7. Matthew 20:6; 22:31; 24:36; 27:46; Mark 12:26; 13:32; John 16:10, 11; 17:20; Acts 21:25; 1 Corinthians 7:1, 25; 8:1; 12:1; 16:1, 12; 1 Thessalonians 4:9; 5:1.

Conclusions

The strongest and most compelling biblical reasons for preferring
a pretribulational interpretation of the rapture have been offered
here. Pretribulationism most consistently fits the biblical data and
is therefore championed by this writer as the view which best
explains the coming of our Lord for His own.

STUDY QUESTIONS
ON
1 AND 2 THESSALONIANS

1 THESSALONIANS

1:1

1. Paul called himself the foremost sinner (1 Tim. 1:15) and least of saints (Eph. 3:8). Who else had a bad past and yet was appointed by Christ to significant service? Do you find this encouraging? (page 34)

2. Do you habitually think about God in the Trinitarian way that Paul did (cf. 1:5)? (page 36)

1:2—2:16

1. Paul encouraged himself, when at Corinth, by what God had done through him at Thessalonica. Do you take enough encouragement from the past? (page 42)

2. How often do you pray and give thanks to God along with others with whom you are involved in the Lord's work? Should you be doing this more? (pages 42f.)

3. How much do you reflect on God's great love to you personally and your unworthiness of it? (pages 46f.)

4. No doubt Paul and his companions used some illustrations when they preached the gospel to the Thessalonians, but they also illustrated it by the quality of their lives. Which is the more important? (pages 48-49)

5. Do you share Paul's confidence in the gospel, the message of salvation? (pages 48ff.)

6. Reflect on the importance of thoroughly receiving God's word in light of Mark 4:20 (where the word used is stronger than in Mark 4:16) and also, in terms of ministering it (Col. 3:16). How deeply embedded in your heart is God's word?

7. The Thessalonian church had a very wide-ranging ministry, despite its youth. Why do you think the ministry of so many churches is very limited today, especially in terms of missionary outreach? (pages 55-56)

8. Think of and pray for some sceptical non-Christians you know. Have you ever talked to them about the evidence for the resurrection of Jesus? (page 58)

9. Paul writes about covetousness. Read the Ten Commandments in Exodus 20 and consider whether God has a particular hatred of this as He refers to it here in addition to stealing. (page 68)

10. Does Paul's description of himself, as like mother and father to the Thessalonians, raise for you the question as to whether you are warm and responsible in your dealings with younger Christians? (pages 72-73)

11. 'God's glory reflected back to Him by us comes through acts of personal devotion and adoration that are God-directed.' Consider 2 Corinthians 3:18, in its context, as a basic text for this. (page 79)

12. 2 Timothy 3:14-17 and 2 Peter 1:19-21 are regarded as basic passages for our doctrine of the inspiration and authority of Scripture. Do you think 1 Thessalonians 2:13 might be added to them? (pages 79-81)

13. Either from your own knowledge or that of a more knowledgeable Christian, select two areas of the world where Christians suffer persecution for Christ's sake and spend some time in prayer for them. (pages 80-85)

2:17—3:13

1. If we are separated by distance from believers we love, are there ways we can still help and encourage them? How did Paul do this for the Thessalonians and for others? (page 86)

2. Is there a mid-way between minimising and exaggerating the power of Satan? Does Luke 10:18-20 help you to get the right balance? (pages 87-88, 94-95)

3. Paul was concerned about both the belief and the behaviour of the Thessalonians. Are we equally concerned for both of these in ourselves and those for whom we have some responsibility? (pages 93-94)

4. 'Christians who don't experience persecution or affliction are the exception, not the rule.' What does that make you think? (page 93)

5. Can you think of times in your own life or in the lives of Christians you know when, in a time of pressure, good news about other Christians has been an encouragement? (pages 95-96)

6. 'Paul's small, newly trained band of militia had withstood the well equipped and expertly prepared army of hell to win the battle.' Can you think of other examples of this in the Bible? (page 97)

7. Make your own personal list of God's names, adding to it as you come across them in Scripture, and keep the list by you for devotional purposes. You will always find there is a name which shows you how sufficient He is for your every circumstance and concern. (pages 98ff.)

8. Christian love is the product of God's own work in us. Look up Ephesians 6:23 to see to what else is said there. (pages 101-102)

9. Christians do not face God's condemnation because Christ has borne this for them, but they will appear at the judgment-seat of Christ. Have you given enough thought to this? How should it influence your behaviour as a Christian? (page 104)

4:1—5:28

1. Does the concept of the family of God play a sufficient part in your thinking about your local church and your place in it? (page 106)

2. If Paul, as an apostle, could actually command the Thessalonians, how seriously ought we to take his epistles today? (page 107)

3. Do you think God sometimes does not reveal His particular will for our individual lives because we are not sufficiently concerned about His general will for us all, His will for our sanctification? (pages 108-109)

4. In what ways can Christians bear testimony to God's standards for sexual activity in the context of the permissive society of today? (pages 108-113)

5. Carefully study 2 Samuel 11:1-4. What kind of actions and attitudes may particularly incline us to sexual sin?

6. 'Jesus taught that love for one another provided the signature sign of one's Christianity (John 13:34-35).' What other signs have sometimes been mistakenly substituted for this? (page 114)

7. Is it possible 'to lead a quiet life' in an unquiet environment? If so, what are the spiritual principles for such a life? (page 115)

8. The believers in Berea were commended for searching the Scriptures to see if what Paul said was taught in them (Acts 17:11). Do you think Christians use the Scriptures to test what they are being taught by Christian leaders today? Can you encourage it in your church? (page 121)

9. 'The King is coming unexpectedly, personally, suddenly, visibly, audibly, and spectacularly.' Reflect prayerfully on each of these adverbs to increase your own expectancy. (page 122)

10. The Thessalonians 'knew enough of what was knowable to produce a godly lifestyle' (5:4-11). Are you living by all the light God has so far given you in your understanding of His word? (page 126)

11. Is there a place for talking about the Day of the Lord to unbelievers in connection with our witness to Christ? (pages 130-132; cf. 126-130)

12. Do you take seriously enough your responsibility to live a godly life in the face of the catastrophic reality of the Day of the Lord? (page 132)

13. A man who was in a coalmine when all the lights went out said he never realised before how rarely people are in total darkness and how terrifying it really is. Reflect soberly and prayerfully on this analogy of what it is to be without Christ. (page 133)

14. 'Righteous before God by faith and righteous toward men through love.' Can you think of Biblical examples of such people? (pages 134f.)

15. If you are a Christian, reflect with profound thanksgiving on the ten major points of encouragement referred to in paragraph 4 on page 136.

16. If you are a church member, do you esteem your leaders highly? If you are a leader, are you sure you deserve such esteem? (pages 138-141)

17. If you get impatient with some Christians known to you, consider the attitude of Christ to the twelve disciples – and to yourself. (page 142)

18. Read through Colossians and see how often Paul mentions thankfulness or gratitude. (page 143)

19. How marvellous it is to know that God is always consistent with Himself! Read Overview, 'Knowing God' (pages 146f.). Do you think consistency ought to mark Christians too?

2 THESSALONIANS

1:1-12

1. Paul told the believers at Thessalonica that he and his friends were praying for them, and we can be sure they did. Do you ever promise prayer and then forget your promise? (page 155)

2. How striking it is that Paul can write to a whole church and commend their faith and love and patience! Do you think he could write in that way to many churches today? (page 156)

3. 'Suffering for Christ was the standard, not the exception, in Paul's day.' How would you live if this was true today? (page 158)

4. If punishment after death is eternal for the unbeliever, as it is, how should this affect your prayer-life as a Christian? (page 166)

5. Since we will admire or marvel at Christ in His presence, we will hardly be occupied in admiring ourselves. Don't you think that will be a blessing? (page 167)

6. Count the number of times in his letters Paul says he prays for the recipients of the letters. Are you challenged by this? (page 168)

2:1-17

1. Do you test all doctrine by the authoratative teaching of the New Testament? (page 169)

2. Is it bigotry to describe somebody as a false teacher if his teaching is contrary to what is set out with crystal clarity in the Scriptures? (page 170)

3. What truths particularly need constant repetition in the pulpit ministry of a local church?

4. If God will bring to an end the reign of Antichrist and be victorious over all evil, consider the encouragement this gives us in our own encounters with evil. (page 180) Consider especially Romans 16:20.

5. If the fruit of the Spirit (Gal. 5:22-23) furnish the ultimate test of spirituality, does this help us, among other factors, in assessing whether a teacher is a deceiver or not? (page 186)

6. Meditate prayerfully on the wonderful fact that all three Persons of the Trinity are deeply involved in your salvation and move from meditation to praise. (page 187)

7. Do you recognise fully enough that your salvation is all of God, both in terms of Christ's work on the cross and of the Holy Spirit's work within you? (pages 185-187)

3:1-5

1. Paul frequently asked for prayer for himself and others with him who were in the forefront of the spiritual battle. How many such people do you pray for regularly? (pages 188f.)

2. Look up the passages quoted in relation to God's faithfulness and give praise to Him for your personal experiences of this great quality. (pages 190-191)

3. The terms 'love of God' and 'patience of Christ' are indications that 'every virtue we possess, and every conquest won, and every thought of holiness are His alone'. Does this encourage as well as challenge you? (page 192)

3:6-15

1. Why do you think there is so little church discipline today? Can you find reasons for this? (pages 193-195)

2. In verses 6 and 14, Paul makes it abundantly clear that his teaching was to be taken as authoritative by the church at Thessalonica. Do you think modern churches give sufficient practical recognition to his teaching today? What about your own attitude?

3. Paul and his friends were examples to other believers not only in character but in their commitment to work. Could you be an example to others in this regard? (pages 196-197)

4. When you pray for your church leaders, do you pray that they may know the Lord's wisdom in difficult matters of discipline?

3: 16-18

1. Both at the opening and the close of this letter, Paul writes of the Lord's grace. Reflect on this grace as absolutely basic at every stage and in every situation of your life as a Christian.

Christian Focus Publications publishes biblically-accurate books for adults and children. The books in the adult range are published in three imprints.

Christian Heritage contains classic writings from the past.

Christian Focus contains popular works including biographies, commentaries, doctrine, and Christian living.

Mentor focuses on books written at a level suitable for Bible College and seminary students, pastors, and others; the imprint includes commentaries, doctrinal studies, examination of current issues, and church history.

For a free catalogue of all our titles, please write to
Christian Focus Publications,
Geanies House, Fearn,
Ross-shire, IV20 1TW, Great Britain

For details of our titles visit us on our web site
http://www.christianfocus.com

Focus on the Bible Commentaries

Genesis – John Currid*
Exodus – John L. Mackay*
Deuteronomy – Alan Harman
Judges and Ruth – Stephen Dray
1 Samuel – Dale Ralph Davis*
2 Samuel – Dale Ralph Davis
1 and 2 Kings – Robert Fyall*
Ezra, Nehemiah, Esther – Robin Dowling*
Proverbs – Eric Lane
Isaiah – Paul House*
Jeremiah – George Martin*
Ezekiel – Anthony Billington*
Daniel – Robert Fyall
Hosea – Michael Eaton
Amos – O Palmer Robertson*
Jonah–Zephaniah – John L. Mackay
Haggai–Malachi – John L. Mackay
Matthew – Charles Price
Mark – Geoffrey Grogan
John – Robert Peterson*
1 Corinthians – Paul Barnett*
2 Corinthians – Geoffrey Grogan
Galatians – Joseph Pipa*
Ephesians – R. C. Sproul
Philippians – Hywel Jones
1 and 2 Thessalonians – Richard Mayhue
The Pastoral Epistles – Douglas Milne
Hebrews – Walter Riggans
James – Derek Prime
1 Peter – Derek Cleave
2 Peter/Jude – Paul Gardner
Letters of John – Michael Eaton
Revelation – Paul Gardner

Journey Through the Old Testament – Bill Cotton
How To Interpret the Bible – Richard Mayhue

Those marked with an * are currently being written.

MENTOR TITLES

Creation and Change – Douglas Kelly
A scholarly defence of the literal seven-day account of the creation of all things as detailed in Genesis 1. The author is Professor of Systematic Theology in Reformed Theological Seminary in Charlotte, North Carolina, USA.
large format   ISBN 1 857 92283 2   *272 pages*

The Healing Promise – Richard Mayhue
A clear biblical examination of the claims of Health and Wealth preachers. The author is Dean of The Master's Seminary, Los Angeles, California.
large format   ISBN 1 857 923 002   *288 pages*

Creeds, Councils and Christ – Gerald Bray
The author, who teaches at Samford University, Birmingham, Alabama, explains the historical circumstances and doctrinal differences that caused the early church to frame its creeds. He argues that a proper appreciation of the creeds will help the confused church of today.
large format   ISBN 1 857 92 280 8   *224 pages*

Calvin and the Atonement – Robert Peterson
In this revised and enlarged edition of his book, Robert Peterson examines several aspects of Calvin's thought on the atonement of Christ seen through the images of Christ as Prophet, Priest, King, Second Adam, Victor, Legal Substitute, Sacrifice Merit, and Example. The author is on the faculty of Covenant Seminary in St. Louis.
large format   ISBN 1 857 923 77 4   *176 pages*

Calvin and the Sabbath – Richard Gaffin
Richard Gaffin of Westminster Theological Seminary in Philadelphia first explores Calvin's comments on the Sabbath in his commentaries and other writings. He then considers whether or not Calvin's viewpoints are consistent with what the biblical writers teach about the Sabbath.
large format   ISBN 1 857 923 76 6   *176 pages*

MENTOR COMMENTARIES

1 and 2 Chronicles
Richard Pratt

The author is professor of Old Testament at Reformed Theological Seminary, Orlando, USA. In this commentary he gives attention to the structure of Chronicles as well as the Chronicler's reasons for his different emphases from that of 1 and 2 Kings.
hardback, 512 pages   ISBN 185792 1518

Psalms
Alan Harman

The author, now retired from his position as a professor of Old Testament, lives in Australia. His commentary includes a comprehensive introduction to the psalms as well as a commentary on each psalm.
hardback, 456 pages   ISBN 185792 1917

Amos
Gary Smith

Gary Smith, a professor of Old Testament in Midwestern Baptist Seminary, Kansas City, USA, exegetes the text of Amos by considering issues of textual criticism, structure, historical and literary background, and the theological significance of the book.
hardback, 400 pages   ISBN 185792 2530

Christian Focus titles by
Donald Macleod
Principal of the Free Church College, Edinburgh

A Faith to Live By

In this book the author examines the doctrines detailed in the Westminster Confession of Faith and applies them to the contemporary situation facing the church.

ISBN 1 85792 428 2   *hardback*   *320 pages*

Behold Your God

A major work on the doctrine of God, covering his power, anger, righteousness, name and being. This book will educate and stimulate deeper thinking and worship.

ISBN 1 876 676 509   *paperback*   256 pages

Rome and Canterbury

This book assesses the attempts for unity between the Anglican and Roman Catholic churches, examining the argument of history, the place of Scripture, and the obstacle of the ordination of women.

ISBN 0 906 731 887   *paperback*   *64 pages*

The Spirit of Promise

This book gives advice on discovering our spiritual role in the local church, the Spirit's work in guidance, and discusses various interpretations of the baptism of the Spirit.

ISBN 0 906 731 448   *paperback*   *112 pages*

Shared Life

The author examines what the Bible teaches concerning the Trinity, then explores various historical and theological interpretations regarding the Trinity, before indicating where some of the modern cults err in their views of the Trinity.

ISBN 1-85792-128-3   *paperback*   *128 pages*

Books
by
R. C. Sproul
published
by
Christian Focus

A Walk With Jesus

376 pages   ISBN 1 85792 260 3   large hardback

A study of the life of Christ, based on the
Gospel of Luke, divided into 104 sections.

Mighty Christ

144 pages   ISBN 1 85792 148 8   paperback

A study of the person and work of Jesus.

The Mystery of the Holy Spirit

192 pages   ISBN 1 871676 63 0   paperback

Examines the role of the Spirit in creation,
salvation and in strengthening the believer.

Ephesians

160 pages   ISBN 1 85792 078 3   paperback

Focus on the Bible Commentary, useful for
devotional study of this important New Testament book.

The Gospel of God

256 pages   ISBN 1 85792 077 5   large hardback

An exposition of the Book of Romans

THE CHRIST OF THE BIBLE
AND THE CHURCH's FAITH

Geoffrey Grogan

This book is a theological study
In the main, the odd-numbered chapters are theological. The first five of these set out the biblical evidence for our understanding of Jesus, while chapters 11 and 13 reflect on this theologically at a somewhat deeper level.

It is an apologetic study
This is the function of the even-numbered chapters. They deal with the main difficulties that have been and still are raised by those who are interested in Jesus but are not yet committed to him. It is to be hoped that they will also be of help to the committed. Each of these chapters follows the theological chapter most closely related to it.

The book will be useful to ministers and theological students. It has however been written in such a way that many Christians without theological training may be able to benefit from it, plus other readers who have not yet come to personal faith in Christ but are interested enough to read a serious book about him.

304 pages   ISBN 1 857 92 266 2

In this wide-ranging and well-written study, Geoffrey Grogan provides a clear, scholarly and reliable account of the identity of Jesus of Nazareth. The fruit of prolonged thought about the New Testament's teaching, *The Christ of the Bible and of the Church's Faith* is marked on every page by clarity of exposition and reliability of judgment. Here we have a careful and thoughtful sifting of evidence and a steady pursuit of conclusions which are in harmony with it.

While familiar with trends in New Testament studies during the past two centuries, and grateful for the work of fellow scholars,

Geoffrey Grogan has listened first and foremost to the witness of the apostles. He concludes that there is only one answer to the ancient question which Jesus himself asked them, 'Who do you say that I am?'

The result is this sturdy volume. Theological students, Christian ministers and leaders will find it invaluable, but any serious reader to whom Jesus of Nazareth remains an elusive figure will also come to the conclusion that this is a book well worth reading.

Sinclair B. Ferguson
Westminster Theological Seminary
Philadelphia, Pennsylvania, USA

This is an apologetic and theological study aimed at preachers, theological students, thinking Christians and interested agnostics. It succeeds in its aims admirably.

Donald Macleod
Free Church College
Edinburgh, Scotland

This beautifully-written book is a feast of scriptural analysis and argument about our Lord Jesus Christ. With profound learning but with lightness of touch, Geoffrey Grogan discusses all the main lines of the presentation of Jesus in the Bible, and then skilfully relates these to the questions that trouble people today about him. So the book is an attractive combination of Christology and apology – explaining Jesus in a way that answers modern doubts and puzzles, cleverly arranged in alternating chapters. Hearts will be warmed and heads cleared by this book – and doubt and unbelief will be turned into confidence and faith.

Steve Motyer
London Bible College

Territorial Spirits and World Evangelization
Chuck Lowe

ISBN 1 85792 399 5   *192 pages*   *large format*

Over the last decade, a new theory of spiritual warfare, associated primarily with the teaching of Peter Wagner, has become popular around the world. This teaching concerns the role of 'territorial spirits', who are said to rule over specific geographical areas. Along with this theory has come a new practice of spiritual warfare: ruling spirits are named, their territories identified, and they are then bound or cursed. evangelism and mission are then said to proceed rapidly with dramatic results. Chuck Lowe, who teaches at Singapore Bible College, examines the full range of biblical, intertestamental and historical evidence cited in support of this new teaching. He affirms the need to be involved in spiritual warfare, but proposes a more biblical model.

'This is a methodologically-clear, admirably lucid, and mission-hearted challenge; a challenge not merely to our theories about Strategic-Level Spiritual Warfare, but to our evangelical technocratic quest for successful 'method'. Lowe argues that the floodtide of confidence in this 'method' has swept away exegetical, historical and empirical caution, and that it has unwittingly produced a synthesis uncomfortably closer to *The Testament of Solomon* and to animism than to any *biblical* understanding of demonology and spiritual warfare. In place of this questionable construction, with its quick-and-easy answers, Lowe points to the grittier, more robust example provided by James O Fraser, a CIM missionary to the Lisu in China. A great read!'

Max Turner
Vice Principal and Senior Lecturer in New Testament,
London Bible College

'So easily do many accept the new and the novel! To all who care deeply about world mission, Chuck Lowe's evaluation of strategic-level spiritual warfare is a needed clarion call; a call to reject what is built on a foundation of anecdote, speculation and animism, and to walk in the established paths of biblical truth and practice.

'Lowe has set himself up as a target for those who follow the SLSW theology. It will be interesting to see how they respond to this book.'

George Martin
Southern Baptist Theological Seminary
Louisville, Kentucky